Melania and Me

Melania

— and —

Me

THE RISE AND FALL OF MY FRIENDSHIP

WITH THE FIRST LADY

Stephanie Winston Wolkoff

Gallery Books

New York   London   Toronto   Sydney   New Delhi

Gallery Books
An Imprint of Simon & Schuster, Inc.
1230 Avenue of the Americas
New York, NY 10020

First Gallery Books hardcover edition August 2020

GALLERY BOOKS and colophon are registered trademarks of Simon & Schuster, Inc.

For information about special discounts for bulk purchases, please contact Simon & Schuster Special Sales at 1-866-506-1949 or business@simonandschuster.com.

The Simon & Schuster Speakers Bureau can bring authors to your live event. For more information or to book an event, contact the Simon & Schuster Speakers Bureau at 1-866-248-3049 or visit our website at www.simonspeakers.com.

Interior design by Jaime Putorti

Manufactured in the United States of America

10 9 8 7 6 5 4 3

Library of Congress Cataloging-in-Publication Data

Names: Wolkoff, Stephanie Winston, 1971– author.
Title: Melania and me : the rise and fall of my friendship with the First Lady / Stephanie Winston Wolkoff.
Other titles: The Rise and Fall of My Friendship with the First Lady
Description: First Gallery Books hardcover edition. | New York : Gallery Books, 2020. |
Identifiers: LCCN 2020019342 (print) | LCCN 2020019343 (ebook) | ISBN 9781982151249 (hardcover) | ISBN 9781982151256 (paperback) | ISBN 9781982151263 (ebook)
Subjects: LCSH: Trump, Melania, 1970– —Friends and associates. | Wolkoff, Stephanie Winston, 1971– | Executives' spouses—United States—Biography. | Celebrities—New York (State)—New York—Biography. | United States. Office of the First Lady—Officials and employees—Biography. | New York (N.Y.)—Biography.
Classification: LCC E914.T77 W65 2020 (print) | LCC E914.T77 (ebook) | DDC 973.933—dc23
LC record available at https://lccn.loc.gov/2020019342
LC ebook record available at https://lccn.loc.gov/2020019343

ISBN 978-1-9821-5124-9
ISBN 978-1-9821-5126-3 (ebook)

To Melania

— Contents —

Prologue: Just Another Lunch • 1

1. How to Marry a Billionaire • 9

2. Opposites Attract • 27

3. The Campaign Year • 49

4. The Setup • 66

5. Showtime • 130

6. White House–keeping • 155

7. Trial by February • 189

8. The Shutdown • 224

9. Be Best • 245

10. The Takedown • 280

11. Just Friends • 312

Epilogue: I'm Still Here • 337

Acknowledgments • 341

— Prologue —

Just Another Lunch

"*Grab 'em by the pussy.*"

The sentence that reverberated around the world on October 7, 2016. The quote was an excerpt from a recording that became forever known as "the *Access Hollywood* tape," published by the *Washington Post* and aired on NBC News, a month before the 2016 presidential election. It had been recorded eleven years earlier, in September 2005, on a bus taking Donald Trump to make a cameo on the NBC soap opera *Days of Our Lives*. Now infamously, Donald told TV host Billy Bush, "I'm automatically attracted to beautiful. I just start kissing them. It's like a magnet. Just kiss. I don't even wait. And when you're a star, they let you do it. You can do anything. Grab 'em by the pussy."

When the story broke about the tape I was deeply immersed in my oldest son, Zach's, health problems related to his life-threatening food allergies and other issues that required many doctor's visits and therapies. My middle son, Tyler, was transferring to a new school, and my daughter, Alexi, was adjusting to hers. I was inching closer to the signing stage of two partnership deals I'd personally and financially been invested in for years and believed would define the next decade of my life.

So the first I heard of the recording was from Zach, who called me from boarding school and asked, "What do you think about this tape, Mom? Do you think Mr. Trump really said that? I hope Melania is okay. Tell her I say hi." I had no idea what he was referring to. Barron Trump was at the same school as my two younger children. Were all the students talking about it at school, too? Had Barron heard? At dinner that night with my kids, the tape was topic A. I still hadn't heard the entire recording myself or read the transcript.

At the time of the recording, Donald and Melania were practically newlyweds. She was a few months pregnant! I'd never heard him speak that way in my life and it didn't exactly ring true. But his reputation for being a lothario preceded him, so of course it was possible. Wow, was I in for a shock when I heard the video with my own ears. Donald had actually said *that*?! About chasing TV host Nancy O'Dell and manhandling random women?

The words themselves on the *Access Hollywood* tape were offensive, whether or not Donald actually did what he described, but I wasn't completely shocked by them. For more than twenty years, I worked with some of the most influential and powerful male executives in entertainment, fashion, media, and politics—Harvey Weinstein, Charlie Rose, Mario Testino, Patrick Demarchelier, and Russell Simmons—who have now fallen from their mighty tower.

I think the difference between the "guy talk" that I experienced and what Donald said, which really rubbed me the wrong way, was that he was bragging about violating women. I knew how men could talk when they thought women weren't listening, but this was not something you'd expect to hear from a presidential candidate.

Back in the early nineties, I worked in the music business for Ron Delsener, the legendary granddaddy of rock promoters, the boy from Queens who created the concept of massive outdoor concerts in Central Park. Ron had booked all the greats all over the world—the Rolling Stones, Jimi Hendrix, the Beatles, Depeche Mode, Janis Joplin, Simon & Garfunkel, you name it! He talked faster than I did, out of both sides of his mouth, and said things like, "Stephanie, get over here and let's see what you can do with those six-feet-long legs." I was twenty-four at the time. His remarks, said with a twinkle of mischief, were right to my face, not hidden or just with the guys. It was a different era, so I took them in stride—on my six-feet-long legs. (In fact, when I agreed to produce the 58th Presidential Inauguration for our forty-fifth president, I called Ron to see if he'd help me find some musical acts. He made himself available the very next day.) Ron is a bit crass, but he is all heart.

Donald, on the other hand, boasted with the boys on the bus, and then, as soon as a woman came on the scene, they immediately shut up. They knew that what they were saying was wrong. I felt sick trying to explain to my kids why Donald, not only the Republican nominee for president but my friend's husband, a man they'd known their whole lives, had bragged about grabbing women's private parts without their consent.

I was concerned for Melania and worried about Barron, too. But, then again, she had responded to my concern many times over the years with, "Don't be, I know who I married." Very matter-of-factly, she had always stipulated, "Barron is my first priority and he is strong." I always interpreted that as her resigning herself to an unconventional marriage or household and having no expectations of Donald as a faithful husband or doting father. He was a narcissist to the core, but his admitting to the entire world that his fame gave him superpowers to violate women had to have affected her. I would have been horrified if my husband talked about randomly assaulting women—and immediately out the door to a divorce lawyer's office. But Melania's basic instinct and reaction were not those of a so-called normal woman with so-called normal feelings about her far-from-normal marriage. I honestly had no idea how she was handling it.

Out of concern (and some curiosity), I texted her on October 9, "Are you okay??"

The next day, she replied, "Hi, love. I canceled interview tomorrow. If you have time for lunch?"

I figured out she'd planned on doing press about the recording but had put it off. (She eventually did talk to Anderson Cooper the following week in a stiff, toeing-the-line interview.) I was a bit surprised that, in the epic shitstorm the Trump family was in, she'd have time for lunch. But, then again, Melania loved to lunch. Her tone—"Let's do the Mark. I'll make a reservation for tomorrow. I need to leave at 2:30 p.m. to pick Barron up from school at 3:00 p.m. Can you do 12:15?" I was relieved. I had yet to see Melania freak out about anything. But if she were ever going to, wouldn't it be over this?

We had our lunch routine. We alternated between three restaurants, wrapped up in under three hours, and took turns paying the bill. When privacy was the prerequisite, our usual spot was the Mark Restaurant by Jean-Georges, inside the posh luxury hotel of the same name on Manhattan's exclusive Upper East Side. I texted that I was running late. She texted back that she was there already, but not to rush.

When I finally arrived, I hurried through the sparkly hotel entrance and the bar toward our regular table. I didn't notice any Secret Service men or women, but I knew they had to be there. Our table was off to the side against the wall, as private as you could get in this busy restaurant. I wish I'd been on time, so I could have seen the reaction of the other lunch-goers when the most talked-about woman in the world arrived in one of her impeccable outfits with her signature look of a jacket draped across her shoulders and a neat-as-always coiffure. New Yorkers don't often stare at celebrities, and definitely not while dining at the A-list-celeb enclave the Mark, which hosted many of them. But Melania must have made heads swivel that day.

She looked happy to see me as I took my seat next to her, smile, kiss-kiss. It was eerily ordinary, like any other lunch greeting at the Mark, or Cipriani, or Michael's. Just two friends catching up. Nothing to see here, folks.

Melania ordered first: "Grilled salmon, well done; sautéed spinach; and a side of French fries."

I jumped in and said, "Make that two, please. And one Diet Coke, no ice, for her, and a Diet Coke with ice, for me."

After the waiter left, I was looking right at her, listening to every word she said about how busy she was, what Barron was up to, details about her upcoming plans and travel. It was surreal, *too* normal. I started laughing at the weirdness and then, out of the blue, said, "Don't kill me, but I have to ask!"

"Oh boy!" she said. "What is it?"

"How many times have the words 'pussy' and 'president' been in the same sentence?"

She looked at me, her blue eyes sparkling, and then she started laughing—laughing to the point where she needed to blot the tears from her eyes with her napkin. I remember thinking, *Thank God this table is semi-private!* I could just see the "Page Six" headline now: "Melania Trump Laughing Her Ass Off in Public Three Days After 'Pussy' Bombshell."

Just for the record, we weren't laughing off Donald's repulsive comments. Many women would come forward in the following weeks with claims about his groping and assaulting them, but I wasn't aware of any of them on October 11, the day of our lunch. The laughter was more of a release of tension than anything else. As in control as she was, Melania would have to have been made of steel not to feel stress over the tape. Our friendship, the trust we shared, was perhaps the release valve. I was the conduit for her to let go, if only for a few hysterical seconds.

Once we calmed down and wiped away the tears, she got serious. The subject was now open, and she had something to say.

"People want him to get out of the race," she told me.

I looked at her closely. I already knew the answer but asked anyway, "Would he ever walk away?"

"No way, he's not going anywhere!" she said.

I'd read that there had been calls for Donald to drop out of the race from within the Republican Party. Public reaction was split. Trump fans bought his "locker-room talk" explanation. Everyone in my social and professional circles in New York was repulsed by his comments, but they were mostly horrified by just about all that he said and did.

"I don't know what's going to happen," she said. "It's not right, what he said. It's unacceptable. If it weren't for this, there would be no question, he would win."

Throughout the long campaign, Melania had never doubted that Donald would win. This was the one time her faith was shaken.

The bill came. She insisted on taking me to lunch. She signed the receipt and I thanked her for the meal. But I couldn't leave without asking, "Aren't you angry?"

She shook her head. "Nope! He is who he is. I told him that if he ran for president, he had to be ready for everything to be opened up and exposed. His whole life."

And yours, too, I thought.

I asked, "Are you really ready for everything about Donald"—*and you, your past, and your marriage*, I didn't add—"to come out?"

She made one of her favorite gestures, a "That's that!" demonstrated by brushing her hands together. "If it happens, it happens." She meant it when she said, "He knows he better be ready."

I paused, my head down, and ever so slowly looked up and asked, "And Barron?"

Her jaw clenched tightly, and she pursed her shiny lips. She said, "I talk with him and I teach him, with all the political chaos around him, to be strong." She wasn't worried that he couldn't handle it. She told her ten-year-old, just as she'd told me many times, "What doesn't kill you only makes you stronger." And that's how she has lived her life. But had Barron absorbed it? He had led a sheltered life. Was he as tough as his mom? That remained to be seen.

We inched closer to each other, our voices barely above a whisper. She said, "Look, I know what the truth is, and it doesn't need to be explained. Some things don't need to be dignified with an answer."

"I agree with you," I said, "but as First Lady, as a public figure, you won't be able to ignore this stuff." I was trying to tell her in a subtle and polite way she would have an obligation to be a role model to our country and the world.

Without hesitation, she said, "Of course I will!"

How silly of me to think otherwise!

"It's my life," she said. "It's nobody's business."

For her, public disgrace was nothing more than brushing sand off her feet after a stroll on the beach. For me and most others, it would be like drowning in quicksand. I was in awe of her uncrackable composure.

I'd gone to that lunch concerned about how she was coping. But she didn't want or need my, or anyone's, sympathy. "Don't feel sorry for me!" she'd said over lesser slights, such as people calling her a gold digger or a hostage. "I'm *fine*." The press and people all over the world always projected their own emotions onto Melania, assuming she felt the same way they would under the same circumstances.

I'd known all along how impenetrable and unflappable she was, but until that lunch, I had no idea of her grit. Not many people could bear having their lives ripped open and all their regretful, hateful, humiliating moments splayed out for the world to see and judge. Melania and Donald, a perfect match, could tolerate any amount of ridicule and flick it aside. *That's that! If it happens, it happens!* If they could withstand this level of pressure and scrutiny, maybe they *should* be in the White House.

Beneath her focused stare and perfectly crafted smile, she conceals an inexplicable calm that spreads to all those around her, especially to her husband and to her friends. When Donald gets flustered—you can tell because his face goes from tempered orange to bright red—all he has to do is look at her, and he settles down. I've seen it happen across the dinner table, but more tellingly, I've witnessed it at press conferences. She sits in the front row posing, shielded from all sides with invisible armor, her chin tucked tightly to her chest and her eyes staring, deadpan, at a spot on the floor in front of her, but when he stands up behind the lectern, her fearless gaze lifts and shifts into a convincing smile for her man, and he is taken over by calmness. I've felt Melania's calm spread into me when I've been upset and crying. One arched eyebrow or word from her could ground me. From the moment Melania entered my life, I was drawn to learn more about her, and sometimes succeeded. I do know that she is honest, is loving, prizes her privacy above all things, and is faithful to her core values in ways Donald could never be.

We stood up to go. "He's going to win," I said. "And you're going to be First Lady."

We exited the Mark Restaurant through the rear door that leads directly into the hotel lobby, avoiding the onlookers seated at the bar. Muse, her Secret Service code name, was on the move. Her security team appeared suddenly in the lobby and on the street outside, waiting to whisk her away.

In mere weeks, Donald Trump would be elected president. Melania and I would cross the line from friendship to partnership. I would be recruited to work on the inauguration and, after that, in the First Lady's office, where I saw and experienced shocking and terrifying behavior and conduct from people who know better. During my two years in Trump World, I was afraid for myself, my friend, and our country. Suffice it to say, it ended badly for me, and for us.

Melania? Don't worry about her! She's *fine*.

How to Marry a Billionaire

*W*hen I met Melania Knauss in 2003, we were both thirty-two years old and walking the hallways of *Vogue*. I was working; she was visiting. Stars, power players, and models came through the offices all the time. I'd *seen* her before, but I didn't *know* her, yet.

My boss was Anna Wintour, editor in chief of American *Vogue* since 1988, current artistic director for Condé Nast, *Vogue*'s publisher. Anna is universally recognized as the most formidable and influential figure in fashion. She's the creator and the subject of global media coverage, a driver of the industry's economy, and despite her *Devil Wears Prada* reputation, she wields her power for good, raising a fortune for charity and promoting the fashion business around the globe.

Anna would be just as instrumental in the creation of Melania Trump as well.

How did I get to *Vogue*? Right place at the right time.

My first job out of college was at Sotheby's, the famous auction house where collectors and art lovers would come to more than eighty-five live auctions annually. In 1993, I started as a "lobby girl," welcoming clientele and giving them assistance. Within six months, I was the third assistant to then–chief executive Diana Brooks (who would later plead guilty of price-fixing in 2000 with rival auction house Christie's).

In 1998, I was invited to a dinner hosted by two *Vogue* editors, Alexandra Kotur and Kimberly Ryan, for the launch of a new cell phone. I spent a good portion of the evening with them, sharing stories about growing up with two older brothers, playing pick-up basketball games, and then later playing in college. I told them I had a communications and broadcast degree and was interested in finding a new job. They told me about an open position in *Vogue's* public relations department. If I was interested, they said, I should reach out to them. Alexandra gave me her card. When I got back to my apartment that night, I updated my résumé, and the next morning, I called to schedule an interview.

Until that point in my life, I hadn't yet been seduced by the world of fashion or lured into the industry. I cared more about my pants having a thirty-six-inch inseam than I did about the brand or label.

I needed to prepare for my interview. Much research was required before I stepped into fashion's minefield; at that point, I didn't *read* style magazines—I occasionally flipped through them. I knew *about* Anna Wintour, but I had to study and learn *who* Anna was, because truthfully, I didn't know, exactly, what made her "the most influential woman in fashion" or "the most feared."

The day of the interview, I spent more than two hours at Condé Nast headquarters, then located at 350 Madison Avenue. After my human resources check-in and interview, I was shuffled around from office to office, stopping for a while with Laurie Jones, *Vogue's* managing director. Anna hadn't yet returned from her lunch meeting, so I was asked to wait in the reception area.

I was mesmerized and transfixed by the women and men getting on and off the elevators, one more poised than the next. Then I saw *her*. I got a glimpse of Anna as she exited the elevator and disappeared around a corner.

My hands got a little sweaty as I sat there waiting. Like clockwork, Anna's assistant appeared. "Anna's ready to see you now," she said. In her two-inch heels and perfectly hemmed skirt, she escorted me down the long, narrow hallway. Everyone moved out of our way when they saw her coming. The right side of the wall was covered with clothing racks filled with bright colors. The left side was crammed with people trying to get to and from somewhere, all in a hurry. I was taking it all in and captivated by the action. The only time I felt this transfixed at Sotheby's was when I was in the middle of a bidding war during an auction, competing for ownership of a piece of artwork on behalf of a client. I was so caught up in the moment, flying through the hallways, that I didn't realize we'd reached our destination. We stopped abruptly, then stood in the doorway waiting for Anna to look up. On cue, her assistant announced me: "Anna, this is Stephanie Winston." I walked toward her, stopping in front of her desk, a natural barrier between us. It was modern, sleek, and immaculately organized. I noticed a Starbucks coffee cup with her smudged lipstick around the outer rim. I could *feel* her eyes on me, checking me out from head to toe. I looked the part in my blue Ralph Lauren pinstripe pantsuit. My uniform.

Anna stood, and I extended my hand and we shook: firm but not pulverizing. I towered over her. "Hi, Ms. Wintour, thank you for taking the time to meet with me," I said.

She said, "Hello, Stephanie." Cool British tone.

I waited for her to sit back down and then I sat across from her. I shuffled around in the chair for a moment, pulled my shoulders back, and sat up straight, thinking, *No one stays here for long.* The chairs weren't made for comfort. They were sleek and strong—just like her, as I would soon learn.

I knew Anna's time was valuable. I reminded myself to keep it brief, concise, and precise. I'd already passed the litmus test. For starters, two of her top editors had vouched for me, and I'd already been vetted by *Vogue* or I wouldn't have been invited to the dinner for the launch in the first place.

My experience and qualifications were already on my résumé, as well as my professional and personal achievements. So, what did we talk about?

She wanted to know about *me*.

"Tell me about yourself," she said. Without missing a beat, I said, "I stand out from everyone else." The room fell silent. She stared at me, probably waiting for me to finish my sentence. But just as quickly, she asked, "How?"

"I was referring to my height," I replied. This time, the room fell deathly silent. It just popped out of my mouth—a joke at a time like this?! Anna waited for more.

"I like to play basketball, and I'm a black belt in martial arts," I said. I told Anna that I began attending karate classes when I was three and a half years old, with my mom and two older brothers, Gordon and Randall, five days a week. In so many words, I explained how my biological father had left us after his nasty divorce from my mother and it was my karate instructor, Young Ki Hong, who became my father figure and who taught me discipline, respect, and focus.

I assumed she was curious about my last name, so I laid my family's story out on the table.

My mom then married Bruce Winston, son of Harry Winston, of jewelry store fame. Bruce loved Mom and my brothers and me, and we loved him. When he asked me to become his legally adopted daughter, there were no words to express my happiness after the loss I'd felt being abandoned by my father. I said "Yes!" immediately. His name replaced the old one on my birth certificate.

A few other pleasantries followed. Two hours later, back at work in my office at Sotheby's, I answered the phone and heard the magic words, "Anna Wintour would like to offer you the job." I gave my notice and two weeks later, I walked out the door and never looked back.

For my first two years at *Vogue*, 1998 and '99, I was the manager of public relations. I answered phones, took minutes, opened mail, made daily Starbucks runs, and set up PR photo shoots. My first week on the job, I was setting up a wedding shoot at Cipriani Wall Street, for a spot on the *Today* show. I was responsible for the gowns and accessories. After the cameras stopped rolling, my superiors left me there with the twenty-pound steamer, fifteen black garment bags, and all the shoes and accessories to deal with. Before they took off, my direct boss looked at me with contempt in her eyes and a snarl in her voice and said, "Just because you're a Winston, don't think you won't be carrying all of our bags. See you at the office!"

I wasn't born a Winston. Everyone assumed incorrectly that I'd grown up draped in diamonds, and I was labeled as one of *those* girls, privileged, spoiled, entitled. Actually, none of the above was true. I was a worker, not a slacker. That woman obviously knew nothing about me. I hauled everything back to the Condé Nast office building at 350 Madison, no problem, no complaints. Two years later, she was gone, and I was just getting started.

After two years in public relations, I became the founding director of the special events department, which would produce all of *Vogue*'s events and projects in-house instead of outsourcing them. I produced and oversaw the Metropolitan Museum of Art Costume Institute Gala—known as "the party of the year" and "the Oscars of the East Coast"—*and* approximately fifty other events and projects each year for the magazine, including private dinners, benefits, and parties in New York, Paris, and London, plus *Vogue*'s Fashion's Night Out events, 7th on Sale, and the VH1/Vogue Fashion Awards.

During my tenure at the magazine, I got married and had three kids. Juggling a family life and a demanding full-time job was a real pressure cooker, but it was all I knew. Sleepless nights, distinctly unglamorous hard work, and nursing all three babies (not at the same time!) at my desk was just a part of the job. I never sat on the sidelines. I loved a challenge. Under Anna, *Vogue* introduced three spin-offs: *Vogue Living*, *Men's Vogue*, and *Teen Vogue*. I was responsible for organizing the launch event, and several projects for all four titles. The workload was heavy and constant.

People outside *Vogue* noticed my work ethic. I'd get calls about other jobs. I didn't make any major decisions without consulting Anna first. Her opinion mattered to me, and her insight was invaluable. It cost me a couple of opportunities, but I have no regrets whatsoever. (Anna's edict within Condé Nast was famously "No poaching!")

The early 2000s were an exciting time to be working at the magazine—the worlds of entertainment and fashion were merging, and *Vogue* was the epicenter. It was super intense. Anna's editorial vision coupled with her imperial management of the employees and content was the stuff of legend. Day-to-day, *Vogue* staffers were actively engaged like troupers, rolling up their sleeves, no assignment ever too big or too small. You would never hear anyone say, "That's not my job."

The senior staff members, handpicked by Anna, would meet with her daily and often; solutions, not excuses, were expected. She preferred scheduled meetings, but I tended to be a drop-byer more often than not. I would quietly walk up to one of her assistants' desks to ask to be put on the schedule, as if Anna didn't see all six-foot-one of me standing right outside her office doors. Was she "Nuclear Wintour"? You bet she was! Anna was that and so much more. She could also turn an ice storm into a field of sunflowers if she so desired. Her influence and creativity are undeniably what set her apart from everyone else on this planet. Anna's notorious thousand-yard stare isn't *just* a stare. She really is looking that far ahead of everyone else.

Thanks to Anna's mentorship, I had a front-row seat to learn about the business of fashion, publishing, and advertising—bottom up, top down, and every angle in between. You can't sell magazines without a great story, and stories need characters, usually lovely, aristocratic creatures with global appeal who would inspire readers' imaginations and fantasies. Anna had, and has, great instincts for talent and was extremely selective about which personalities to put on the cover and to welcome into the inner circle.

My office at *Vogue* was right across from Anna's and within eye- and earshot of my friend, the larger-than-life editor at large André Leon Talley, one of the fashion industry's top arbiters of style and culture. I hadn't met anyone quite like André, whose flamboyancy was addictive, fierce loyalty was self-evident, and knowledge of the world of fashion and art was contagious. No matter where he was, he always held court, draped in custom-made silk caftans adorned with gold braid and wearing crocodile shoes custom-made by Manolo Blahnik. Anna relied on his advice, and I admired his extraordinary ability as an editor and was in awe of how he balanced his spiritual, ambitious, and eccentric lifestyle. From the moment we met, he took me under his wing and helped me navigate the land mines—from seating-placement dramas to wardrobe malfunctions—that awaited me.

One afternoon, I saw Melania Knauss was at the office, having a private meeting with Anna. Part of my job was to know all the players, to research them and learn whatever I could about them. I needed to know more about Melania than I already did, which was that she was the Slovenian model girlfriend of Donald Trump. I knew more about him, of course, the businessman who loved to see his name in print and on the sides of buildings. They'd been together for three years, during which time she had gotten her green card and moved into the penthouse of Trump Tower. Trump and Anna were friendly—they had met over the years at New York society events. His daughter Ivanka, his favorite, had even been offered a job at *Vogue* after she graduated from Wharton.

Donald needed the perfect setting to roll Melania out of relative obscurity, and what better than the city's biggest, boldest spotlight, where the fashion, entertainment, and media universes collided—the Met Gala. The event was the ultimate setting for the who's who; not just anybody could make a grand entrance.

Melania was no industry power broker, but Donald was. Did he somehow convince Anna to turn Melania into the magazine's shiny new object?

Before her *Vogue* makeover, Melania was a very pretty young woman who seemed like she was playing fancy dress-up—more a brunette Marilyn Monroe than a Jackie O. After Melania's makeover, André's achievement, she was transcendent, high fashion, editorial worthy. The makeup. The hair. The jewels. She truly was ready for her moment. I was an innocent bystander for her makeover to a small extent, in that she and André were photographed together by Patrick Demarchelier for a *New York* magazine article titled "The Charity Ball

Game," which featured my work on the Met Gala and all of *Vogue*'s labors to jigsaw the event together.

Melania was sweet, gracious, and smiley. André and I agreed, "We like her." We started taking Melania to lunch together at Michael's, the see-and-be-seen midtown restaurant, where André would hold court. We talked about what (and who!) was hot and what was not. She accompanied him to many of the right cultural events he'd been invited to attend while sculpting her image. As her stepdaughter Ivanka Trump wrote in her 2009 self-help book, *The Trump Card: Playing to Win in Work and Life*, "Perception is more important than reality. If someone perceives something to be true, it is more important than if it is in fact true. Let the other guy think what he wants. This doesn't mean you should be duplicitous or deceitful, but don't go out of your way to correct false assumptions if it plays to your advantage." Perception means *everything* to this family. Melania became André's plus-one. He brought her to a Martha Graham performance, so she was suddenly perceived as a woman who appreciated modern dance, even if she had no idea who Martha Graham was before she arrived. Suddenly, Melania was invited to Fashion Week shows and being photographed with André and Anna around town.

The timing was not coincidental. Two thousand four could have been called the Year of Trump.

On January 8, 2004, the first episode of the first season of *The Apprentice* aired on NBC. The creator and producer, Mark Burnett, a former British paratrooper and onetime Beverly Hills nanny, cast Donald, the man who'd declared bankruptcy four times and would do so twice more, as a brilliant businessman, richer than God, "a real American maverick tycoon, who will say whatever he wants," Burnett told the *New Yorker*. "He takes no prisoners. If you're Donald's friend, he'll defend you all day long. If you're not, he's going to kill you." And this friend/killer became the host, the boss, of a competition show where aspiring businessmen and -women schemed and fought each other for his approval. A suit-and-tie cage match. Americans couldn't get enough. The show was an instant cultural phenomenon. Trump's brand went from has-been to superstar. As many would say later, his name recognition and TV stardom were the reason he was so popular with the voting base that elected him as the forty-fifth president of the United States.

I have only recently learned that Melania appeared on one of the first episodes of the show, giving a tour of the Trump Tower penthouse to some contestants (including a very young Omarosa Manigault Newman). The penthouse's design aesthetic: The Palace of Versailles. As the contestants marveled at the gold everything, one said to her, "You're very lucky."

Melania's reply with a smile: "And he's not lucky?"

Touché. She knew the value of her beauty. She wasn't lacking self-esteem; I'll give her that.

I never watched *The Apprentice*. While swaths of the country were tuning in every week, getting prepped for the Boss's eventual presidential run, I was deep in preparation for the upcoming ball only four months away. The Met ball was always on my mind. I called it "my baby," and I lived and breathed it all year long. I've chased runaway peacocks through the Temple of Dendur and coaxed a wasted Johnny Rotten of the Sex Pistols to sit down and shut up, among thousands of other miracles of diplomacy working with oversized egos and high blood-alcohol concentrations. I loved my job. The nine years I produced the gala were the highlight of my career. I was addicted to the feeling of accomplishment I got every time I pulled a happy ending out of a pit of chaos.

Mixing and matching stars from the worlds of fashion, entertainment, sports, finance, and government, along with C-suite types, top execs in corporations and institutions, was part of the job. Beyond the glamour of it all, the bottom line mattered most—it was financially beneficial for the museum. I was very flattered to read what people said in a 2008 profile of me in *Avenue*. Harold Koda, the institute's curator in charge, said in the article, "[Stephanie is] straight-talking, yet always charming. And she effortlessly balances the needs of the museum with the evening's more creative impulses." Anna called me

"General Winston," saying, "[Stephanie] marshals her troops, and leads the charge. It takes a year of planning to make the evening happen, and Stephanie never misses a thing. She pays attention to every single last detail." That was my life at *Vogue*: excitement, drama, pride, and joy, and so, so, so many dresses.

Without question, the gala was the mountaintop—fashion's Mount Everest. My days were filled with conference calls, rapid-fire email exchanges, and back-to-back meetings. The 2004 theme was "Dangerous Liaisons: Fashion and Furniture in the Eighteenth Century," so I anticipated lots of crystal, silk, décolletage, hoops, and, probably, wigs.

As we neared the Costume Institute G-Day, the offices at *Vogue* were like Grand Central Terminal. The staff, a.k.a. "Anna's Army," and I were managing the hysteria, the frenzy, the opulence, and diva behavior straight out of *The Devil Wears Prada* (I knew author Lauren Weisberger well); if their body was taking up a seat at the gala, it was my job to know everything I could about them. My own office was cyclone struck. Guest lists, production materials, piles of color-coded Excel spreadsheets. The garbage overflowed with seating charts, dried-up Sharpies, and crumpled Post-it notes (blue for men and pink for women).

The guest list of seven hundred was star packed. It included Madonna, Mick Jagger, Jennifer Lopez, Scarlett Johansson, Prince Charles, Natalie Portman, Serena Williams, and Renée Zellweger, to mention a few. The wait-list had more than two hundred people, all of whom were dying to attend and willing to pay thousands per ticket. (In 2019, tickets were $35,000 apiece, and a table for ten people ranged from $200,000 to $300,000.) I played an integral part behind the scenes in raising money for one of the only self-funded curatorial departments at the Metropolitan Museum of Art, and in transforming a New York City philanthropic event into the global cultural event of the year. During my tenure, the millions we raised paid to maintain and renovate the Costume Institute. I'm proud of that.

People who could easily afford to buy tickets *begged* to purchase

them, but it was by invitation only. Donald always stuck to the minimum with two $1,500 individual tickets—the cheapest available—as
did his daughter Ivanka, then twenty-three. Donald intended to use
his golden ticket to "win" the Met ball that year. But to do so, he
needed a masterstroke that would raise his and Melania's stars above
the rest. He needed Mark Burnett, the TV producer who'd already
given him a comeback and turned him into a star. No one knows how
to grab attention like Burnett, producer of *The Apprentice*, *The Amazing
Race*, and *Survivor*, and later *Shark Tank* and *The Voice*. Both Donald
and Mark believed in taking action and letting the results speak for
themselves. I believe that, together, they mastered the art of seizing the
moment and came up with a story line for the red carpet that night—
Donald and Melania Get Engaged! A Mark Burnett Production.

But first, Melania needed to look the part. Fortunately, they already
had the perfect *Vogue*-approved gown checked off their list.

In celebration of the December 2000 issue of *Vogue*, featuring
Nicole Kidman on the cover, Anna had hosted the premiere of Baz
Luhrmann's *Moulin Rouge!* at the Paris Theater in New York City. The
evening was my responsibility, as Melania would say, "from A to Z,"
including the screening, a performance with cancan dancers, a dinner, and, finally, an auction at Brasserie 8½ on West Fifty-Seventh
Street, right around the corner from the theater. Anna, the visionary
extraordinaire, never *just* threw a party. There were always many layers
to her events, like a napoleon. And the endgame was much sweeter.
It was almost always about raising money for charity. I asked eight
designers—including Helmut Lang, John Galliano, Oscar de la Renta,
and Dolce & Gabbana—to create garments reminiscent of what belle
époque courtesans wore, which we would auction for the benefit of
the Council of Fashion Designers of America/Vogue Fashion Fund.
All the items were magnificent, but the pièce de résistance was a one-
of-a-kind black gown by Donatella Versace.

Thankfully, I knew how to run an auction by the time I left Sotheby's.
After working for Sotheby's president, I was promoted to manager of
client services and then became a member of the Sotheby's Private

Client Group, where I worked with clients on purchasing and consigning in all collecting categories. I was involved in several high-profile auctions, such as the Duke and Duchess of Windsor auction and the Jacqueline Kennedy Onassis estate auction, which raised $34.4 million, luring thousands of bidders who wanted a piece of Camelot for themselves—a glass, a photo, a car, a rocking chair. *Time* came to Sotheby's for a story on the auction and my photo ran in the magazine.

Compared to those enormous productions, auctioning eight custom-made garments would be a piece of cake. But I did plenty of reconnaissance anyway. I'd learned the importance of knowing who I was dealing with, the personalities, the likes and dislikes, and the size of their egos. To guarantee a bidding war for each garment, I would play to the bidders' vanities.

I worked with Baz Luhrmann and his team to set up a ministage. For spectacle and glamour, I asked Hugh Jackman to serve as auctioneer. Thanks to some pre-auction calls I made, the bidding got heated between Donald Trump and Harvey Weinstein, then a movie producer (and now, infamously, a convicted rapist), over that Versace dress. Donald walked away with it, much to Harvey's disappointment. I think Harvey had intended to give it as a gift to Nicole Kidman.

Melania didn't wear the black Versace gown in public in 2001, 2002, or 2003. It was as if they were saving it for a special occasion, when *everyone* would be watching . . . like the Met Gala in 2004, when Donald was on top of the ratings.

The production continues . . .

The Fifth Avenue stage was set with a sprawling red carpet. Donald knew that the party inside the museum wasn't nearly as important as the stairs leading into it. That stretch of Fifth Avenue on the first Monday in May is priceless real estate. If you were seen and photographed there, you were "in." You'd made it. That was a matter of fact. Having invested only $3,000 in tickets, Donald would get invaluable and priceless publicity, using the paparazzi and journalists covering the red carpet to bestow superhuman powers on him—and his woman—as they ascended the steps.

The players were in costume and makeup—Melania in her Versace, styled by André, Donald in a black Brioni tux. As they stepped out of their limo into the spray of photographers, Donald announced to the press that he'd proposed on the way over and told Melania to show off her brand-new fifteen-carat (per the *New York Times*) $1.5 million Graff diamond ring. (The price was controversial. The *New York Times* reported in 2005 that Trump paid only half price for it. In 2018, *Forbes* said that Donald had lied about getting a discount at all.)

Most of the guests at the party were oblivious to Donald's proposal until the following morning, when it was splashed across the front page of the *New York Post*, the daily paper owned by Donald's buddy Rupert Murdoch, who did his part in the whole production. Gossip columnist Richard Johnson wrote, "Melania wore the bauble, mingling happily with hundreds of guests who didn't notice the massive sparkler on her left hand." At the event, I heard someone refer to the ring and say, "I guess dreams really do come true." Diamond aside, all I could think about was how radiant Melania looked. André must have sprinkled pixie dust all over her.

That Monday in May, a star was born.

No, I take it back. A star was *made*.

It took a lot of work by a lot of willing, and some unknowing, cohorts, but Melania's coming out was perfectly choreographed. She was thrust onto the fashion world's most iconic stage. Her unveiling was *Vogue* ready. The world got a good look at Donald's intended, and they liked what they saw.

You could call it a magic moment. Or you could call it making a deal. Donald had, as he would say, turned dealmaking into an art. This deal was, he would give Melania the fashion world's answer to the Olympics. She gave him . . . companionship, arm candy, someone whose body parts he could brag about on Howard Stern's radio show, someone to put him in the middle of a pseudo–model sandwich with his daughter Ivanka on the other side. By getting engaged to Melania, Donald would be seen by his middle-America audience as a good man, a decent fellow, the marrying kind. She wasn't so naïve as to think that their relationship didn't serve a purpose for each of them. But, as I'd come to see as our friendship grew closer, theirs was a kind of love, nonetheless. From that night on, the newly engaged couple's social calendar was full. They went to the CFDA Fashion Awards at the New York Public Library and the Whitney Museum of American Art's annual gala.

The more time I spent with Melania, the more I genuinely liked her. Being with her was like having the sister I never had before—but a really confident, perfectly coiffed, ultimate older sister. In her world, nothing was a big deal, and everything was just as it should be. Just being with her made me feel good. She had her shit together! She was all about her family—Donald, Barron, and her parents—and herself. I was attracted to her directness. Despite her thick accent, she always got her point across, with a look in her stunning blue eyes, her magnetic smile, or a graceful gesture. Later that summer, in July 2004, André was on assignment to escort Melania to Paris Fashion Week and help her find a wedding gown. In a sit-down interview with Robin Givhan, fashion critic for the *Washington Post*, he said "Melania was very impressive" as they hunted down wedding dresses at couture houses. "She was not the arrogant Mrs. Trump. . . . We went to a fabulous dinner at Valentino's chateau . . . I was sitting next to Melania and she was so impeccable in her manners, in the way she spoke to people, and she was so charming."

Melania chose a couture bridal gown, a sixteen-foot veil, and a thirteen-foot train designed by the House of Dior's John Galliano (it's been reported that Donald paid $100,000 for it). Per *Vogue*, the white duchesse satin gown required nearly three hundred feet of material, took a thousand hours to make, and required five hundred and fifty hours of labor just to do the hand-stitched embroidery with more than fifteen hundred crystal rhinestones and pearls.

Mere days after the triumphant season-two finale of *The Apprentice*, the next production from the dynamic-duo hit machine was *Donald and Melania Get Married! A Mark Burnett Production*.

I received my Tiffany & Co. engraved wedding invite and was

amused that the wedding would be on my birthday, January 21. I'd heard rumors that Donald's intention was to throw a lavish, over-the-top extravaganza, and through endorsements and sponsorship deals, discounts and bartering, he would somehow turn a profit. He made a million-dollar deal with Getty for the photo rights, which the company could turn into huge profits by selling images to magazines and newspapers around the world. The *New York Times* reported that Trump bartered for discounts from jewelers, caterers, and florists in exchange for being a part of the high-profile wedding.

My husband, David, and I flew down to Palm Beach for the wedding, met up with some of our friends, and saw Anna, Shelby Bryan, and André there. I wore a strapless floor-length gown with gold-leaf details on ivory chiffon by my friend Hervé Pierre, then the artistic director with Carolina Herrera, who designed several of my Met Gala dresses (and is currently Melania's stylist).

I heard that, at the pre-wedding dinner for Donald's special guests, the groom spent most of his time with Mark Burnett (of course) and casino mogul Steve Wynn, who has since stepped down as chairman and chief executive of his company, Wynn Resorts, over decades' worth of sexual misconduct allegations.

In the morning, while Melania got ready for the wedding, Donald played a round of golf with his son Don Jr. and *Access Hollywood* host Billy Bush. On the links, he allegedly said, "I keep forgetting I'm getting married today."

The service was held at Bethesda-by-the-Sea, the 1925 Gothic Revival–style Episcopal church in Palm Beach. The vibe outside was circus-like, pure spectacle, with celebrities in black tie wall-to-wall and hundreds of fans lined up outside the church to catch a glimpse of the magic couple and their famous friends. Camera and recording devices were banned among the guests to prevent any photos from being leaked. Rumor had it that Donald had tried to make a deal to broadcast the wedding live on TV, but Melania had put her foot down.

Melania's sister, Ines, was the maid of honor. Don Jr. and Eric Trump were the best men. Mark Burnett's seven-year-old son, Cameron, was the ring bearer. Two memorable moments at the service: when Donald recited the vow to honor and obey, for richer or poorer, everyone laughed, and when pre-Jared Ivanka read some scripture.

The more than four hundred guests included Prince Albert of Monaco, Derek Jeter, former New York mayor turned Trump "personal attorney" Rudy Giuliani, Russell Simmons, TV news host Matt Lauer, Kelly Ripa, Tony Bennett, Barbara Walters, Simon Cowell, Katie Couric, Paul Anka, Shaquille O'Neal, Kathie Lee Gifford, P. Diddy, Usher, Heidi Klum, Arnold Schwarzenegger, and the Clintons.

After the ceremony, we celebrated at the Trumps' 20,000-square-foot, renovated-for-$35-million, ballroom at Mar-a-Lago, Trump's Palm Beach, Florida, resort. The reception was the first event held there. The décor was as expected: garish, gold and frills, chandeliers everywhere, and a spotlight trained on the Trump family crest. When we walked in, I remember saying, "Oh my God." The flowers, thousands of them, were incredibly beautiful. It was just so much extreme, competitive-energy opulence, like, "My ballroom is bigger than yours!" As we circled the room, taking it in, we heard snippets of conversation like, *He got a deal on that, I heard he got the flowers for free, It's so over the top, but I kind of love it.* People joked about the extravagance, but with affection, as if Donald were in on the joke. André was in his element, cutting through the crowd, listening to the ladies, looking at what they were wearing, having a great time.

There was no sign of future enmity between some of the wedding guests and the groom. Although it's hard to imagine now, in 2005, Donald seemed like a harmless egomaniac. He wasn't yet the divisive force he is today. I can't say whether Bill and Hillary Clinton genuinely respected Donald Trump then, but they showed up and ate roast beef and lobster rolls, *that Trump said Jean-Georges Vongerichten provided for free.* They drank the Cristal champagne we heard had been donated. Billy Joel serenaded the guests with "Just the Way You Are" and made up lyrics about Trump to the tune of "The Lady Is a Tramp." It was a joyful celebration. There was a sense of being at an Event, capital E. My group and I had a blast. My husband is such a great dancer, and whenever I can relax and let him lead, we have the best time. The set-ting was so surreal, it felt like we were on a movie set like Fred Astaire and Ginger Rogers.

Melania and Donald skipped a honeymoon. He told the *New York Post*, "I don't want to go anywhere else because this is the best place to be." Instead, he played golf at his resort, while Melania could probably have been found in her favorite spot at Mar-a-Lago: a treatment room getting a facial from facialist Tammy Fender, whose holistic, botanical products Melania relies on heavily.

As incredible as it might seem, Melania's "I made it" moment was still yet to come. Her ultimate validation and glory, what every "model" dreams about, came when she was featured on the February 2005 cover of *Vogue*, photographed by Mario Testino, the only bride in full wedding regalia in the magazine's 115-year history to date. The billion-dollar bride bounced *Million Dollar Baby* Hilary Swank from the coveted spot. Along with the cover, the magazine devoted fourteen pages to a feature by fashion news director Sally Singer called "How to Marry a Billionaire." (I remember reading that headline and think-ing, *Ouch*.) Sources said the cover coup was dependent on Melania's revealing the dress prior to the big day, which she had clearly agreed to. The story covered the nuptials as well as the "apple of Don's eye," the "smashing 34-year-old Slovenian," and her yearlong journey to her "American-royal wedding."

André reflected on the wedding in 2017 in that same interview with Robin Givhan: "I've never seen any woman except Melania Trump who can walk for hours or stand in four-and-a-half-inch sti-lettos. She wore them in her wedding all through the night."

And the fairy tale continued the following year, with the next logical chapter: *Donald and Melania Have a Baby! A Mark Burnett Production.*

In 2006, pregnant with Barron, Melania was photographed for *Vogue* by famed celebrity portraitist Annie Leibovitz. In the photo that ran in the magazine, Melania wore a gold bikini and gold paint on the steps of Trump's private plane. Donald sat in the front seat of a $188,000 Mercedes-Benz SLR McLaren nearby. Leibovitz was later quoted at one of her book signings: "[Melania] brought that gold bikini. You have to understand Melania loved taking that picture. Trump was blasé about where he should be. I didn't make it up. I met them on the tarmac, the plane was there, and I saw the graphics of the stairway and I put Melania in it and the rest is what it is. They loved that."

Before she met Donald, Melania was single, striving, with an uncertain future. Ten years later, she was polished, married, a *Vogue* cover model, a mother, and an American citizen. Ten years after *that*, she became First Lady of the United States.

Looking at Melania's transformation from a distance, I can see clearly how many players and influencers were involved in her seamless creation.

Millions of Americans watched *The Apprentice*. Donald was a household name, a flashy brand like no other. And he needed a woman who looked and played the part and let him be the star. He used his ace in the hole, Anna Wintour, to bring Melania up to snuff. He used *Vogue*, a distinguished brand, to create a star—not just Melania, but himself as well. If his bride was a *Vogue* cover model, it legitimized him, too. The Trumps resembled a close enough version of the true product to convince people who couldn't tell the difference.

Donald, who has been called "the King of Bling," taught Melania how to master the *perception* of prestige and influence. Rolex, the luxury timepiece brand, is called "the King of Watches." Donald is a Rolex man. He owns a gold Rolex President, the same watch that was worn by Lyndon B. Johnson.

I was there at the beginning. I witnessed the transformation of Melania from gold plate into twenty-four-karat gold. I believed she had the heart to match, that she was genuinely caring and loving and worth all of our attention. Throughout our early friendship, she lived up to what I saw in her. Watching her now, and seeing that only the gold shell remains, I have to wonder if that's all she ever was, and I was the sucker who bought the fake watch on the street corner.

— 2 —

Opposites Attract

When Melania and I were first becoming friends, I thought we complemented each other, like Lucy and Ethel, or Snooki and JWoww. Essentially, our differences attracted us to each other and were the reason we became so close and our interactions seemed effortless.

Our different values, backgrounds, outlooks, and philosophies kept us enthralled. It was a friendship of endless discovery, especially since she kept so much of herself private.

The first difference I noticed between us was that Melania carried herself with real confidence from the inside out, while my confidence was sporadic, frequently outweighed by insecurity.

As soon as she stepped into the *Vogue* offices, it was as if she was in the movie *Aladdin* and her genie was taking his bride on a magic carpet ride. Her relationship with Donald *was* life altering for her. It catapulted her from "model" to "MODEL." Thanks to him, she actually had the magazine covers and photo shoots she would claim that she'd always had on her efforts alone.

Exuding confidence was paramount. She wanted to appear assured, mysterious, and strong to the outside world, and she did. I saw those qualities in her and was hooked. When she looked in the mirror, she probably saw what everyone else did. Her Confident Melania self-image and her true self, I believe, are one and the same.

The true self in my mirror, the one precious few really know, isn't nearly as confident and strong as I might appear to be. I have doubts, insecurities, self-esteem issues I can't hide from. My friends know when I'm not feeling my best. Melania would never let anyone see her vulnerable.

From that first day, I envied Melania's confidence and her ability to put herself first. For a people pleaser like me, I was fascinated. I always got sucked into other people's needs and wants. She never apologized for putting her needs first. Over the years to come, I'd hear her say, "Pleasing anyone else is not my priority!"

Life Philosophies

Philosophically speaking, Melania seemed to follow Plato, the Greek philosopher, who believed in the control and mastery of emotion. He described emotion and reason as "two horses pulling us in opposite directions." Not saying Melania is always reasonable, but her first instinct is to suppress emotion.

My first instinct is to wallow and/or bask in my feelings, and to express them. If I tried to suppress my emotions, I might explode. I prefer the philosophy of Plato's best student, Aristotle, who believed that it is essential for a good life to learn to experience a full range of emotion. Which I would, and Melania could work her magic to calm me down with a look or a comment. I felt like I needed her. And I was only too happy to help her when she needed me.

My "glass half-empty" pessimism would get the best of me, and her "cup runneth over" optimism would be there to pick me up. I admired how she always stayed levelheaded and in control. Her even keel brought the best out in me.

Self-Care

I have a tendency to put things off. Not work or family stuff, but what I need to do for my own health and wellness—for example, making and keeping doctor and dentist appointments. My nails? Bitten to the quick. Hair? I go for months without a cut. I end up hiding my roots with TopSecret Hair Fibers.

Melania takes *extremely* good care of herself, inside and out. Especially out. She rarely left her Trump Tower penthouse without an immaculate outfit. She has a glam squad at her beck and call, although she does just fine without them. She's mastered the art of Melania, always seeming perfect, model-like. She would rarely let someone see her without a full face of makeup and a perfect do. Don't bother asking her for tips, though. She won't share which cosmetics brands she uses.

I remember one lunch at our favorite restaurant, Harry Cipriani, located near Central Park, off the lobby of the Sherry-Netherland hotel in New York City. I ran in late, as usual, lugging my purse with me. I might as well have been carrying around my kitchen sink, it was such a mess. I saw her through the glass door. She was already seated at our table, front and center, cool as a cucumber.

Melania and I did our usual round of "sweeties," kisses, and hugs. Then I dropped my bag on the floor.

Her eyes widened and threatened to pop out. "Don't put your bag on the floor! Put it on the chair. What's *in* there?"

Uh, Post-it notes with scribbles I couldn't read, old insurance claim forms I needed to mail in, receipts, tickets, candy wrappers, makeup I never wore, a hairbrush I never used, a few hair scrunchies, a dozen pens and Sharpies, my agenda, notepads, a can of Coke Zero, and a bag of dried mangoes. Your basic mess.

Melania's purse was always pristine, and she treated it with gentle care. At times she only had her green American Express on her, sans purse. My bags got a daily beating and showed it. She understood that I carried my life in my bags, but she wrinkled her nose at how disorganized they were.

"How do you find anything?"

"Well, I use my hand like a claw, see, and just grab what I can and see what comes up." I demonstrated and came up with a handful of already-chewed hard gum nuggets wrapped in scraps of paper. "It can get kind of sticky, though . . ."

She looked at me with great bemusement.

Careers

Melania's career is to support her husband. I have worked since I got out of college. The milestones have been my job at *Vogue* and being the founding fashion director at Lincoln Center, where I produced Mercedes-Benz Fashion Week with IMG Fashion, a job I accepted at Anna's suggestion and that I dutifully held for several years. When I got caught up in the politics between IMG Fashion and all the various constituents at Lincoln Center for the Performing Arts, I felt like my hands were tied. Anna gave me the best advice. "Leave," she said. And I did.

I created my own consulting company, SWW Creative, where I worked with clients and companies including Hermès, American Express, CAA, Mattel, and the New York Knicks, to name a few. I was removed from the headaches of working for a large corporation and gained freedom that allowed me to produce and work on several TV and film projects, including The Style Awards with Penske Media Corporation and the feature films *37: A Final Promise* and *Inside Game*, something I'd always been interested in pursuing.

Melania's career has been patchy. She modeled, as we have all been told ad nauseam, in her late teens and early twenties. To me, she sometimes referenced her background in design, but fleetingly. She studied architecture at the University of Ljubljana but dropped out after her freshman year to sign up with an Italian modeling agency. "Her career as a model officially began in 1992 when she won second place in the 'Face of the Year' contest," according to an article by Gerardo Reyes for Univision News. Melania rarely spoke to me about her modeling career in Paris and Milan from 1992 to 1996, after which she moved to New York.

Reputable modeling jobs were set up for her after Donald came into her life in 1998. She stopped working entirely when Barron was born in 2006. Four years later, in 2010, she sold the Melania Timepieces & Jewelry line on QVC. At the time, she told me excitedly that she had "meetings, so many meetings, about this and that," and that she had drawn some sketches for the line. Although QVC sales were brisk, that venture ended after one season. A couple of years later, she developed a skin-care line and heavily promoted Melania Beauty Caviar Complexe C6 in 2013 on *The Celebrity Apprentice* and *Good Morning America*, but due to a series of lawsuits between the owners of the company she was working with, the line wasn't made readily available in stores.

In all fairness, Melania was only twenty-eight when she met Donald, and she was very well aware of what he wanted—and didn't want—in his third wife. He wasn't the kind of husband who cheered on his wife's career. Melania told me the secret of her long marriage to him is that she is completely different from his other wives. Unlike Marla Maples, Melania didn't pressure him emotionally. Unlike Ivana, Donald's first wife, who ran one of his Atlantic City casinos and sold jewelry and clothes on QVC for a decade, Melania didn't pressure Donald for things to do.

As a publicity and marketing expert, I was confused about why Melania didn't use the name Trump to sell her products. She said, "I want it to be mine." She'd spent a decade on Donald's arm by the time she launched her brand. Perhaps she was ready to stand on her own? Did she believe her own hype, that her celebrity would be enough to move product? She insists that she was always a "top model," even *before* she met Donald, and was a one-name icon like Cher or Beyoncé. All she thought she needed to do was slap a big letter M on a pump bottle, and it would fly off the shelves.

But still, why *not* use the Trump brand for that extra nudge? Perhaps she wasn't telling me the whole truth. It was entirely possible that Donald didn't allow her to use his name. After all, another female family member had a lock on Trump-branded women's products. Ivanka had sat next to Donald in the boardroom on *The Apprentice* and *The Celebrity Apprentice*, and brand integrations were a hallmark of the show. Ivanka had launched Ivanka Trump Fine Jewelry in 2007 and become the name and face of the Spa by Ivanka Trump in Trump hotels in 2009, and she would launch her apparel and accessories brands in 2011. In a battle of the brands between Melania and Ivanka, with Donald/Daddy keeping an eye on the bottom line, it's obvious who wins.

Relationships

I had the same boyfriend from my junior year in high school through my years in college at Fordham and Loyola universities. In my early twenties, I decided to expand my horizons. My husband, David, likes to tease me and say, "She dated an Alex from every country, who spoke every language, and who came in every size . . . mainly short." (In reality, it was only two guys named Alex.)

The story of how David and I met is pretty cute, if I do say so myself. Unbeknownst to us, we had three mutual friends, Andrea, Mitch, and Jeff, who didn't know each other. One afternoon, Mitch called David at the office and said, "Hey, check out my girlfriend in *Time* magazine." It was a close-up of Mitch's girlfriend and me. The two of us were bidding for clients during the Jackie O auction.

"That's great!" David said. "Who's the good-looking broad next to her?"

We played the telephone game for six months. After having dinner with Andrea, I realized the David she'd been trying to fix me up with was also Jeff and Mitch's David, who'd left ignored messages on my answering machine. I ran home and called him back. It all felt serendipitous and predestined. We got married four years later, March 18, 2000, at the Pierre Hotel, with three hundred of our family and friends—including Anna and André—in attendance.

I've had to attend a lot of gatherings and events throughout my career, but given the choice, I would have gladly stayed home and cuddled on the couch in our apartment with my hubby and our children.

Melania has never been much of a party girl, either. Her former manager Paolo Zampolli once told the *New York Post*, "She only went to movies by herself and to the gym. This is a woman who modeled for Camel cigarettes on a huge billboard . . . but stayed home all the time." I believe it. The Melania I know preferred to sit around the penthouse in her Trump bathrobe or to march around with weights on her ankles, pumping her pink dumbbells. I visited her at Trump Tower more times than I can count. I have lived in my current apartment (five blocks from her) for six years, and Melania has never stepped foot inside it. One evening, we were texting, and I wrote, "Why don't you just come over?" like you'd say to any close friend. She laughed at the insanity of that idea, as in, "Yeah, like *that's* going to happen," and demurred. She is a "come to me" person.

It's been reported that Melania had dated a Slovenian while in college. I'm only aware of a previous boyfriend in Paris or Milan. She "dated" before Donald, of course. Her former roommate, photographer Matthew Atanian, told *GQ* that when Melania first arrived in New York at twenty-six, "she didn't go out to dance clubs; she'd go to Harry Cipriani for dinner at ten and be home by one. Men she would go out with tended to be wealthier, the industrious, European type. They were Italians, playboys. But they'd go out for dinner and she'd be home before [I] was."

Melania and Donald met not-so-cute. As the story goes, the then–twenty-eight-year-old model caught the eye of the world's greatest self-promoting real estate developer in September 1998 at a party during Fashion Week at the Kit Kat Club in Times Square, when he was still married to his second wife and dating Norwegian cosmetics heiress Celina Midelfart. As soon as he spotted Melania, he zeroed in on his future bride.

People often ask me what it's like to go on a double date with Donald and Melania. But that assumes that they are a normal couple that does normal things, like meet friends for dinner or go see a show. Of the few times the four of us were out together—never a double date; always with others at a charity event—the men talked about real estate and golf. Melania essentially *listens* when she goes out with Donald— because of his monologuing, it's nearly impossible for anyone to get a word in. If the two of us were seated next to each other, we would talk, but Donald had a tendency to rope her back into listening to him, as in, "Hey, baby, did you hear that? Hey, baby, am I right?" Melania never pushed Donald to spend more time with individual couples. They both liked going to openings and events to get their picture taken.

David, on the other hand, tried to avoid the red carpet as much as possible and doesn't like to "do" fancy parties that feel like more work after work. He prefers having dinner alone with me or with our close friends, hosting at home, and going to concerts and sporting events.

Friendships

Melania and I showed up for each other at personal events. She came to my surprise fortieth birthday party at MoMA; I went to her baby shower. But our friendship was lunch based. Since Melania didn't go out at night unless it was with Donald, she relied on midday meals for her social life. I kind of hate going out to lunch, since it eats up your whole workday. But if it weren't for our monthly lunch dates, Melania and I would not have become good friends. She preferred to meet on the early side, at twelve thirty, so she'd have time to pick up Barron at school at three, which she very rarely missed, and when we were together, she always offered to take me to pick up my kids, too.

A couple of times I asked her if I should invite mutual friends Rachel Roy or Pamela Gross, and she said, "Let's just do us." I had her undivided attention when I unloaded about whatever work crisis was getting me down. She listened intensely, making eye contact the whole time, as though she couldn't tear her gaze away from my face. No over-the-shoulder peeking for her. Her responses to my stories— frowning at the right moment, laughing loudly at my lame jokes—

came off as spontaneous and genuine. After one such lunch, she said with cute syntax, "Still laughing from our laughs."

We traded off paying. "It's my turn" implied that there would be a next time, and there always was. We formed an unspoken understanding that our time together was precious and needed to be protected and nurtured. Melania chose me for my company, our conversations, the way we made each other feel. No deadlines with her. Only heart outpourings (mainly mine), some serious moments, always laughs and lunch.

I thought she was smart, genuine, trustworthy, and grounded. She gave really great commonsense advice. I would tell her about a tiff with David, say how I'd gotten mad at him for playing golf on Saturdays. She'd say, "Just let him do what he's going to do. Why get in a fight about something that won't change?" It sounded like brilliant insight at the time. This piece of advice came from her own life experience and how she'd managed her own marriage. And it seemed to work for her. Can you imagine the number of men in America who would like their wives to take this kind of advice?

Any intimate question about her marriage was deflected by her seamlessly turning the chat back to what was going on with my husband, my kids, and my career, about which she was endlessly fascinated. I was all too happy to gripe about my work and have someone on the outside (but interested in) the biz to listen to me, assure me, and put me at ease. To the many, Melania is glacial, impenetrable. But to the few, she was warm and sweet, and I was her girl.

Giving

Humanitarianism is about promoting human welfare and making a positive difference for all of society. I learned about the joys of charity work from my mother, who sits on numerous philanthropic boards. Since *Vogue*, I have felt compelled to give back, donating my time and money, in particular, in areas that have impacted my own family deeply, like supporting research for food allergies, sitting on the advisory board of the Sean N. Parker Center for Allergy & Asthma Research at Stanford University, and supporting the Child Mind Institute. A constant thread in my emails with all of my friends was my asking them to donate to a charity auction. To Melania's credit, she always came through, gifting a meal at the Trump Grill or a round of golf at a Trump property. I never saw Melania or Donald simply write a check, as most of my friends and contacts did. That wouldn't have been visible enough. If they were going to give something away, people had better know about it. Although they were always invited to these charity auctions, they rarely attended them.

When she did come to an event by herself (also rarely), Melania walked in with her head up and an "I'm above all of you" attitude. She wasn't intimidated by the celebrities and power players on the guest list because she didn't give a damn about impressing anyone. Unlike most people who go to parties, Melania was not there to make friends or to network. She showed up because she wanted to (or Donald did). If she wavered about going, she didn't go.

I invited her to my farewell lunch from *Vogue* at the Trustees Dining Room at the Metropolitan Museum of Art, hosted by Anna Wintour and Emily Rafferty, the museum's president, when I resigned from the magazine in 2009. I'd been in charge of nine Met Galas, had three kids by then, and needed to slow down. Anna said, "She never lost sight of her mission: to enable the dinner to be the most fabulous event of the year, any year, in New York, so that it could raise much-needed funds to help the museum. At the last count, in Stephanie's time working on the benefit, that has meant approximately forty million dollars."

It was a beautiful party, and I was honored that so many of my friends and colleagues came to send me off. I placed Melania next to André, so she'd be comfortable and happy. She sent me an email the next day, saying it was a beautiful luncheon, that she was so happy to be a part of it, and that I looked fantastic. "If you have a second, please mail me the names of PR that you think will be great for my timepieces and jewelry line," she put at the end. "Thanks a million."

This dynamic emerged, that I was the giver in the relationship. Melania was the receiver, always looking for more. It started small, with her asking for recommendations for assistants, housekeepers, designers, florists. Even when she was thanking me for including her or helping her, she'd slip in a request for something else. At the time, it didn't faze me.

In 2010, in order to give them the best possible seats, I hosted Donald and Melania at my table at the Met Gala. As soon as Donald sat down, he asked, "Where's Anna's table?" Real estate was everything to him, and if he wasn't seated close enough to Anna, well, he wasn't happy about it. Anna was strategically seated on the other side of the room.

That same year, Melania asked for me to serve as a reference by putting my name on Barron's application to the school my boys attended. She said, "You are my best and first choice." I agreed to do it, of course, although Barron never went to that particular school.

She enlisted longtime Trump attorney Michael Cohen to help with Barron's admissions, too. He was extremely well connected on school boards. Slavishly devoted, Cohen did help Melania get Barron into Columbia Grammar & Preparatory School, which two of my kids eventually attended as well.

One day, Melania emailed that she'd dropped off Barron and spotted my middle child there. "I saw Taylor today," she wrote. "I called his name, but I don't think he recognized me."

Maybe because his name is *Tyler*, not *Taylor*. She spelled and pronounced his name incorrectly for ten years, and I never corrected her and neither did Tyler. She saw it spelled the right way in my texts, emails, and party invites but stuck with her variation. What could I do? I chalked it up to the language difference.

In 2012, Melania asked me to write a letter on behalf of her sister, Ines, who was applying for an O-1 visa. She sent me a sample letter and wanted me to write something similar.

I looked up what an O-1 visa is. It's for "individuals with extraordinary ability or achievement." To qualify, per the US government website, "the beneficiary must demonstrate extraordinary ability by sustained national or international acclaim and must be coming temporarily to the United States to continue work in the area of extraordinary ability."

This was a different kind of visa than the "Einstein" EB-1 Melania had received for "extraordinary ability in the sciences, arts, education, business, or athletics through sustained national or international acclaim," which specified, "Your achievements must be recognized in your field through extensive documentation. No offer of employment is required."

So what was Ines's area of extraordinary ability in which she would "continue to work" in the US? I had no clue.

Melania sent me a recommendation letter for Ines's application written by someone in the Trump Organization, describing her gifts in the "field of design." Mystery solved. The letter I read said, "I got to know Ines more thoroughly and I learned what a talent and visionary she is in the field of design. I heard her ambition and passion for design the more we spoke, and I realized her talent needed to be utilized immediately. As my real estate projects continue to continually develop, there is always a need for a true artist to finish the project and complete the details. The Organization enjoys a superior reputation and hires only the best and most talented staff to maintain and enhance its brand image." It went on and on. The letter writer said that Ines did work on a commercial property, but I have no idea if that was true.

I wrote my own letter, signed it, and emailed it back to Melania. I never asked her about it again. Ines got her visa and now lives in New York.

In 2013, I got an email from Melania's assistant asking me to make a call to get the Trumps invite-only tickets to the Met Gala. Didn't she know I hadn't produced the event in years? I couldn't help her. A few weeks later, I followed up and asked what she was wearing to the event, and she said, "We decided not to attend." Even to me, she fudged. The truth was, they couldn't buy or steal tickets. But her implication to me was that they had chosen not to attend. I didn't challenge it. I accepted her for who and what she was, regardless of what anyone else thought about her and her husband. I knew a Melania that no one else did, the warm, laughing softie with flashing eyes who made me feel safe.

I gave her the benefit of the doubt, and she took it.

Parenting

In 2013, I had to close my doors at SWW Creative. Zach's illness became more severe. My son was my priority, and I shifted my focus toward his care and research into uncharted territory for food allergies. I dedicated a lot of my life to learning about, supporting research into, and helping to find a cure for food allergies through trials, clinics, collaborations, and partnerships.

I invited Melania to attend an event I was hosting that I'd been working on for quite some time and she knew was important to me, to raise funds for food allergy research. She wrote that she was not available that day. I thought that was a bit abrupt, especially compared to the no from her stepdaughter Ivanka, who wrote a heartwarming note about my son and a long explanation saying that she was out of the country on the date in question.

Ivanka and I knew each other from the Met ball and other connections around New York. In 2013, David and I had dinner at her and Jared's modernist apartment—I loved it. We had a nice evening. After dinner they took us to peek in on Arabella Rose while she was sleeping. It was really kind of sweet.

Melania and Ivanka got along okay. Pre-election, Melania talked about her relationship with her husband's adult children as cordial, comfortable. From what I understood, Melania was accepted by Don Jr., Eric, and Ivanka. She hadn't broken up their parents' marriage, after all. She said that while they were growing up, they came to her for advice.

As for why Melania was uncharacteristically terse with me whenever I invited her to my food allergy fundraisers—she didn't go to any of those events—I found it weird, but I didn't push it.

"I'm so tired," I texted her after one particular event.

She replied that she didn't know how I "did it," and reminded me to take care of myself.

"I wish I had the time!"

"Schedule it!"

In January 2014, Zachary entered a clinical trial at Stanford University School of Medicine, and within three months he had already developed some immune tolerance. Melania checked in, texting weekly, sometimes daily, "How is Zachary feeling? How are you?" She remembered my birthday and wished me a "joyous and magical day! 🎉 🎉 🎉 🎈 🎈 Love you! Miss you! Let's get together for lunch soon! ❤️ ❤️ ❤️" Emojis could have been invented just for Melania and me. Those tiny little symbols said it all without having to *actually* say it, and when they came from her, they had special meaning.

In early May, I sent a photo of Zach holding a peanut M&M to family and friends that said, "Zach is HOLDING and EATING (under strict protocol) the foods he is allergic to. We all know that this is not a cure yet but a way to a 'normal' way of life where our children can go to restaurants, play dates, sleepovers, vacations and so much more." To Melania, I added a personal note: "Hi. I can't believe I haven't seen you in so long. How are you? Barron? DT? I am free whenever you are . . . I am back and forth to California every two weeks for Zach's medical trial. If you're interested would love for you to join me. XOXOXO."

Everyone else who saw that photo wrote back with great joy and excitement. When Melania replied *nine days later*, she didn't mention Zach, just tried to set up a lunch. I was hurt but I chalked it up to the reality that people are busy. I never placed any expectations on replies to emails (because I am the worst at replying and feel terrible about it).

Melania is private about her relationship with Barron, not wanting to share parenting challenges, while I am unabashedly open about being a helicopter mother. Zach has courageously overcome many health issues, but still needs a lot of my attention. I hover in protective mode. I do it with Tyler and Alexi, his younger siblings, as well. I share an extremely close bond with all three of my kids, in which there's an open line of communication, and feelings are shared and listened to. Our snuggle time, TV time, and dinner time is what I look forward to at the end of each day.

Melania is oddly secretive about her son and her experience with motherhood. If Barron got sick, she wouldn't mention it or she'd say he was feeling better once it was all over. When I complained about breastfeeding my kids—Zach for six months, Tyler for five, and Alexi for only one because I tore my C-section stitches running up the steps of the Met to get to a meeting with Anna and had to go on antibiotics—Melania didn't hop in and say, "Oh, yeah, breastfeeding is a killer!" as many women would. She just listened to me and laughed. The one time she opened up about anything childbirth related was when I told her David was in the delivery room each time. Melania revealed that Donald wasn't within two hundred feet of her delivery room. She wouldn't allow it!

It takes a village to raise children, and I am so grateful to all of the people who've helped me raise mine. I wouldn't have been able to do so, and have my career without them. Melania and I both agreed that our parents were lifesavers, and I was lucky to have my in-laws, too! Melania has perpetuated the myth that she never hired a nanny when Barron was young and that she waited to start her businesses until he went to school. But even Donald admitted that the Trumps had help. "Yes, there is a young woman, someone who works with Barron," he told the *New York Post* in October 2015. There was always someone there—the cook, Melania's assistant, and a lot of the time, her mother—to watch him. Now, at the White House, Barron hangs out with the Secret Service agents.

For two years, our kids coincided at Columbia Grammar & Preparatory School and loved it. When friends asked Melania how Barron was doing in his classes, she would say, "He's great." "Any issues?" they'd ask. "Nope!" she'd say. "He's just a boy. All the normal stuff." It didn't matter what was going on.

What's Melania like on a playdate? This is another question I get a lot. Barron's playdates were *his* playdates. Melania didn't sit around watching the kids play. Nor did she entertain the mothers who arrived and wanted face time. Many moms tried to finagle playdates. Few succeeded. I'd often hear moms at school say, "Melania and I are such good friends. I went over there for a playdate and we hung out for hours." When I'd see Melania and tell her I was happy to hear she was branching out, she'd laugh. "Oh, sure!" she'd say. It just wasn't true. Even though the vast majority of parents at Columbia Grammar are Democrats, Melania was inundated with requests after the election. She didn't change her tune. "Barron decides who he plays with," she'd say. "The playdate is not for me." Barron's isolation is a function of his parents' fame and values. Melania, fiercely private, has taught him to be the same way.

He was something of a prankster. Once, Melania and I took a stroll around the Residence. In the Lincoln Bedroom, I asked her, "Doesn't it fill you with awe to think of who has slept in here? And I don't mean Ivanka and Jared." (They had held a Shabbat service in the room the day after the inauguration.)

Melania told me a story about how Barron had secretly placed a recording device in the Lincoln Bedroom and timed it so that it made ghost moans and noises when a friend of his was in there. Melania thought it was so cute. "He's so funny!" she said.

Melania's Childhood

We all know Melania grew up in Communist Yugoslavia, now Slovenia, in a town called Sevnica. Considering that she told *GQ*'s Julia Ioffe in 2016, "I love my childhood. It was a beautiful childhood," it's just plain weird that she *never* talked about it with me. I was naturally curious about what it was like to grow up in a Communist country. I figured that if she wanted to tell her stories, she would eventually. But since she never picked up the conversation about her childhood when I shared details about mine, I let it go. I was raised that it's rude to pry.

You can go online and read the curated version of her past, the things she and a select group of approved sources—including me—have revealed, with a heaping pinch of salt. I can tell you what I've personally observed about her family relationships, having spent time with Melania and her parents in living rooms, cars, and planes.

Melania's father, Viktor Knavs (Melania changed "Knavs" to "Knauss" when she started modeling), is a sweet man, but I wouldn't characterize their relationship as super close. When Melania and her mother go back to DC after a vacation or weekend at Mar-a-Lago, Viktor sometimes stays in Florida to play golf. Father and daughter are not physically affectionate (not at all like Ivanka and Donald). Since Melania provides for her family, she and Viktor have a bit of a role reversal going on. She makes the rules. I imagine it wasn't that way growing up, but it is now.

The first time I met Viktor, I couldn't help noticing he resembled Donald physically, girth, height, and constant suit and tie. The two men are only five years apart in age. During his working years, Viktor was a dealmaker, selling used cars at a government-owned company. Basically, Melania's father was a lot like Donald.

Also like Donald, Viktor had children by multiple women, fathering Melania's older half brother, Denis Cigelnjak, with a woman not his wife. When Marija Cigelnjak told Viktor about the pregnancy, he allegedly urged her to get an abortion. She had the baby anyway. Viktor denied that the boy was his, and the mother took him to court. A blood test confirmed his paternity, and Viktor was compelled to pay child support until Cigelnjak was eighteen, but he refused to meet or acknowledge him. Melania has never met her half brother either. When Ioffe asked her about him, she said the story wasn't true. The reporter produced court documents, and Melania backtracked, saying she misunderstood the question, that her father was a private person, and, essentially, to back off. So that's one family secret Melania protected. Perhaps she learned to keep her mouth shut about her family while living under an oppressive government as a child, when one wrong word could get someone thrown in prison. Or maybe she just likes to withhold.

Melania and I are also both super close to our siblings; they're our trusted best friends. I have met her sister, Ines, but even upon threat of death, I couldn't remember a thing about her. I've heard she is a homebody. She flies so far below the radar, many people are surprised to learn that Melania has a sister at all and that they have a tight relationship.

We are also both incredibly close with our mothers, whose unconditional love is what keeps us emotionally satiated and whose support keeps us dependent. We don't keep secrets from our moms; they know *everything*, the good, the bad, and the ugly. Her mom, Amalija, is just as chic as her daughter, always kind, polite, and sincere. When they're not together, she and Melania talk every day. I've been on long car rides with Amalija, whose English is about as good as my Slovenian. Our conversations went like this:

"Melania is doing so great as First Lady!"

"Yes." Smile, nod.

"Barron seems really great, too."

"Oh, yes." Smile, nod.

Amalija is a constant calm and steady anchor at home for Barron, who speaks Slovenian fluently. (They all converse in Slovenian when together, often in front of Donald.) Her presence in his life gives Melania great comfort as she travels and attends to Donald.

Melania also looks after her parents' appointments and health care in the US. It's a big responsibility, one she shoulders without complaint. That said, when the Knavs are in a different city, Melania is happy to have some breathing room. Who can't relate to that? She's like Marlene Dietrich. She *vonts* to be alone.

My Childhood

Growing up, my extended family numbered only fourteen people. With my immediate family of five, I grew up in the Catskills, in upstate New York. My parents fought constantly. It was a bad marriage. My brothers, Gordon and Randall, and I were the reason they stayed together as long as they did. Mom was tenacious about getting us out of the house and fostering our independence. I was twelve years old and the last one to leave home to go to boarding school. Boarding school was the best decision my mom could have made for the three of us. As for my paternal grandparents, our relationship was severed during my parents' divorce. My father told his parents, "It's either them or me." They chose their son over their grandchildren. And then there were eleven family members. Mom married Bruce and we were twelve. When my maternal grandparents and my aunt Shirley passed, that left us with nine, including my mom's younger sister, my Aunt Roz, my uncle Martin, and my two cousins, Brandon and Devon. Today, I'm happy to say we are more than a bunch, at twenty-two. And I feel that we have a strong family.

Mom was our source of love and strength, a supermom parenting by herself with an emotionally distant husband, an only child whose family operated lucrative egg farms in New York State. He was miserable about following in his father's footsteps and longed to be anywhere else than there with us. Mom expected Gordon, Randall, and me to always rise to the occasion, to be the best at everything we did. B's were unacceptable and C's were forbidden. "You could be president one day," she would say to each of us.

Mom lived with a perpetual sense of danger. She was born in Germany in 1947 and resided in a displaced persons camp in Zeilsheim, eleven miles west of Frankfurt. Bobie Ethel and Papa Joel, her parents, managed to survive the Holocaust when six million others didn't. Their stories about the concentration camps were harrowing; their experiences were a huge burden to bear. My mother told me that toward the end of Bobie's life, as she was tucking my grandmother into bed,

Bobie said, "I cannot take it anymore, the nightmares and visions of the camps." She'd told me once, "I was shuttled into the back of railcars filled with horseshit, just like cattle, and when we arrived at the camp we were pulled from the cart and pushed to the left or right side. My mother knew her fate and forced me to go to the other line, leaving her and my two sisters. They were carted away to the crematoriums."

Papa was a gentle soul. An intellectual. He had a farm and did real estate investment. He worked seven days a week. Papa told us, "I had seven sisters; all were killed. I saved myself once by lying with the dead. We waited for the dogs to finish eating. Maybe there was something left."

Telling their stories would take a book. Heartbreak was evident, but they were valiant to go on with their lives and raise their children. We saw Bobie and Papa almost daily, and if they didn't come over, Mom would speak to them throughout the day. They were tough, with pure, loving souls.

Even though I was the youngest and the only girl, I was never treated like a precious little princess—I was just one of the boys. No pigtails or Barbies for me—I liked Tonto and Bruce Lee. My brothers and I bickered, threw punches, and broke a few toes kicking each other and a nose or two wrestling around. Teasing me was their idea of fun.

The three of us attended public grade school together and were bullied, mostly because we were Jewish and had a nice house. Our father said we had to learn to defend ourselves. It would have been nice to have had a dad confront the culprits of our bruises, but his words did lead us to karate class, for which we are grateful.

Mom, my brothers, and I practiced Tang Soo Do five days a week and became black belts. The *dojang* became our home away from home. Eventually, we all became black belts and were left alone. ("Your mom's a black belt, too?" Melania asked when I told her about it. She couldn't believe it!)

My brother Randall was a successful child actor who did a lot of commercials and eventually starred in some TV shows and films. Mom and Randall traveled often for his auditions in New York and

Los Angeles. Our father went away often, too, but I didn't know where. I was left in the care of Bobie and Papa, which I loved.

The last time I had any real interaction with my father was at my high school graduation from Suffield Academy. I had my diploma in hand and was looking forward to the celebration ahead. And then he dropped the D-bomb. "No matter what, I'll always love you. Your mom and I are getting a divorce," he said. Although I was never close to my father and didn't like the way he treated our mother, I was still rocked by a sense of loss.

I spent the summer after graduation in Ohio with a friend from school. Our mornings consisted of five a.m. wake-up alarms, followed by a six a.m. dash out the door to work at McDonald's. We manned the register and flipped burgers by day and got stoned by night. Two months and sixty pounds later, I returned home to New York City to be with my mom.

The next morning, I took my first subway ride to Fordham University in the Bronx, where I interviewed and was accepted. I enrolled, made the basketball team as a walk-on, and eventually received a full scholarship playing Division I basketball for the Fordham Lady Rams. I wanted nothing from the man I'd once called my dad. I had to make my own way in the world; it was a given.

My grandparents' histories with the Holocaust terrified and shaped us as a family more than anything else. My motivation to succeed as an athlete, as a student, and later in my career came from their inspiration. I have tried to match their fortitude and resilience by putting challenges in front of myself to learn what I can endure and overcome.

When I got married and became a mother myself—and proudly added to our tiny family—I was immediately immersed in Zach's food allergies and the severe anxiety it caused for him, and for all of us. If he ate the wrong thing, he would become dizzy, break out into hives, wheeze for breathe, and his face would turn a purplish red. We've had to inject him with his EpiPen *too* many times and rush him to the emergency room, with Tyler and Alexi anxiously awaiting to hear from us that he was safe. When Zach was ten, it got to the point where he was afraid to leave the house and be exposed to something that might kill him. Watching my husband, David's, love and patience with Zach was bittersweet, since I don't recall receiving either from my father. I married a far more loving and caring person than my father could ever be. Could Melania say the same?

Our backgrounds, relationships, and life experiences are so different, and yet, Melania and I bonded as women, daughters, mothers, and New Yorkers. Our common ground and devotion to each other were enough to keep our friendship going and growing. But I never thought it would change into anything bigger than a mutual admiration society of two.

I was wrong about that.

— 3 —

The Campaign Year

On June 16, 2015, Donald and Melania descended the golden escalator into the lobby of Trump Tower, where he announced his candidacy for president. It had all the hallmarks of a classic Trump spectacle. It was a flashy, splashy show. David and I watched it on TV, completely surprised. We had no idea about his intention to run. David's impression was that Donald was doing it as a business ploy, a way to prove how well he could get publicity while in the midst of his contract negotiations with NBC. Many pundits agreed that the whole campaign, from the very first time he uttered the phrase "build a wall," was an investment in his future earnings as a TV star, real estate mogul, or whatever other plot he had on his mind. I had to agree.

Melania, on the escalator, literally and figuratively, was just along for the ride. She had been asked what kind of First Lady she'd be back in 1998, when she was just the girlfriend, and replied that she'd be traditional, like Jacqueline Kennedy. An attractive, supportive wife.

I wondered if my friendship with Melania would change now that her husband had finally, after years of talking about it in the press, decided to run.

This could be interesting, I thought.

Parallel Reality

I kept track of the campaign when I could. Melania's texts kept coming, nearly every day, about the kids and her summer travels. On July 21, 2015, a month after Donald's announcement, she wrote, "DT crazy busy. Me and B[arron] have relaxing summer." Three weeks later, on August 11, from the Trump resort in Bedminster, New Jersey: "Donald is in Michigan. It's so gorgeous out. Just got back from swimming. Wish summer would last forever."

It was almost like her husband wasn't running for president, or saying "They're bringing in drugs. They're bringing crime. They're rapists" about Mexicans, or commenting that Fox News host Megyn Kelly had "blood coming out of her wherever."

Into the fall and winter, we resumed our monthly lunches and talked about our kids' schools and Halloween costumes, and our families in general. She barely spoke about the campaign at all. When she went to New Hampshire for the Republican primary in February 2016, she didn't text about the excitement of the campaign or Donald's groundswell of support. She wrote about the weather, saying that it was cold and snowy. *Breaking news!*

When I asked her about the hotel, she said that she brought her own linens, pillows, and terry robe. She always did.

In late February into early March, she texted me the chronicle of her kidney stone's long journey to freedom while not once mentioning the heated debate that week between Donald and Florida senator Marco Rubio about whether Donald's hands (and other parts) were unusually small. It really felt like they were living in parallel realities.

Melania's emails and texts to me increased in quantity that year. More lunch-date requests, more favors. Reporters needed sources for their articles about her. No one in her family spoke fluent English, so they were out. As for friends, she handpicked a very select group of us, each one blindly faithful to her.

On November 18, 2015, she asked me to talk to writer Alex Kuczynski for *Harper's Bazaar* and I agreed. "Thank you!" she replied. "I know you will say great things. Watch 20/20 Friday. Barbara Walters interview. Pink dress! 😀 😀 😀 🖤 🖤 🖤" She was very excited about that dress. The interview was almost beside the point.

I asked her, "What would you like for me to say?"

She texted me some guidelines about the upcoming interview. I was to say that she and Donald met fifteen years go. That she was born in Slovenia. That her sister and parents wanted to have a private life. That it was her decision not to be a part of the campaign. That she was devoted to raising Barron. That she'd had a successful business and was now "enjoying life" and being a mom. The "enjoying life" part was evident. "Thank you!" she texted. "I am in Caribbean. So gorgeous. Just want to stay here."

Here's how Kuczynski quoted me: "According to Stephanie Winston Wolkoff, a fashion-industry consultant who has known Melania for nearly 20 years, Melania's even keel is part of what makes the Trump marriage work. 'Donald is always full speed ahead. It is constant with him,' she says. 'But Melania went into the marriage understanding who he was, and she is accepting of him.'"

"Perfect!" Melania said.

I was enlisted again in May 2016, to talk to *DuJour* reporter Mickey Rapkin. By that point, Melania had been the target of a lot of media attacks about her family, how she'd gotten her visa, why she wasn't more present on the campaign trail. She told me to tell Mickey that all the stories written about her were inaccurate. "Not many people know me and have [a] wrong picture of me," she said.

That wasn't going to work with a reporter, but okay. I would be Melania's good soldier. Sure enough, he wrote about every speck of dirt he could find, but he did give Melania plenty of room to talk about Donald in similar terms to those in which she'd spoken to me privately about Barron ("boys will be boys").

From Rapkin's article: "She uses that same phrase—'Men will be men'—when asked about Donald's old appearances on Howard Stern's show, which had recently resurfaced online. Stern once asked if Donald would stay with Melania if she suffered a horrific car accident, and he replied: 'How do the breasts look?' A similar vibe was conveyed when Trump came out onstage at a town-hall meeting at the University of Pennsylvania in 1999 and shouted, 'Where's my supermodel?'"

My contribution was preapproved by Melania: "Don't underestimate her just because she is quiet and reserved. There is virtue in the fact that she appears to be quiet and isn't on the front lines constantly saying, *Hear me, see me.* But she's very confident in her viewpoint. She does not agree with everything that [Donald] says or everything that's being done, but she believes in the greater good. They are a power couple. They are each other's teammate. He's out there. He has so much going on. It isn't about her yet. She has always said, when and if the time comes, she will step up. She's a wife and a mother until that day comes."

She thanked me for speaking to the reporter, and texted often about how much she valued our friendship and loved me. She always asked about my kids. I asked her for a similar favor, to talk to a *Hollywood Reporter* journalist who was writing a piece about the Met Gala. I thought she could recount some of her experiences there or describe her favorite gown. She didn't reply to my request all day and then wrote that she hadn't seen it because she was in the spa, taking some time off so she could relax. "Not in the mood to talk to HR," she said. I didn't push it. She could have done what she'd always done with press inquiries and just emailed her response. But Melania does not do what she doesn't want to do, period.

Whenever I thought about the possibility of Donald's winning the election, I (now regretfully) brushed aside his divisive rhetoric and deplorable behavior, like mocking reporters or other candidates (and their wives) because of their physical appearance. Instead, my mind immediately went to what Melania could do from atop the highest, broadest platform on Earth, and what good *I* could do as a private citizen if she became an actively engaged First Lady who wanted to effect change and allowed me to give her advice. We could do a hell of a lot.

From the very beginning, Melania told me her initiative as First Lady, if that position became a reality, would be about helping children and families. We began what would be a two-year-long mission to make a profound impact in that area. She wanted to focus it on cyberbullying. I thought she'd need to broaden the scope. Her heart was in the right place, but her messaging was off. How could Melania get on a soapbox about cyberbullying when her husband was Public Enemy Number One on that score? It was as if she had no idea what he was tweeting.

While he was crisscrossing the country, she stayed home at Trump Tower or went to their other residences in Palm Beach and Bedminster. She would text me from various locations, writing nearly identical notes, like, "In Palm Beach. Wish to stay here. So gorgeous!" or "In the Caribbean—so gorgeous! Just want to stay here." It seemed like she wanted to be anywhere *but* the campaign trail. She didn't register an iota of the excitement that Donald clearly felt at the rallies.

Many times, while I visited her at Trump Tower or shared a car with her, Donald would call her from Ohio, or Nevada, or Michigan, to check in. She'd answer with a breathy "Hello?" He'd say, "Hey, baby, did you see my speech?" She would give me a knowing look and adoringly tell him, "You did a great job, honey!"

One evening, we were on our cell phones talking for hours while he was at some rally. She lost track of time and didn't watch a minute of it. The landline rang, and when she realized it was Donald calling she said, "Oops, I forgot to watch his speech!" We laughed that she'd missed him on TV entirely, but she was off to answer his call and, I'm sure, to praise his performance to the skies.

Melania's Convention Speech

One of Melania's rare campaign appearances was in April 2016 in Milwaukee, Wisconsin, where she was going to give a speech. She texted me on April 4 that she was headed to Wisconsin, and hated traveling alone in bad weather. She was anxious about her speech. "The more I think about it, the more knots I have in my throat," she said.

"You will be fine. Take deep breaths and close your eyes."

"I am doing that a whole day already!" she said.

She managed to deliver her rally speech, which I assume she wrote herself. It closed like like a love poem:

He's a hard worker.
He's kind.
He has a great heart.
He's tough.
He's smart.
He's a great communicator.
He's a great negotiator.
He's telling the truth.
He's a great leader.
He's fair.
As you may know by now, when you attack him, he will punch
*   back ten times harder.*
No matter who you are, a man or a woman, he treats everyone
*   equal.*
He's a fighter.
And if you elect him to be your president, he will fight for you
*   and for our country. He will work for you and with you and*
*   together we will make America strong and great again.*

Look, she wasn't in an editorial meeting at the *New Yorker*. She was addressing a crowd of supporters who hadn't come to listen to her. She kept it short and simple.

Donald applauded her when he came onstage and said to her, "So beautiful."

She smiled placidly. From the way she inhaled sharply, she knew she had delivered. Despite what you may have read, Melania had told me many times that she wanted Donald to win.

One appearance Melania could not get out of was the July 2016 Republican National Convention in Cleveland, Ohio. Not only would she have to show up and sit through so many speeches, she'd have to give one herself, as would all four of Donald's adult children.

On June 28, she told me, "Miss you. Working on my speech for the convention. Love you."

That sent a chill down my spine. Melania had good ideas, but she was not a native English speaker or skillful writer. I called her and suggested she work with a professional and mentioned the name of someone I knew. I followed up with a text: "Do you want me to introduce you? I will never bother you, but I am here for you and would love to help you and guide you. You know you can trust me and I know I can trust you. I love you and all I care about is making sure you are protected and ready."

She replied with the usual "love you" and "you're the best." But she said she didn't want to talk to my guy "for now."

Three weeks later, she came out of the shadows and had her moment in the spotlight. My family and I watched her speech on CNN. I wasn't such a fan of her fluffy white dress with Popeye sleeves by designer Roksanda Ilinčić, but I was pleased with her delivery—I thought she came across as poised, confident, and warm. The press reported rhapsodically that Melania had insisted on writing the speech by herself, which I didn't believe. She probably did a draft, but someone else's hands had been on it.

We all know what went down within hours afterward. A political journalist named Jarrett Hill noticed that passages in Melania's speech were practically word-for-word identical to a 2008 convention speech by Michelle Obama. The next day, I texted Melania, "Do not listen to the noise. But from now on, I want to read the speeches. I mean it . . . the heck with all of them."

It wasn't quite an "I told you so," but I had been suspicious about why Melania was allowed to work on her own speech for even one minute. You'd think someone would be paying closer attention to the woman who could be First Lady.

Unlike, say, Ivanka, who probably had the top five people on the campaign working on her speech with focus group vetting and multiple full-staff rehearsals, Melania had no one in her corner. She didn't have a handpicked, loyal communications team backing her up. One could say that since she didn't participate in the primaries, it stands to reason that none of the campaign staff knew her well or cared that much about her. But Melania was going out on that stage as the wife of the nominee. Out of the most basic respect and consideration, someone of high caliber should have helped her, or at least read her speech or done due diligence by running it through a plagiarism search program on the Internet. Melania was treated like a second-class citizen and her speech was an afterthought, dashed off.

She replied on July 20, "Don't worry. Liberal media bashing. Nothing new. It is not the first time or last time. Love you!"

But . . . the media was only reporting the truth. The plagiarism was undeniable. The real story was how the Trump campaign could ever let this happen. Trump surrogates like Sean Spicer went into overdrive to defend Melania, making all kinds of excuses, even saying that the lifted paragraphs weren't all that original in the first place. The "official story" was that Melania had given Obama's speech to her collaborator, a Trump Organization ghostwriter named Meredith McIver, for inspiration, and somewhere along the way, those passages made it into the final draft. McIver took all the blame and offered to resign from her long-standing job at Donald's company. He refused to accept her resignation.

If you're caught plagiarizing in school, you get in trouble. But no one really suffered from this incident. No firings. No public flogging.

How did Melania *really* feel about the incident?

She was not all that humiliated. Any other human would have been. But she doesn't do shame. She *was* suspicious that the plagiarism had been left in on purpose. *Someone* in Trump World didn't want Melania to shine. We talked about who that might be. Who stood to gain by making Melania look bad? Our conversations were guarded, and she kept it light, as always. But it seemed to her, and to me, that the plagiarized speech was like drawing first blood between rivals. Or was it a warning that Melania should stay in the background?

The Naked Photos

It's believed that Melania was so mortified by what happened at the convention that she brushed her hands off and said "That's that" about doing another damn thing for the campaign. In truth, she did take five giant steps back, but not because she was mortified or embarrassed. It was obvious no one had her back, so this gave her an excuse to stay in the background. She used her "devastation" to beg off any further duties, and no one, not Hope Hicks or Kellyanne Conway or even Donald himself, was in any position to convince her otherwise.

She was happy.

She was relieved.

She was back at home.

Back with Barron.

In her bathrobe.

With a smile on her face.

Ten days after the convention, Melania was in the hot seat again. She couldn't avoid it, even sequestered in her penthouse.

Rupert Murdoch's *New York Post* ran a nude photo of Melania on the cover with the leering headline "The Ogle Office." The pictures (more were published inside the paper) had been taken in 1996, when she was twenty-five, and had run in *Max*, a French men's magazine, in 1997. As awkward as it may have been for Melania to explain to Barron why Mommy was nude on the cover of a tabloid, I'm sure one part of her looked at the images and thought, *Damn, I look good.* Many a woman would be publicly outraged but privately gloating.

As soon as I saw the paper, I texted, "Hi. WTF! I just saw the Post. Want to talk?"

She wrote back immediately, "Not surprised. They would do anything to bash me. No worries. Not first time. Will not be last. Have a thick skin. Liberal media making big deal of nothing. One day story. Love you."

But . . . the *Post* wasn't the "liberal media."

Trump and Murdoch have a bromance. It was rumored, and

widely acknowledged within Trump circles, that Donald himself was responsible for his pal media mogul Rupert Murdoch's learning about the existence of the photos. Why do it? Perhaps Donald just needed to move the national conversation away from whatever incendiary tweet he'd posted that day. Or to change the conversation from Donald's indiscretions. Or he had to back up his frequent claims of her being a "top model." (She'd already been outed for the claim in her bio that she'd graduated from college with a degree.) Or maybe he thought his campaign needed to show America exactly what he was getting into bed with (on the nights they were in the same city), (on the nights they were in the same room), (on the nights they were in the same bed).

As far as I know, Melania never forgave Rupert Murdoch. Knowing how the press operated, I spent the weekend at my in-laws' home in Quogue, locked in my bedroom, researching *Max* and those who've graced the cover, to legitimize it as a real fashion publication and not just some spank mag. My kids banged on my door, asking me to come outside and join them. Instead, since Melania didn't have anyone on the campaign team she could trust, I stepped up and wrote a memo for her in case the press asked her to defend herself, not that she needed to say anything.

To: MT
From: SWW
Date: July 31, 2016
Re: Max Magazine

FACTS THAT YOU CAN SAY
"I HAVE WRITTEN MYSELF":

- Supermodels and celebrities have graced the cover of MAX magazine.
- All of the most coveted photographers, such as Mario Testino, Terry Richardson, Helmut Newton, Annie Leibovitz, and Richard Avedon, photograph models in the nude.

- All of the most magnificent museums celebrate the beauty of the human form.
- Nudity is an expression of one's self. You are confident and strong. Empowering.
- You are a kind, intelligent and beautiful woman who is being portrayed as someone who is unqualified to become the First Lady. You welcome the challenge and stand tall.
- You have nothing to be ashamed of and you have nothing to hide. You were a model and were fortunately at the right place at the right time.
- Life is about embracing the unexpected moments and living every moment in the moment. When you became Mrs. T, you had to adapt to the world Mr. T. lived in, and you did so in a sophisticated and elegant manner. We all go through transformations when given the opportunity to do so.
- You should not be scrutinized and polarized because you met and married DT. You were a model. On the go. Living in the moment. HE picked YOU. He was a real estate tycoon and celebrity.
- You live your life caring for your immediate family.

Along with Melania's talking points, I included a 1996 *Max* cover with future French first lady Carla Bruni (Sarkozy) without a shirt on. The memo was the first I'd write for Melania's defense against the media and the first where I gave her language to say that she had written herself. In the White House, my ghostwriting for her would become a daily part of my job.

I sent her the memo in the early morning, and within hours, Trump advisor and speechwriter Jason Miller went on CNN's *Reliable Sources* and said, "These were photos that are twenty years old, before Mrs. Trump met Mr. Trump. They're a celebration of the human body as art. There's nothing to be embarrassed about with the pictures. She's a beautiful woman."

My talking points exactly. I could help my friend, keep my privacy, and protect her. It seemed like the perfect combination since nearly everyone I knew in fashion, entertainment, and the media hated the Trumps with a passion. I didn't hide my feelings for Melania or that I was helping her from my friends. But I did want to retain a degree of anonymity out of respect for her.

Several weeks after the *Post* covers (there was a second one, with pictures of a naked Melania in an embrace with another nude model), a Maryland blogger named Webster Griffin Tarpley posted an article alleging that Melania's modeling agency in Europe was actually a high-end escort service. A couple of weeks after that, on August 20, 2016, British tabloid the *Daily Mail* published an article online with the headline "Naked Photoshoots, and Troubling Questions About Visas That Won't Go Away: The VERY Racy Past of Donald Trump's Slovenian Wife," which echoed Tarpley's claims. She sued both, with a vengeance, and they retracted.

Still, Melania's nude pictures and all that escort smoke hinted at the very real possibility that perhaps she had other secrets yet to be revealed.

By August 21, she was way over it. She texted from Bedminster: "How are you? How is Z? DT and B won parent/child [golf] championship. So boys are happy. Lunch? The Mark?"

Charlie Who?

Designer Rachel Roy and I have been friends for years. We worked together on many projects, and I included her in symposia and helped her on her presentations and installations during Fashion Week. We saw each other on joint family vacations, hung out, had dinners. We had a normal friendship, like any two women. I was the connective tissue between Rachel and Melania, and, through me, their relationship went up a notch. Rachel sometimes joined us at lunches and on group texts.

On September 8, 2016, Rachel, Melania, and I had a lunch date at the Jean-Georges restaurant at the Trump International Hotel & Tower. I remember Melania wore a cream Balmain jacket and looked like she was floating on air. She was happy that day, the vexing summer behind her, Barron back in school. She could relax with her two pals over a great meal.

Jean-Georges Vongerichten himself stopped by our table in the middle of the restaurant to say *bonjour* and give kisses all around. Every person in the restaurant seemed to watch the interaction, including a swarm of ten Secret Service agents in black that dotted the periphery of the restaurant. We were conscious of being the center of attention, so we leaned forward with our elbows on the table, our three foreheads practically touching, and talked in giggly whispers so no one could hear.

We gossiped and discussed the business Rachel and I were trying to get going, but we kept bringing it back to the obvious, saying, "Holy shit. Can you believe you might be First Lady?"

Melania laughed and beamed and said, "I know, right?" She was just enjoying a lighthearted moment with pals. If she was worried about the election, which was two months away, she gave no sign of it at all.

I needed the friendly distraction, too. Work was busy, deals were pending, and my kids' health issues were flaring up. I didn't want to bring any of it up at lunch. This meal was about fun. I needed a break, if only for an hour.

After we finished, we exited the restaurant, still inside the narrow entryway, and began our goodbyes. "Wait," Rachel said, "get together! We need to take a picture!"

The three of us scrunched together, posing for some selfies, while I snapped away.

We were all in a giddy mood and started to do what we called the Melania pose, fixing our hair, acting up. In that state of mind, it was all silly and hilarious. When you get Melania laughing so hard she cries, it's impossible not to feel joy deep in your heart, and all three of us were basking in friend love.

When we left, Escalades were lined up all along the curb, swarming with security. It was a shocking reminder that the woman we'd just been taking duck-face selfies with was under constant 24/7 protection by people with guns.

Our text exchange the next day was strictly middle school:

MT: So much fun 😎
RR: I'm still laughing about our selfies. 😄
SWW: Love, love, love.
MT: 🖤 🖤 🖤
SWW: Charlie's Angels have nothing on us.

Election Night

The first time I voted in a presidential election was in 2016. Two reasons I hadn't voted before: (1) I knew nothing about policy. If you asked me the difference between Barack Obama's and Mitt Romney's stances on immigration or to explain their economic plans, I would not know where to begin. (2) I fell exactly in the middle between Democrat and Republican. On some issues I care deeply about, I would never vote Republican. I'm conservative in other areas and can't in good conscience vote Democratic. Unable to choose, I just couldn't pull the lever. I know that people have fought and died for my right to vote, and it was wrong of me not to perform my civic duty. I was patriotic in my support of American charities and local causes, but my activism was apolitical. My humanitarian work wasn't about left vs. right or red vs. blue. It was about right vs. wrong.

But on the morning of Tuesday, November 8, 2016, I performed my civic duty with excitement. David and I voted together. Like him, my mother, and my in-laws, I voted for Trump. I was aware that the vast majority of my fellow New Yorkers had probably voted for Hillary Clinton. New York City was a Democratic stronghold and Clinton's home base. The fashion and entertainment industries in particular were actively supporting Hillary Clinton. I understood why my colleagues and city were loyal to her and that if they knew I'd voted for her opponent, they might have some choice words for me. I pushed aside all of the Trump hate around me and voted for my friend's husband.

On election night, colleagues and friends were celebrating at the Jacob K. Javits Convention Center on Eleventh Avenue in Manhattan, where Clinton was expected to break the figurative glass ceiling by becoming the first woman president in our nation's history.

I was in midtown, at Pietro's on East Forty-Third Street, with my husband, kids, and in-laws, celebrating my father-in-law's birthday. Our plan was to bring the kids home, change, and head out to the New York Hilton on Sixth Avenue for the invite-only Trump election-night party. Melania and I texted early and said we'd see each other there.

After dinner, we headed back to our apartment, went into the playroom, and turned on the television. I was like a nervous schoolkid, unable to keep still. David and the children were in and out of the room, but I didn't want to miss a moment. Donald was winning states that Hillary should have won, but his victory was not guaranteed.

David came to sit next to me with a big grin. He said, "If we're going to go, we should leave in about thirty minutes."

I leapt up, filled with excitement, and started clapping. "Yes! Let's go!"

Zachary and Tyler looked at me like, *What's wrong with you?* Alexi couldn't wait to help me pick out my outfit and get ready.

"You'll see, he's going to win," I said. With that, I strutted out of the room, down the hall, and into my bedroom with Alexi.

I stared at my closet, not sure what to wear. Automatically, I grabbed my red Altuzarra suit, thinking, *It's perfect. American made. Good start.*

"I love it, Mommy," Alexi said, "but that's a lot of red."

I wasn't sure if it was *too* red, but I knew who would know.

I called Rachel in Los Angeles. "Hi," I said. "I'm on my way to Trumpland."

She said, "Shut up! You're a good friend to show support."

We talked over each other, laughing. Every other word out of our mouths had four letters.

Rachel agreed with Alexi that my outfit was way too loud, too obvious, and advised I should wear something "neutral." I wore a cream pussy-bow blouse and a black suit with white stitching.

"Love you, honey," I said. "I will call you from there."

"Don't forget to take selfies!" Rachel said.

David and I taxied to the Hilton at around ten p.m. Our family friend Steven Mnuchin, Trump's campaign finance chair, came out to meet us and take us to a private reception. The place was packed with Trump supporters. At first, not all of them really believed he'd win. But as the night wore on, with more and more states turning red, Trump's victory seemed inevitable. The excitement level got higher and higher. At 2:30 a.m., Wisconsin went for Trump, pushing him over the line of the 270 electoral votes needed for victory. Clinton conceded at 2:35 a.m. on Wednesday morning. When news of that rolled through the crowd, the Hilton erupted. I was cheering along, jumping higher than most, even in my heels. Underneath the pulsing energy of the crowd, I was quietly, privately, proud and thrilled for Melania. I remember thinking that hers was a great American immigrant story, and certainly one of the most unique.

Victory had been declared, but there was no sign of the victor. The crowd didn't seem to know what to do next. I texted Melania, "People are starting to leave! What are you doing?"

She replied, "We're on the way!"

I shouted to David, "They're on the way!"

A few minutes later, the Trump family arrived at the Hilton and took the stage. I was cheering from below, videotaping their entrance and Donald's acceptance speech, while commenting on a group text with Rachel Roy and Melania.

Rachel, who was watching on CNN, texted, "DT is amazing! MT is so beautiful! Speech very Donald who we all know and love."

I scoffed at her flattery. (Rachel was a lifelong Democrat.)

"Our work is just beginning. Let's be the change we want to see in the world. Let's work for women and children." Rachel again. She'd been involved in children's causes at the United Nations and worked closely with Deepak Chopra on them. I couldn't have agreed more. Melania, with our help, could shine a light on the needs of child refugees and so much more. Unlike Rachel, though, I knew that as soon as a friend asked Melania to get involved in a business-type partnership, she would bristle. It was too close for comfort, not her style to mix the two. I'd never done it. And now Rachel was promoting her agenda and advocating for a role before Melania had even left the Hilton stage.

I wrote, "Here we go, girls. We're going to laugh a lot." What I thought of as a sign-off.

Rachel kept going: "This shit is crazy. You have always been this role. You have lived it. You got this! Saying a prayer for Donald's safety!" Melania has always been the role of First Lady? Really? Twenty years ago, she had been a barely-getting-by model in Paris. Thirty years ago, she'd lived in Communist Slovenia. Rachel was a bit overexcited.

I tried to get to the heart of the matter. "We love you. Strong support."

Melania finally texted back at four a.m., "Love you both."

The next day, Rachel asked to meet Melania and her mom for a celebration lunch in NYC or DC. Melania's answer: "I need to see my schedule," to which Rachel replied, "Yes, Madame President. No pressure ♥."

I'm not sure it ever happened. Melania does so hate to be asked for anything.

— 4 —

The Setup

*I*magine if your close friend suddenly, unexpectedly, became one of the most powerful, influential women in the whole world. What could she, and you, do from atop that mile-high platform? End violence against women? Fight hunger? Promote literacy? Melania was in a position to do something incredible. I was awed by the possibilities.

So, what was the problem?

Her husband, Donald Trump, was the problem.

Melania was automatically an extension of him. She had never really established her own identity, and—no fault to her—she was just fine being Mrs. Trump. But now she was going to be First Lady, and "just fine" wasn't going to cut it. She'd need an identity makeover.

She knew this truth and she needed someone to help get her there. I was the person she asked to join her on this journey. She knew I was loyal, to a fault, and that I had no ulterior motive other than to do everything in my power to help her succeed.

No Big Deal

We'd been texting, and she knew how excited I was for her, but I couldn't wait to tell her in person. She invited me to visit her at home in Trump Tower, just two days after the election. Whenever I hung out with her in the penthouse, I entered the building from the residence side entrance on Fifty-Sixth Street between Fifth and Madison. I only used the main entrance to Trump Tower, on 725 Fifth Avenue, when I was meeting someone else from the family, for business.

I assumed the lobby would be swarming with Secret Service. Not a one! On the way up to the penthouse, the elevator operator and I chatted about election night. He was animated, smiling and laughing. I'd been riding the high for days, buoyed by the win.

As soon as I stepped off the elevator, I was greeted by a security man and his magic wand. After a quick screening, he waved me through. I walked up to the penthouse's gold-and-diamond front door and rang the doorbell. Daga, the housekeeper, was always there to greet me, and she smiled and said, "Good to see you. Mrs. Trump will be right down."

I walked into Melania's living room as I'd done many times before, my heels drumming on the marble floor, the gold spiral staircase glinting in the sunlight from the floor-to-ceiling windows. I sat on the couch and waited. I always waited. I'd just assumed Melania enjoyed making her grand entrance, or else why wouldn't she already be downstairs, knowing I was on my way up?

Melania descended the stairs. She looked perfect in a sweater and brown leather pants, not a hair out of place, as if it were just another day in her life, another afternoon catch-up with a friend. From my perspective, the disconnect between what had happened in her life and how she was acting caused a glitch in my brain. Donald had won, and Melania was going to be First Lady, right? It had happened, right? This wasn't some parallel dimension where Melania was just First Lady of Trump Tower?

She greeted me with her perfect smile. I made a mental note to go see her dentist.

We hugged and kissed. I was giddy. "You're First Lady! I want to hear everything!" I said.

She laughed but waved it away as if it were no big deal.

I remember thinking, *How do you even begin?* The magnitude of her new role was overwhelming, but she seemed unfazed.

We talked about what a future move to DC would entail, how busy she was.

"When do you move to Washington?" I asked.

"I'm not doing that yet."

What? "What do you mean?! You have to!"

"I'm not going to just get up and go." Brush of the hands, that's that. Melania had spoken. "I'll go," she conceded. "But not until Barron is done with school."

"How's Barron taking all this?" I asked.

It seemed like just yesterday Melania had told me that Barron had worn a suit and tie to school. He was dressing "just like his dad." The other kids laughed at him. Melania had told him, "Don't listen to any of them. Be strong."

She said Barron was fine. "I just have so much to do," she said. "Big move!"

"Think of all of the amazing things you'll be able to do," I said.

"So busy," she said.

"Who's helping you?" I asked.

"It's being arranged," she explained. "I'll have someone."

"You'll only have one person?" I asked. Bewildered. Flabbergasted!

I couldn't help myself and asked, "How many does Ivanka have?"

"Who?" Melania said. "You mean *Princess*?!" We both bellied-over with laughter.

Melania and Ivanka were never that close, and the distance between them had been growing all year. The Trump family dynamic was complicated, and I didn't pretend to know exactly how it worked.

But I did know that Ivanka was always a daddy's girl, and I could only imagine what that would mean as she assumed the role of the First Daughter. Ivanka made herself the stand-in for Melania during the campaign, serving as her father's surrogate, attracting female voters. Would that continue? How involved would she be in the inauguration or the White House? Most relevant to me was how Ivanka's undefined role would affect Melania.

The cold war between the two of them was just beginning.

It was getting late. "I hate to go," I said, "but Zachary's on his way home."

"Say hi to everyone," she said. "Can you meet me on Monday?"

We had so much more to talk about. I would reach out to my designer colleagues to help dress her for the presidential inauguration. I had no clue how many outfits she'd need, or for what events.

Melania walked me to the front door and, with a smile, said, "You'll come with me?"

Just as I'd done so many times over the years, I said, "Of course," without an inkling of what I was saying yes to.

I paused and looked back at her, and said, "To DC?" No response. "What will I do?"

"There is so much," she replied. "We'll figure it out."

With a hug and kiss on both cheeks, I walked out the door, excited and extremely nervous in a way I'd never felt before.

"I'll see you on Monday," I said. "Can't wait."

In hindsight, with all my heart, my soul, every fiber of my being, that one time, I wish I'd said "no."

Sixty-Nine Days Until the Swearing-In

I spent the weekend thinking about Melania and her newfound power and whether I could help her harness it for good. I asked some of my friends about the possibility of my working with Melania in the White House, and they all said, "DO NOT work with the Trumps, Stephanie! *ANY* of them!"

My sixth sense warned me not to trust the Trumps. But my heart said, "Melania is not really one of them. She's one of us."

Sixty-Seven Days Until the Swearing-In

On Monday, November 14, 2016, I went back to Trump Tower to see Melania. I prepared a list of designers that I thought would look magnificent on her.

"Michael Kors!" I said to her. It seemed like a natural fit.

She frowned at me and said, "Are you kidding me?" She didn't believe that anyone would make her clothing because of Donald.

If I could just get the point across that she was different from Donald and had her own initiatives to do good, I felt I could sway them. Wouldn't it be an honor and a privilege for any designer to be asked to dress the future First Lady of the United States? I soon came to realize that that was not the case. I found myself frequently asking for a favor, not offering one. More often than not, I was answered with a "no."

She didn't want to discuss fashion at the moment. *Huh?* I thought to myself. *Isn't that why I'm here?*

"Over the weekend," she told me, "the family got together and talked about all the stuff we have to do. Donald and all of us talk—about the planning of the inauguration."

"How exciting!" I quipped.

"Donald said they needed someone with expertise to plan the inauguration," she said. "I mentioned you, and everyone, including Ivanka, said, 'Oh, yes, Stephanie!'"

I didn't know what to say at first except "Wow!" And then "What does that even mean?"

"I don't know the details," she said.

"But," I said, "I'm here to help *you*, first and foremost."

Melania was so nonchalant. She wanted me to help her and also consider working on the inauguration. "You can do both." No big deal.

It didn't seem like a favor, but an honor. I guess I interpreted it as any producer would: Does it get any bigger than this?

I hadn't the first clue what I was getting myself into.

Okay. Donald and Melania, as well as Jared and Ivanka, knew my résumé. They also knew I was a workaholic perfectionist. Donald knew Melania and I were close.

"You'll get a call from Ivanka later," she explained. "She makes the official ask. She's going to want to say it was her idea to ask you."

Implying . . . Ivanka wanted to take the credit for asking me to work on the inauguration.

"I don't think I'd even consider working on this inauguration if you hadn't asked me yourself," I said.

She knew that very well. So did they all.

"After you talk to Ivanka, let me know what she says," said Melania.

We were just two friends, hanging out. I did feel a shift in the tenor of our relationship, though. Melania was breaking her rules. The invisible wall between friendship and partnership was coming down between us for the first time.

Our eyes locked, my heart raced, and, in that moment, I knew I was going undercover to be Melania's eyes and ears—*her spy*, keeping her informed and up to date on the family's planning of the inauguration.

I was about to take on this huge new responsibility that I knew nothing about. I left Trump Tower soon after, excited and mystified.

I told David what had happened, and he seemed to think what she'd asked me to do was a very big deal indeed—not just helping her choose some outfits or plan a couple events. I started to catch on later when Ivanka called, as expected, that evening.

"Hello, Stephanie," Ivanka trilled. "The family met earlier this week and we unanimously agreed that we wanted you to be involved in the planning of Dad's inauguration!" She said she would introduce me to Tom Barrack Jr., chairman of the 58th Presidential Inaugural Committee (PIC), who would be my boss. I would be his senior advisor. She and her father had a relationship with Barrack already. So did her husband, Jared Kushner. Donald had asked Barrack to help bail out Kushner to prevent a foreclosure on 666 Fifth Avenue, a building Kushner bought in 2007 at the top of the market, just before the Great Recession. Barrack had come to the rescue.

The hooks were in from the moment Melania told me about that family meeting. Ivanka's official "ask" was just a formality.

Ivanka's introductory email to Tom Barrack said: "Stephanie would be great for you to speak with about the planning of the inauguration—as mentioned, I have no doubt she will be invaluable to you!"

When Tom and I connected, he really buttered me up. "I am so happy to meet you electronically! Ivanka has spoken so highly of you, and we are really in need of high-level event and marketing expertise. You are the living legend in that regard!" During that initial exchange, he assured me that I would be responsible for the thematic elements of the events and said, "There's a whole team to execute, you'll have oversight on the creative process."

I googled my soon-to-be new boss and learned he was the billionaire real-estate financier Thomas J. Barrack Jr. Born the son of a grocer, he was now the founder, president, and CEO of the investment firm Colony Capital, Inc. As I sat there digging deeper and deeper, I was fascinated by the companies and industries he acquired, merged, intersected with, commingled, partnered with, and collaborated with. In 2005, he graced the cover of *Fortune* beside the headline "The World's Greatest Real Estate Investor."

I was surprised I'd never heard of him in the entertainment industry. He should have been on my radar—there were so many crossovers with *Vogue*. He's one of the biggest low-profile "insiders," involved in film, fashion, and entertainment. In December 2010, Tom led a group of investors, including Colony Capital and the Qatar Investment Authority, along with construction magnate Ron Tutor, to purchase Miramax for $660 million. He was also behind Michael Jackson's 2009–2010 comeback tour. Once Michael committed to that, Colony Capital agreed to bail out his Neverland Ranch and arranged for Anschutz Entertainment Group (AEG), the concert promoter, to stage his comeback and relaunch his career. (Unfortunately, Michael Jackson died from an overdose, and the tour didn't happen.)

The pieces of the puzzle were starting to come together. Now I understood that he amassed his fortune bailing out so-called distressed celebrities. He bailed out famed photographer Annie Leibovitz from ruin, buying out her debt for $40 million. He is also one of the winners of the US housing crisis, which washed away the life savings of millions of people. Barrack is drawn to the inefficiencies of businesses and distressed companies and turns them into investment opportunities.

When I mentioned the inauguration to friends, they reacted as if I'd enlisted in Satan's army. "But this isn't about Trump or the administration, it's about making America proud," I said—and believed it! I thought I was doing my patriotic duty.

They said: R.U.N.

Sixty-Five Days Until the Swearing-In

On November 16, I entered Le Bilboquet, a Manhattan bistro, my head spinning with ideas and my belly full of butterflies. I scanned the restaurant for a bald, tan, fit, and well-groomed gentleman.

Tom saw me before I found him, and our eyes locked. He'd commandeered a corner table. Another man was with him, his backpack on a chair. The backpack made me think this guy was Tom's assistant.

Tom and I shook hands and then the other man introduced himself. "Rick Gates, nice to meet you," he said. Rick was the deputy chairman of the PIC, second in charge.

First impression: Tom and Donald were nothing alike. Donald was a man of prose. He talked in rambling, often incoherent sentences. Tom was a man of poetry. He spoke in metaphor and imagery. "Each detail of the inaugural week will be perfectly strung together, to create a seamless canvas of harmony, inclusion, and democracy, as we come together as one nation and honor that quintessential and uniquely

American tradition of the peaceful transfer of power," he said. As he spoke, his hands flew around him, precisely synchronized with every expressive word.

Tom glanced over his shoulder, measuring the distance between the tables around us, and in a New York minute, we were huddled elbow to elbow. His voice dropped a notch. "No one thought the boss would win, so there's no team in place. We need you! Your expertise! Rescue me!" he said.

Rick clearly stated there were companies in DC that would be providing services and that had been involved in planning the presidential inaugurations going back to Harry S. Truman.

Tom said "the boss" hoped I would be able to "elevate the creative design elements with glamour and elegance"—to provide my "vision" and "sprinkle" my "special brand of magic" on a couple of events and one dinner hosted by the PEOTUS (President Elect of the United States) and Mrs. Trump.

His confidence, charisma, and enthusiasm—and his faith in my abilities—drew me in. I accepted Tom's offer to be his senior advisor, and we agreed to discuss my contract and fee once I had a better idea of the scope of my work. We parted with firm handshakes. I felt excited but a bit shaky, still unclear about what I'd just signed on to do. What I did know was that if I hadn't said yes to Tom, Melania would have had little to no idea what was being planned, how it was being executed, or who was doing what, and how it would reflect on her. It was her right to know, and it wasn't like Ivanka, Thomas Barrack, or Donald was going to keep her up to speed.

Sixty-Two Days Until the Swearing-In

Emails were flying back and forth between me, Rick, and Tom's assistant. Information wasn't being openly shared. It all became too political so quickly. I was in a league I knew nothing about, so I turned to a friend and colleague whom I trusted and whose insight and political experience, having been senior advisor and speechwriter for British prime minister Tony Blair, would provide me with invaluable advice, direction, and insight: Jon Reynaga, cofounder of Tiny Horse, an entertainment company with expertise in live TV events and digital shows. Tiny Horse's clients included CBS and ABC. Jon knew politics.

"Besides the swearing-in, what happens at an inauguration?" I asked.

Jon said, "Sweetheart, you have no idea what you're getting into."

I most certainly did not.

Fifty-Eight Days Until the Swearing-In

Tom was developing a road map, and I was on board. He left early in the morning (he was forever on a plane, forever fundraising) and by nighttime he'd already texted: "Had a great working night with Steve Wynn [then a Las Vegas casino and hotel owner] and I think we have a great game plan that I want to craft with you, which gives us one big event on Thursday night, one big event on Friday, a free concert in the Mall on Thursday, and that's really it the president and the first lady have to worry about. Whatever you want to craft for a luncheon on top of that is extra."

That sounded like plenty to me and more than I'd signed up for, but my sleeves were rolled up and I wasn't going to back away because he added a "free concert."

The scope of work was expanding. "It sounds like I'm going to need to assemble a team?" I asked.

"Yes," Tom responded.

"I need to make some calls to some of my colleagues," I said, "with production, branding, and creative expertise."

"Sounds good," Tom said.

Then I inquired, "Who do I speak to about my contract?"

Tom said, "Sara Armstrong is CEO. Rick will coordinate all for you. I'm meeting with Burnett as we speak at the Soho House."

I hadn't yet heard the name Sara Armstrong, PIC's CEO, but I guess I hadn't needed to since Rick was "coordinating" my contract for me.

Fifty-Seven Days Until the Swearing-In

On November 24, Rick sent a long email about how the Trump inauguration would be "charting new territories . . . we have *carte blanche*," but he still hadn't sent me any information about previous inaugurations, logistics, run-of-shows (the timeline with minute-by-minute detail of an event's schedule), vendors, venues, caterers, or suppliers. He attached some links and advised me to "watch the attached videos and build out."

I asked Rick how the PIC financing was going to work. "You don't need to worry yourself with that," he said. "Tom and I are handling all of the finances. PIC's finance team is already up and running."

"What about using my personal Wi-Fi?" I asked. "I'm concerned due to the nature of this information regarding timing and logistics of PEOTUS and Mrs. Trump."

"It's fine to use your personal Wi-Fi network," he said. "It is some encryption, although as we know anything is hackable these days." That made me feel assured—*not*!

The next day, I called Melania and said, "I can't put my finger on it, but things don't *feel* right. I'm not sure why they haven't sent me guidelines, and no one seems to think your safety is a priority."

Melania told me not to worry. "We have security," she said.

I wasn't referring to the Secret Service—more like cybersecurity.

It took a week of asking but Rick finally sent me a few documents. The first Excel spreadsheet I opened was the organizational chart of all the people on the PIC, thirty-eight staffers. Tom's name was at the top left. Except for Rick, listed second in command, and CEO Sara Armstrong, I hadn't heard of any of them. Back to Google. Many of them were a part of the RNC.

On the right side of the org chart, my name was at the top, right next to . . . *Mark Burnett*! We were listed as special advisors for inaugural planning. Underneath our names there was an entertainment committee listed, packed with heavy hitters, top execs from Sony, MSG, and Imagine Entertainment.

I called Melania and told her the great news. "Tom has put together a stellar group! Did you know Mark Burnett was working on this?"

"Really?" she said. "I didn't know."

Rick forwarded me a legal outline, addressed to Tom Barrack, from Katie Walsh, the RNC's chief of staff, and Cara Mason, its finance director, describing the role of the Presidential Inauguration Committee as "a privately funded, nonprofit, nongovernmental, partisan organization that represents the interests of the president-elect and plans and executes most of the inaugural events." It went on to outline the overview, donations, initial letter filing with the FEC, reporting requirements, time and proposed schedule, budget, personnel and organizational chart, finance structure, and proposed finance packages.

Rick also emailed me a memo about making the inauguration a "Sea to Shining Sea" tour. They wanted Donald and his entourage to motorcade from the Pacific to the Atlantic over a period of two or three days.

Donald couldn't walk down Fifth Avenue and the PIC was proposing to have him travel three thousand miles on unsecure routes in three days? Was this a joke? Less than a day later, the Sea to Shining Sea idea was scrapped.

The final attachment from Rick was a tentative schedule of events. I wasn't sure what I was looking at since there were twenty-two events listed. I wondered if Rick had sent me the Trump family's personal schedule of events by accident. But why would he even have their schedule? It didn't take long before it clicked: of course, the family was getting in on the celebration. The PIC's suggested list included events hosted by Ivanka, Don Jr., and Eric and his wife, Lara. With a red Sharpie and a yellow highlighter, I reviewed the list, jotted down lots of questions, and made tons of notes to self, including "Find out who is producing and executing all of these other events." I was responsible for two balls and supposedly the most exclusive event, the Candlelight Dinner, the *only* dinner hosted by President-Elect and Mrs. Trump, to be held the evening before the swearing-in. The Sponsors' Reception and the Underwriters' Luncheon with the president-elect and vice president–elect were both big-ticket items! Major donors could pay millions for packages consisting of VIP receptions and priority booking at premier inaugural hotels. Each event had a date, a host, a location, and a number. I figured out that the number represented the ticket price (as part of a donation package). Tickets for the Victory Reception, hosted by Reince Priebus, went for $100,000. The Leadership Luncheon at the Trump International Hotel, hosted by cabinet secretaries, went for $1 million. Quite the price difference. A few of those tables would be hosted by the Trump children.

This was supposed to be the "People's Celebration." I emailed Rick, "What tickets are available to the public? Where can someone purchase tickets to the balls?" Could an average American afford even the least-expensive ticket? He responded, "Find attached a document that outlines the ticket prices for the official inaugural balls for each of the years going back to 2001, with comparative prices, ranging from free to $175."

He also told me, "Don't worry about ticket pricing."

"What about hotels?" I asked.

The PIC and RNC were handling that, too.

I went to meet Melania at Trump Tower at 3:00 p.m. We sat together on the living room sofa, and I handed her a copy of the event schedule. We stared at it simultaneously. I'd never set foot in any of the DC venues being suggested for inaugural events and I'd never been to an inauguration, so this was as new to me as it was to her. "I prepared this venue guide with pictures of each venue and its location, capacity, AV capabilities, preferred vendors, and catering services," I said, handing it to her.

We sat there speechless.

Neither of us really had any clue of what was going on yet.

"So," I read aloud, "the first event listed is for a Ladies' Luncheon, hosted by Ivanka and Lara, tickets for five hundred thousand to one million dollars apiece."

Melania looked surprised and said, "That's news to me."

I agreed and replied, "It was to me, too."

Halfway down the page, Melania was listed with Donald, hosting the Candlelight Dinner on January 19, 2017, for tickets at the $1 million donor level.

"No one told me they're using my name to raise money," she said, miffed.

I explained, "Donation packages for one million dollars include six tickets, and for five million dollars include twenty tickets, to the Candlelight Dinner."

"So, *anyone* can buy tickets to attend *my* dinner?" she asked.

"I guess so," I replied. I reached into my folder and pulled out several pages. "Here are the donor packages." Anyone could buy their way in.

"Rick has also made some suggestions about your grand entrance," I continued. "Instead of you and Donald walking out from behind a curtain, he wants you to rise up from underneath the stage."

Totally amused and with eyes squinting, she asked, "What are you talking about?" I waved my arms up and down and said, "Like in a cloud of smoke and *poof!* You and Donald magically appear?" We laughed so hard at that.

"Seriously?" she asked.

"Sounds like a Mark Burnett production to me!" I laughed.

"I want you to send Rick a photo of the stage from my convention speech," she requested. "I want the stage to look like that one."

I almost choked on my own saliva. Luckily my face was looking downward into my notebook as I frantically jotted down, "Send Rick a picture of the stage Melania stood on," and thought to myself, *When she delivered her plagiarized speech rumored to have been penned by Rick Gates.* I don't think she gave it a second thought, and I wasn't going to remind her. If she was happy, then I was, too. She and Donald wanted the same aesthetic at all of the events, especially for their iconic first dance at the Inaugural Ball. "A classic, sleek, modern feel, you know what I mean?" she said. I did. Classic, sleek, and modern, like her.

I pointed to the next event listed on the schedule.

"What's the Ivanka Trump/Leo DiCaprio Environmental Ball?" she asked. It was listed at the National Portrait Gallery.

"Maybe Ivanka is really thirsty for Leonardo DiCaprio," I said.

"Give me a break!" she replied.

"Do you know about Don Jr. and Eric planning something called Camouflage and Cufflinks?"

"What's that?"

"I have no idea," I said. "Does Donald hunt?"

"No!"

Ivanka, Lara, Don, and Eric were hosting events. Did they think *they* were elected? And does all the donor money go to pay for these events? I just didn't know.

"I'm sure Donald doesn't even know about all these events," Melania said.

"Oh, wait, there's another event with your name on it. Your first weekday in the White House, on Monday, January 23, you're hosting a staff appreciation reception at the White House."

"A what? For who? Who is asking?"

"Maybe this one's the traditional event Rick told me about," I said. "I think you and Donald host it to thank the staff for all of their hard work through the campaign, transition, and inauguration. Let me look into it further and get back to you."

"I'll be back in New York," she said. "Cancel it!"

When I later relayed that news to Tom and Rick, they were not pleased that I'd shared this information with Melania.

Fifty-Six Days Until the Swearing-In

As soon as I got home, my next call was to Jon Reynaga. "Hey," I said. "You are *not* going to believe who's on the PIC org chart!"

"Who?" he replied.

"Mark Burnett!"

"What?!" He wanted more details, but I couldn't give him what I didn't have. I explained the lack of communication and the delay of information. He'd already been advising me on Melania's messaging and transition. "Rick sent me a list of twenty-two events and documents from the RNC," I told him.

"Girl, what are you talking about?" he asked in his posh British accent. "Have you lost your mind?"

"I only agreed to oversee a couple of events and a dinner hosted by Melania and Donald," I explained. "So I don't know who else they have involved.

"There's a lot more going on than I know about," I told him. And I wasn't just referring to the number of new events that had popped up out of thin air and were now on my radar. "I'm going to DC," I continued. "Please come with me." I sensed he'd jump at the chance to work with Burnett.

He made no promises but agreed to come to Washington and check it out with me.

He sent me his hourly rate and some terms for services and fees, but I told him I wasn't asking him to commit to anything. I said, "Let's first go to DC and take it from there," and he agreed. We needed to see for ourselves what the PIC had already been planning. Depending on his level of interest, his role, and the scope of the work, Jon would discuss his contract directly with Tom, Rick, and the PIC.

I texted Melania, "Jon's coming to DC with me to check out what's going on and look at venues!"

She sent, "❤️ 🙏 ❤️ 🙏 ❤️ 🙏."

"I got my contract too," I wrote, "but the PIC made it out to 'Stepanie Wilcox' 😂 They don't even know how to spell my name right!"

Rick said he'd fix it and get it right back to me.

Fifty-Three Days Until the Swearing-In

Rick had planned two days of back-to-back meetings for us with members of the PIC's senior staff, who'd update us on the scope of work and present us with key information, planning already underway, timelines, and budgets.

Our journey began on November 28. I flew to DC with Jon Reynaga and a few colleagues from my *Vogue* days, whom I promised would remain nameless. The five of us arrived at Ronald Reagan Washington National Airport at 9:28 a.m. The deputy directors of the PIC's special events team, Lindsay Reynolds, a nice teacher from Ohio, and Ramsey Ratcliffe, a self-described "neutral gal" and former RNC Director for Finance Events, were waiting for us at the airport in two sparkling SUVs. With open arms and smiles, they were ready and eager to whisk us away to show us around town, but first we made a quick stop at the hotel they'd booked for us, the Trump International Hotel.

I'd only been to DC a few times before and hadn't toured the landmark buildings that held our nation's history, like the Smithsonian, the National Portrait Gallery, the Library of Congress, and the John F. Kennedy Center for the Performing Arts. Despite my mounting anxiety about how much work we had to do, I was inspired by the places we toured.

Inside the rotunda of the National Archives Building, I stood inches away from the Constitution, the Bill of Rights, and the Declaration of Independence. Only a piece of glass separated me from these founding documents. I stopped to reflect on the magnitude of that moment and was overcome with feelings of awe.

I had a lightbulb moment but no phone service. I excused myself and stepped outside into the chill, and I called Melania. "I'm touring venues in DC and I can't begin to tell you how exciting this is for me to be standing in the vaults of the National Archives." Each location was enticing and as magical as the next. I said, "I'm like a kid in a candy store!"

We'd been speaking a lot about her initiative, but we hadn't yet figured out how she would launch and be actively involved in bringing awareness to the importance of overall well-being and the pledge to oneself to be ethical and respectful.

"This is it!" I said. "It's perfect."

"What's going on?" she asked.

"You'll soon have unlimited access to every historic building, each one with its own treasure trove of history," I said. "And using this historical backdrop for delivering your message will be so impactful." My head was spinning with limitless possibilities.

Melania was a treasure, too, and I wanted the world to see how special she was.

Later that evening, Jon recapped the day in an email and signed off with three words—Who *Is* She?—our joke, what he and I called each other, but then it became the unspoken question on the PIC people's lips when they met me. He tacked on a PS: "Burnett may want to do an *Apprentice* reunion with normal and celeb contestants supporting different candidates, a show of people coming together?"

I laughed, assuming that he was joking. Did he know something about Burnett that I didn't?

Fifty-Two Days Until the Swearing-In

At seven thirty a.m., Jon, the others, and I met in the lobby of the Trump International Hotel. We headed downstairs to the Adams Room for part two of our "kickoff" meetings and site visits. I was looking forward to putting a face to the names and meeting other members of the PIC's team.

Listed at the top of the agenda was Rick Gates, PIC's Deputy Director, Sara Armstrong, PIC's CEO, and her senior advisor, Jeff Larson. In addition were Director of Budget and Treasury Heather Martin, Director of Public Events Ryan Price, and his deputy, Tim Tripepi, who were overseeing operations and budgets for all of the outdoor events.

Jon and I were prepared to discuss the overall theme and ideations,

like unity and "With the People, Making America Great Always."
We didn't get anywhere with that.

In addition to the nuts and bolts we were expecting to hear about,
the agenda was packed with logistics, graphic elements for digital and
printed materials, credentialing protocol, invitations, ticketing, communications, brand guidelines, vetting, and much more, all in addition
to a list of events that was almost sixfold of what I'd been told about. I
was curious to find out who was producing them all.

Under the headline of outdoor events, the "official public events"
were listed, including the parade route and bleachers, live-streaming,
entertainment and concerts, balls, and fireworks. Hargrove, the events
company we were meeting later to "sign off on," had already started
building the viewing stand for the President, First Lady, and their
family and guests to sit comfortably during the parade.

The scope of this job and our involvement grew exponentially
overnight. The PIC looked to us for our experience and expertise.
What were we going to do, walk away?

The clock was ticking. I had to leave with Lindsay and Ramsey for
one last day of venue and site visits, keeping in mind the thematic and
visual elements of the events I was thinking of creating.

"We just have to divide and conquer!" Jon said, and stayed back at
the hotel to dive into the production and media elements.

Later, Jon, my team, and I were asked to join Rick, Lindsay,
Ramsey, and the others from the PIC for lunch to meet the executives from "Team" Hargrove, the "full-service provider" that would be
"providing services."

We were relieved to hear "full-service provider." The PIC told us
they were "considering" hiring Hargrove as the general contractor to
facilitate and execute all the moving parts of the inauguration, but
wanted our "input" and "approval."

"Sure!" I said. "We'd love to meet them." But we were under the
impression we were meeting other vendors, too. "Are we meeting with
anyone else?" I asked Rick.

Rick was working on that . . .

Jon and the team met up with me for lunch in the back room of the Charlie Palmer restaurant. Carla Hargrove McGill introduced herself and her executive team, welcomed and thanked us for the "opportunity" to present their ideas, and said they were there to win us over. And they did. It was a shop started by her father in 1946, and they'd been the events company involved in planning every presidential inauguration since 1949. It was a one-stop shop. They'd provide *everything*! Their presentation was very impressive indeed, and Rick Gates gave the final vote of confidence, saying he'd worked with them successfully before, and with no other options and no one else to meet, Hargrove it was.

Later that afternoon, Hargrove's vice president of events, Ron Bracco, sent the PIC a budget estimate based on their experience from previous inaugurations, cc'ing Tim McGill, CEO of Hargrove, and his wife, Carla Hargrove McGill, Hargrove's president, all of whom we'd met earlier. Rick sent me the proposed budget (it was in excess of $29 million) and asked, "What do you think?"

I told him I couldn't answer that question until I reviewed a detailed and itemized budget, and asked him to forward it to me.

He replied, "No additional attachments." I wondered who had financial control of the event budget. Who was calculating it? Who was determining the expenses?

This was beginning to sound like what nightmares are made of, but I wasn't ready to hit the panic button just yet.

Upon closer examination of the contract, I saw, in fine red print, "drafted on November 20," which was eight days before we stepped foot in Washington, with some portions already approved by Sara. Asking for our thumbs-up seemed to be a mere formality. It was already a done deal. Why the charade? Why make it seem as if we had a hand in Hargrove's approval process?

I was still waiting for Rick to introduce me to the other event companies he'd mentioned earlier: Freeman, Encore, and PSAV, the full-service in-house creative and technical production company for all Trump properties. (In 2018, PSAV acquired Hargrove.)

* * *

Back at the hotel, Jon and I rehashed our day, and he filled me in on his meetings with Rick at the Trump International Hotel. He said they had discussed the broadcast production components.

"Broadcast of what?" I asked.

"The concert and balls!"

The scope of the contracted work I was brought in to provide and had asked Jon to help me with was consulting, creative, and executive production services, basically "above the line" production work. We quickly realized that in order to pull this rabbit out of the hat, the PIC was going to need a team with extensive production and entertainment experience, and it didn't seem like there were any staff or vendors for us to work with, especially for the large-scale broadcasting events. This is when the PIC asked us to also assume "below the line" production responsibilities, from designing to building the stages, hiring the contractors to sourcing vendors, and booking performers to dealing with TV networks.

Was Burnett in or out? We couldn't get a straight answer.

Jon and I quickly realized the depth and scope of this project would be far greater than any of us could have imagined, and we'd never envisioned we'd have to start from the very beginning—no past inaugural broadcast plans, no prior floor plans, no run-of-shows. There was no margin for error.

Luckily, Jon and his Tiny Horse partners, with loads of broadcast, production, and digital experience, said, "We're in!"

Thank God.

Later, I was working in my room, and I must have dozed off on the bed. My computer, still on my lap, pinged with an incoming email from Rick to Ivanka Trump, cc'ing me. "Hope you are well. Tom asked me to send you the current schedule of events that the family will need to attend during the inauguration. We have been with Stephanie in DC for the last two days working on finalizing the events and venues.

I highlighted the events in yellow that the family will be expected to attend," he wrote.

Why on earth is Rick sending a tentative schedule to Ivanka before Donald and Melania have seen it? Has Ivanka been elected president?

I sent a hasty reply to Rick: "Why did you send Ivanka the schedule?"

"Ivanka wanted the schedule," he said. "Tom asked me to send it."

Ivanka had asked Tom and Rick had complied. The food chain couldn't have been clearer. Ivanka was at the tippy top. Their priority was the First Daughter.

"PLEASE do not send this to anyone else," I implored Rick, copying Tom. "We are not ready for anyone else to see this. We have due diligence to discuss."

Tom's reply: "We have budget to discuss."

I waited a bit to calm down and then emailed Ivanka at one thirty a.m. "Ivanka, hi. We will speak tomorrow, but [the schedule] is still too premature to share with anyone. I will walk you through it when we talk. Have a good night."

Before shutting my eyes, I forwarded Melania Rick's email to Ivanka. Ivanka had her insider source, and so did Melania. The more Melania became dependent on me as her confidant and advisor, the more I committed to having her back throughout the transition period, from election night to the swearing-in ceremony and into the White House, and through the launch of her initiative. I became a double agent of sorts, which was thrilling and also terrifying, because spies usually end up gagged and immobilized.

Fifty-One Days Until the Swearing-In

I called Melania with the good news: "Jon's all in!"

"That's great," she said. "Is everything else okay?"

I couldn't answer that question, so I told her so. "I just don't know yet. On the drafted schedule, there are three events slated to take place at the Trump International Hotel." I didn't believe it would be in the family's best interest to have the Candlelight Dinner and champagne toast at the hotel, unless, of course, Donald was covering the costs.

"I don't know anything about that." That phrase was fast becoming her refrain.

I presented my suggestion. "I think Union Station would be spectacular for the Candlelight Dinner!"

Melania asked, "Inside the train station?"

"Yes, right inside," I said. "It's grand and magnificent."

"Send me what it would look like," she said.

One more item for my to-do list. With as much pixie dust as I was apparently expected to have on hand, there wouldn't be enough to do this on my own. I thought to myself, *Boy, did I screw up by agreeing to get involved and work on any of this.* I still didn't have a full grasp of what *this* was. Who was putting all of these events together? And how did they all end up on my lap all of a sudden? (Ultimately, there were a total of eighteen events; several were canceled, thank God.)

Rick wanted to know what I thought about Hargrove's budget.

Outrageous, I maintained, doubting the budget we saw was what Hargrove had charged Obama.

Jon understood and expressed the same concerns, but we didn't feel we could walk away. With our take-no-prisoners attitude, we felt it our "patriotic duty" to help with the inauguration—that the ceremony represented the "best of American democracy," namely, "the peaceful transition of power," and we would figure this out.

I called Tom and asked, "Twenty-two events, live TV broadcasts, and $29 million?"

"The timing and number of broadcast selections is subordinate to my selection of venues, events, and the programming of them," he replied, unfazed. "We need to be definite, concise, and understandable in what we ask from [Hargrove]." He told me to focus on the original three events, not the broadcast, and "if you want to oversee these other events too," they weren't going to turn me away.

Later that day, Rick Gates reached out to make sure I was okay and sent me an urgent email: "Will MT [Melania Trump] participate in a lady's luncheon or host an event as First Lady? Will she want to attend the wreath-laying ceremony—tradition is that she should. Will she be willing to attend the Military Ball—very big deal to the military. How does she want her name to appear on the program? Melania K. Trump or Melania Knauss Trump?"

He'd gone straight to me to ask about Melania's schedule. This was significant because it meant he and Tom knew how close Melania and I were. We'd preferred to keep it on the down-low, so I could watch out for her best interests and feed her info on the sly, but it didn't take long for them and the PIC staff to figure out that whenever Donald complained about something he'd heard from his wife, the intel had come from me originally.

As for how her name would appear on the program, Melania said, "I want to be listed as First Lady Melania Trump."

"That's your official title but not until *after* the swearing-in ceremony," I said.

"Then call me First Lady–Elect."

"We can't do that because you weren't elected."

"That's what I want."

"Karen Pence is using Mrs. Karen Pence."

She didn't care. "First Lady–Elect!" became her mantra whenever programs and invites came up. This was one of the only times she didn't get her way. She was listed as Mrs. Melania Trump.

Tom was on his way to Los Angeles to meet with Burnett to talk about getting A-list performers for inaugural events. We were in New York that day, and Rick organized a teleconference at Tom's office at Colony Capital at 712 Fifth Avenue with several top entertainment executives. The LA group talked a big game. Exactly what we expected. We had Mitch Davis, Clive Davis's son, on the line.

Mitch said he'd prepared a "talent grid" that listed artists and their affiliation with the GOP and/or Donald Trump, if any. If we could get two or three of these acts—Aerosmith, Carrie Underwood, Celine Dion, Kelly Clarkson, Kiss, the Killers, Meat Loaf, Mavis Staples, Pat

Benatar, and Lynyrd Skynyrd, to mention a few—it would blow people's minds. We had our doubts, but Mitch tried. He was put between
a rock and a hard place.

After the meeting, Jon texted, "Mark Burnett is NOT working on
the production of the concerts at all, so we 100% must enlist Hargrove
or another vendor to do it." *Shit. Easy come, easy go.* I wondered how he
found that out. No one told me.

Next up on that very long day, I met with Melania at Trump Tower,
carrying bags and boxes so she could review and sign off on menus,
décor, paper stock. I was weighed down by anxiety, too. Melania knew
that the scope of my responsibilities had increased many times over.

"We don't have any A-list performers locked in, or B-list for that
matter," I said. "We don't even have an office to work in! I have at least
ten people in and out of my apartment all day. It's not fair to David
and the kids. And can you please tell me *why* Rick Gates has an all-
access badge to Trump Tower?"

"He does?" she asked.

"He took us to Don Jr., Eric, and Ivanka's office suite. He knew
where the security button was located. We all just walked right in."
In Don Jr.'s office, Rick made himself right at home and sat down in
Don's chair.

"Really," Melania said, seeing that I was getting upset again. Her
voice was a balm. I felt better just being in her presence.

We had a lot to go over. We sat down at her dining room table
and spread out all of the printed material for her review. She told me,
"When Donald comes home, I want you to tell him what's going on."

An hour later, he walked into the dining room as chipper as could
be. "Hi, baby," he said to Melania.

She was looking at Pantone colors but flashed him a quick smile.

"Hello, Stephanie. How are you?" he asked.

I began to stand and he said, "Stay, sit, sit. *Time* magazine—I'm on
the cover again!" He was the 2016 Person of the Year.

Melania laughed and said, "Oh, Donald. That's great!" Her tone was
coquettish, hyperfeminine, an open invitation for him to keep going.

He said, "I've been on the cover a dozen times already."

I said, "Donald, you're going to be the president," implying that his new job was a bigger deal than a magazine cover.

He said, "Yeah, right! Great!" and then continued to describe the *Time* cover, and the one before, and the one before that. After ten minutes, he said, "Wow, you ladies look like you're busy! Look at all of this."

Melania said, "So much to do. We are so busy, but no worries."

"That's my girl!"

Melania leaned her shoulder into mine. "Tell him," she said.

"It's nothing," I said, but he wouldn't let me chicken out and waved for me to speak. I exhaled. "Honestly, the PIC is a shit show. They are disorganized, incompetent, and can't produce the material we need. My team's been working around the clock and we can't get the answers we need and we're not really sure who to turn to."

"What about Tom?" Donald asked. We both knew Tom was spending most of his time fundraising.

"I met Sara Armstrong, the PIC CEO," I said, "but she's not *really* in charge. She's just there to sign off on budgets."

"So who is in charge?" he asked.

"I've been working primarily with Rick."

"Rick who?"

From the corner of my eye I could see Melania's back stiffen.

"Rick Gates," I said.

Donald exclaimed, "Rick?! Rick Gates?! Who's Rick Gates?!"

Was he serious? "He's the deputy chairman of the inauguration," I said.

Melania shot him a *C'mon* smirk.

Donald's reaction was so visceral. Was he telling me the truth? I'd bet my life on it!

"Oh, *Rick*. Rick Gates!" Donald paced himself into a tirade. "That son of a bitch stole seven hundred fifty thousand dollars from me. I'm going to sue him! He's the one . . . It had to do with Don McGahn."

Now I was totally confused. Who was Don McGahn? Did this

have to do with the campaign? The transition? A lawsuit? What was it with these people and lawsuits!

Donald stopped pacing and stood in front of Melania and me, his face scarlet. If I hadn't known so much about food allergies, I would have thought he was going into anaphylactic shock.

"*Give me your phone!* I'm calling Tom Barrack. I want Rick fired right now! That bastard. He stole my money!" He reached out to take my phone.

I looked to Melania for help. If Donald called Tom from my phone, I'd be the biggest tattletale on the block.

"Tom will kill me for saying anything," I said. "Donald, please, no, you can't."

"Melania!" Donald roared. "Call Tom. Use your phone!"

Melania did what he asked. I'm sure Tom thought Melania was butt-dialing him, but he answered.

"Tom," Donald said, "I'm here with Stephanie and Melania."

Those words alone were the kiss of death.

I felt nauseated and texted Tom, "URGENT. I am at DT house."

Donald was hopping mad and going off the deep end.

"Tom!" Donald yelled. "I want Rick *FIRED*! What's he still doing around?"

I wished I hadn't said anything. I was nervous knowing that I'd stepped on Tom's toes and ticked him off by telling Donald and Melania how I felt working with the PIC.

Donald hung up the phone and looked like he needed to blow off some steam.

"I'm going upstairs," he said.

As Donald exited the dining room, a young man walked inside the apartment carrying a brown paper bag. Donald asked him, "What are you doing here?"

A bit shaky, the man said, "I'm delivering your turkey sandwich for dinner, sir."

Donald grabbed the bag and told the kid to sit down. He looked like he was just out of college. The president-elect said to him, "You're in charge of the inauguration now. Stephanie, fill him in. Tell him what he needs to do."

I couldn't tell if Donald was serious about tapping the twenty-five-year-old body man to be the new deputy chairman of the PIC—and that's what made it terrifying.

The guy stared like a deer in headlights. Melania and I looked at each other like, *Do you want to start or should I?*

She said hello to him and he nodded. I introduced myself and he said, "Nice to meet you. I'm John McEntee." He was petrified.

"Have you ever produced an event before?" I asked. "Run an organization?"

He just shook his head. You could see sweat bubble on his brow. "I don't understand," he said. "What just happened?"

I gave McEntee a brief rundown of the inauguration and told him, "Let's keep this between the four of us for now, okay?" After he left, McEntee later told me, he fled straight downstairs to the campaign office and recounted his version of the whole story to Trump advisor David Bossie. (John McEntee became Donald's personal assistant, his body man, and accompanied the president everywhere. Whenever John and I saw each other, we smirked at our inside joke about that night. He was eventually fired from the White House, in March 2018, for online gambling and tax issues, but he went straight to a job at America First Policies, a 501(c)(4) nonprofit raising funds to promote Trump's agenda for 2020, where so many ousted Trump White House staffers landed softly after their expulsion. In January 2020, he was back at the White House, as director of the Office of Presidential Personnel.)

Fifty Days Until the Swearing-In

At 5:43 a.m., Tom texted me, "Wheels down! Seeing JK [Jared Kushner] and then will call you! Saw Showstoppers [the lavish Vegas act] at

Wynn [hotel and casino in Las Vegas] with Steve [Wynn] last night! It was perfect! Still sick about Rick."

I was supposed to meet Rick that morning. Did he know he'd been fired yet? For that matter, did he think I was the cause? "Do I meet with Rick?" I asked Tom.

Tom wrote, "My advice is to be very careful and probably leave this alone. He is trying to figure out why this happened. He had had quite a bit of contact with DJT before he moved over to us without incident. In fact, DJT was quite kind to him! RP [Reince Priebus] has told him [Donald] that he also is quite confused and that this was *not a result of the Don McGahn $750,000 issue!* . . . I am meeting with JK at 7:15 and will call you when I'm done."

Did PEOTUS know who Rick Gates was or not?

Tom and Jared's meeting must have resolved things, because Rick was still the deputy chairman of the inauguration, just no longer working for the PIC. He was now working at Colony Capital. He just couldn't show his face around Donald anymore.

"All cleared up," Tom texted me. "Unfortunately, [Donald] has the wrong Rick. My advice would be to stay away from this because nothing good is going to come from it!"

Another thing to "stay away" from.

(The mystery was eventually solved. There was, of course, only one Rick Gates. Donald genuinely appeared not to know him—at least that's the interpretation I got—and Tom and Reince were convinced that Donald must have been thinking of a different Rick.)

"I want nothing to do with this," I told Tom. "I have a job and I am doing it. If it's the wrong Rick, then tell DT [Donald Trump] when you see him."

Around this time, I was talking to someone on the PIC about Rick Gates, and she told me that he had been Trump's deputy campaign manager, brought in by (convicted felon) Paul Manafort, and that he'd stayed on after Manafort was fired. Was Donald that clueless? Was someone pulling Rick's strings?

Ivanka reached out again that day, asking for an updated schedule.

Barron was in the news again. YouTube videos showed him nodding off during his father's speech on election night. What ten-year-old kid doesn't want to be asleep at nearly three o'clock in the morning? I heard Melania's words in my head: "Give me a break!" I was upset for Barron, a kid I'd known since his birth, and angry for Melania.

Melania wanted to put out an op-ed asking the nation (and the press) to uphold the long-standing tradition of respecting the privacy of the president's young children. It started, "Today, First Lady–Elect Mrs. Melania Trump released the following statement . . ."

Jon read it and asked, "Who drafted this? Sounds like Rick! She is not the First Lady–Elect. She doesn't hold an elected position but a ceremonial one. Protocol office will know but until she becomes FLOTUS, I think she is officially called 'Melania Trump, the wife of President-Elect Donald Trump.' Basic mistakes like that cannot be made! And seriously, someone who knows the protocol should be checking this for her. The tone sounds cold from a mother."

No one, except for me and my team, was looking out for Melania's best interest whatsoever.

More responsibilities were added to my plate every day. I was at my wit's end and flooded with stress hormones. On top of the inauguration, where I needed staff to help manage and execute all that was being asked of me with a tiny team, no budget, and no contract, I was also helping Melania by giving her advice, meeting with stylists and designers, and creating exclusive editorial content with media companies for her.

Almost daily, I went over what I'd seen and heard with Melania and reviewed her schedule. The Chairman's Global Dinner was not on it.

"Don't you think you should go?" I asked.

"I'm not changing my plans," she said. "This event was not on my original schedule, and I did not plan for it. Donald can go if he wants. I've got too much to do."

Steve Wynn's Showstoppers was booked for Tom's event's entertainment. Since we were having so much trouble securing talent, I thought Showstoppers could perform at one of the balls, too.

Rick Gates, Hargrove execs from DC, Wynn's team from Las Vegas, and Production Resource Group (PRG) worked together to bring Steve Wynn's Showtoppers from Vegas to Washington. The show was scheduled to finish its Vegas run on December 31, 2016. The inauguration was three weeks after. Rick was told performers would need to be paid during the interim, at a cost of $350,000 per week. A million-plus dollars to pay people to do nothing, and then a fee for the actual performance, along with travel and accommodations. Final pricing had to be worked out with Rick, Tom, and Wynn.

Steve Wynn decided Showstoppers and Alabama would perform *only* at the Chairman's Global Dinner at the Andrew W. Mellon Auditorium on January 17 as the kickoff inaugural event, but we were still going to see about one of the balls. That morning, Hargrove submitted a $2.75 million budget for the stage decking, stage décor, and technical production requirements at the Mellon Auditorium. By evening, I saw almost the same budget, line for line, on PRG's letterhead. WTF was going on?

Forty-Nine Days Until the Swearing-In

Ivanka asked me to come to her office in Trump Tower to discuss her women's lunch or dinner (scheduling was still up in the air). She asked, "Can I suggest that you work with Abigail [Klem], president of my company, and Rosemary [Young], head of marketing, to brainstorm this event further?" She was sunshine and kisses, as always. "My preference [for the dinner] is Wednesday the 18th," she said, and added, "My interest in hosting depends on the quality and theme of the event." Get off your high horse! Why was I doing this event in the first place? What she told me she wanted was "an incredible group of female entrepreneurs and thought leaders." What I wanted to say to her was, "You mean Hillary Clinton and Michelle Obama caliber?" I bit my tongue. She then said, "I'd also like to integrate young girls into the program." Then there was a big but: "Only if we can make it an impactful event" would she "love to do it." Ivanka enlisted not only Abigail and Rosemary, but also Reince Priebus and Katie Walsh, cc'ing them on the email. Wow! Ivanka had leverage. "You should be in good hands but please let me know if you don't get the direction that you need from Reince and Katie, and I will step in," she said. Oh, and one last thing she said: "It would be great to have a cross section of industry and also invite top female cabinet members."

After we discussed the event, her team asked my advice on their marketing strategy to help her separate from her apparel and jewelry brand businesses. The messaging had to be right—that she was leaving her companies in good hands while she moved to Washington, DC, even though she'd claimed publicly she wasn't going to be involved in the White House. Having me meet with her team and asking me for non-inauguration strategy blurred the lines, because I was technically working for the PIC. But this was a familiar situation since I was also an unpaid advisor to Melania. I tried to be helpful. Ivanka sent me a nice note after the meeting, saying, "Thanks, Stephanie. Looks like [the women's lunch] is going to be a special event! So glad you are involved."

But . . . why was the PIC planning an event for Ivanka *at all*? And how had I gotten roped into it?

Tom texted, "How was your meeting with Ivanka?"

The two of them were as tight as an apple and its peel.

"We have so much to do for each of them," he wrote, meaning each of the Trump family members.

I replied, "We needed talent, catering, invitations, guest lists, security, floor plans, tents, *everything*." Nothing seemed to be coming together, because no one and nothing were ready to go, or existed.

I'd sent Melania a vision board of Union Station, the historic train station transformed into a glamorous party space for the Candlelight Dinner. "It's great!" she said. The renderings she'd received were inspired by the breathtaking décor at the 2005 Met Gala in the

American Wing, which I'd worked on with David Monn, the extraordinary event designer.

I told Rick, "After seeing the many other venues available to us, why use the Trump Hotel unless they are giving it to us rent-free? I really would like to discuss moving the Candlelight Dinner to Union Station. Thoughts?"

"Great!" Rick replied. "Union Station is a beautiful venue. Also gives us more space. I like the idea. I think as long as we do some sort of event at Trump Hotel, we will be good."

At least the day ended on a bright note when Rick emailed, "Michael [Alpert, of Ashkenazy Acquisition] gave the PIC Union Station to use rent-free!"

"Amazing!" I replied. "It's the perfect spot."

Forty-Eight Days Until the Swearing-In

My first text to Tom that morning was "This is so unsettling . . ."

Team Hargrove was on its way to meet with us in New York City at Colony Capital. I texted Tom: "I do not like being involved in crosshairs or intrigue. What we are doing is so historic that I can't believe people are taking advantage in such a crucial time for our country. Everything's become a big mess . . ."

Tom found himself reassuring me constantly. "Just spoke with the big man. We have a change of plans, which is going make our life much easier. On my way to the office."

I wondered what "the big man" (Donald) had to say.

Central command was my dining room table. We needed an office! The PIC's offer to lease us a space a few blocks from Trump Tower in a barren room where we'd be required to build out offices and pay rent seemed wasteful, so we turned it down.

I took my request to Rick again, who then asked, "Would Trump Tower be okay? Or do you want something away from TT?"

Of course we wanted to work from Trump Tower. Why would we want to work anywhere else?

Rick introduced me to Brad Parscale, the "digital director" who was "largely responsible for the great win." Brad was Jared Kushner's all-things-digital genius and would eventually become the campaign manager for Trump 2020; he initially said he could allocate office space on the fifteenth floor to us. We walked through the empty floor in Trump Tower. "It's a bit of a mess," he said. "The campaign team just moved out." I didn't care what it looked like—there were offices and there was space.

After I left, Parscale reached out to Jared: "What is this whole thing about?" he'd asked. "Stephanie Wolkoff wants the campaign to pay for six to ten people on the campaign floor?"

What? I'd asked nothing of the kind. Why was this so hard? Trump Tower was full of empty offices and conference rooms. I had seen them with my own eyes. We couldn't use just *one*?

Jared said, "They should be paid by the inauguration. This isn't campaign related."

Tom explained to me, "[There's a] battle on the finance side. The transition team and campaign are raising money against us [the PIC] on DJT's Victory Tour. This is very harmful to PIC fundraising."

These details were above my head, and frankly not my responsibility. All I knew was I. Just. Needed. An. Office. Tom texted me to "STAY AWAY!" So we did.

A week later, free of charge, we started using his conference room at Colony Capital at 712 Fifth Avenue—a hop, skip, and jump from Trump Tower. Phew.

Forty-Seven Days Until the Swearing-In

Jon suggested we combine our professional strengths under one umbrella. "We'll call it WIS Media Partners," he said. "WIS" was a reference to our joke "Who Is She?" Tiny Horse, the media company Jon cofounded with his partners Melanie (Mel) Capacia Johnson, Owen Leimbach, and Kyle Young, would partner with SWW Creative (me) to work together producing the events of the 58th Presidential Inauguration.

Rick told us all to contract directly with the PIC. Tom reminded me to keep my contract "simple."

In coordination with the PIC, I'd have general oversight of the creative and design development of the inauguration. Jon, Mel, and other executives from Tiny Horse would oversee the operations, communications, TV broadcast, and digital rights deals, as well as executive produce the broadcast components.

Forty-Six Days Until the Swearing-In

We had a meeting scheduled with Mitch Davis, hoping to get some good news on performances. Our list of entertainers: *zilch*. Trump needed a Hail Mary or the Godfather, and we got them both with Mark Burnett and the team he recommended.

December 5, 2016, was a *big* day. Jon flew to New York with former vice president of Tiny Horse, C. J. Yu. "C. J. is the best!" he said. "He worked for Burnett."

Jon, C. J., and I met at my apartment, and then the three of us joined Rick to visit Mark Burnett at his vast apartment at the Ritz-Carlton Hotel. Mark welcomed us with open arms. Even though C. J. had worked with him before, for some strange reason they acted as if they vaguely remembered each other. I felt like I was the only one not in on the joke.

I found Mark to be magnetic, gracious, and enthusiastic. I opened my presentation book and showed him what we were planning for the overall theme. He said, "It's incredible! Brilliant! You've got fantastic ideas, elegant Stephanie." Like Donald, Mark liked to put an adjective in front of your name and *voila!*, instant brand. So, to him, my brand was "elegant SWW." Really, he gushed.

There we were, sitting with the king of broadcast himself. And Burnett had some good ideas up his sleeve! He knew just the right people; Chris Wagner and Jim Roush of the Roush Wagner Company (RWC), award-wining television broadcast producers who could manage everything, were his go-to people. The PIC could finally exhale because they now had access to a top-of-the-line team of professionals whose credits included such notable productions as the Academy Awards, the Golden Globes, and the Emmy Awards, and reality TV shows like *American Idol, The X Factor, Shark Tank, The Voice,* and the MTV Music Video Awards. Their experience producing logistically complex live events in an efficient manner and on budget was invaluable due to our limited time frame. Burnett was our savior, going back and forth from LA to New York, and staying in communication with the executive producers and in close proximity to me.

All the while, as this was happening, I was working with Melania on her transition, initiatives, and styling, too.

Forty-Five Days Until the Swearing-In

Thanks to Mark Burnett, at last we had a great team with experience on top TV shows and live events. Chris Wagner and Jim Roush incorporated Inaugural Productions (IP), a.k.a. DC Productions, and subcontracted top-tier executive TV producers; communication and digital consultants; and skilled technicians to deliver the broadcast productions.

Our responsibilities grew tenfold. But we believed that with our combined extensive production experience and strong ties to the entertainment and fashion community, Inaugural Productions and WIS Media Partners were going to pull this off!

In an effort to maximize the PIC's resources and economies of scale, WIS was also asked to assume oversight and management of some internal and external coordination between the PIC and many of its different vendors, including Hargrove, Design Cuisine (a catering company), and Amaryllis (a floral design company), to name a few. I was like a piece of chewing gum, getting stuck between budget reviews that I ultimately had no authority to question or approve. I stretched as far as humanly possible, and in every direction, trying to be heard. I didn't have the power of the pen, so, at the end of the day, it was all a masquerade. Little did I know then how this would come to haunt me later.

IP's $25 million broadcast production budget was preapproved by Thomas Barrack and PIC CEO Sara Armstrong, along with the PIC finance team, the PIC's treasurer, Douglas Ammerman, PIC's budget director, Heather Martin, and, always in copy, the RNC's Jeff Larson.

Things seemed really complicated. Operating Agreements, Scope of Works, Master Service Agreements, proposals, and vendor budgets flooded my inbox. So many different versions, with revisions and comments, that it was impossible to keep track of them all. To me, contracts are like gobbledygook. Thankfully, I had learned an invaluable lesson from Melania: I told everyone to "speak to my lawyer."

Jon sent me an email letting me know WIS Media Partners LLC was incorporated to develop, produce, and manage the events of the 58th Presidential Inauguration. I was a part of WIS's senior level executive design and supervisory team.

After the PIC realized it could not deliver the broadcast production PEOTUS had envisioned and relayed, PIC asked WIS to assume this responsibility as well. For the production and broadcasting of the live performance events, WIS contracted IP for the Make America Great Again! Welcome Concert, a two-hour live event to take place on January 19 at the National Mall, plus a two-hour live broadcast of the musical performances, speeches, and presentations that took place at the Freedom and Liberty Inaugural Balls on January 20. This was all under the oversight of WIS Media Partners.

As WIS's oversight grew, I made myself very clear to Jon. "I will not assume the financial responsibility," I told him. "I'm not okay with this." I didn't have time to read the scope of work. Jon needed to, as I said, "speak with Tom and Rick to make sure the agreement is between you [Tiny Horse] and the PIC, not you [Tiny Horse] and SWW!" And to Call. My. Lawyer.

Jon replied, "That's easy BUT let's discuss. I think there are significant benefits to you to make it all under SWW."

With all the crazy numbers swirling around, that was the last thing I wanted to do, so I immediately reached back out to my lawyer Larry, a partner at Grubman Shire Meiselas & Sacks, P.C., who told me, "Your partner's [Jon's] legal team represents him, they don't rep you! Have him call me."

So I told Jon, "Call Larry!"

Jon was calling and emailing me nonstop. "Are there any updates? We need to sign the Operating Agreement today. Please advise."

I emailed my lawyer and said, "My biggest concern is that if millions are going into WIS, and we are paying IP, I do NOT want to be financially responsible. I am ONE person and Tiny Horse is a major company."

Larry replied, "I am growing concerned about these people, the way they are pressuring you to sign in this manner. I want to understand why they need this. You need to be sure the agreement is right and not be pressured into signing when it's not quite ready."

This legal dialogue continued for weeks. Larry reached out again and again to Jon, Mel, and their legal counsel and said, "Will someone please forward a copy of the agreement for our review? There is no attachment on the emails we are receiving."

Why didn't the PIC just pay Inaugural Productions directly? Their fee comprised more than 90 percent of our budget. It seemed odd that WIS subcontracted them when our staff retained less than 5 percent of the budget. Shouldn't they have subcontracted *us*?

I didn't like that WIS was front and center, but, to make matters worse, there was a new effort in place by all parties to lower WIS's profile and push SWW to the front of the line. The more I fought and resisted, the more I felt like a target.

After being repeatedly told by my partners that I was overreacting and that it was "easier this way" and "better for me," my answer was always the same: "Please run it through my lawyer." To this day, my lawyer has never signed off on this arrangement.

In addition to thinking about the big picture, I was focused on the tiniest details, like fonts. I had invitations to source and samples to approve. I tried to get the MAGA font from Brad Parscale, but he always lost my emails. Melania put me in contact directly with Rhona Graff, senior vice president at the Trump Organization, Trump's gatekeeper, the woman who knows all. Within minutes, we had the goods. FYI: the font is Berthold Akzidenz Grotesk Bold Extended.

The barrage of emails and "action items" never stopped. Rick sent me tons of emails, always in need of immediate attention.

The action items from Rick that day were all about the swearing-in ceremony.

For example, he wanted me to ask Melania if she had any suggestions for the swearing-in; the only thing we knew for sure was who would administer the oath of office to President-Elect Trump. That one was easy. Since John Adams in 1797, it had been administered, with few exceptions, by the chief justice of the Supreme Court. I asked Melania which Bible(s) the president wanted to use. A single Bible or stacked? Which on top? Open or closed? Who would deliver the invocation? The benediction? Were there musical selections? Poetry readings? Who would perform the national anthem?

I had no idea what Donald wanted, and he probably didn't either!

Melania's reaction to all of these questions was, "You have to speak with Donald."

I was on a mission to find out the answers, and that I did. For the Bibles, he chose his childhood Bible, given to him by his mother in 1955. "I want to use the Bible my mother gave me," he told me. "It's inscribed." I actually teared up. The second Bible on the stack would be the one Abraham Lincoln used in 1861. Tom Barrack told the *Times*, "[Trump] is humbled to place his hand on Bibles that hold special meaning both to his family and to our country." The only other president besides Lincoln to use that Bible? Barack Obama.

Forty-Four Days Until the Swearing-In

Talent was a must! The messaging "Donald's the biggest and best talent!" was wearing us all out and certainly not attracting other talent.

Inaugural Productions took the lead, with WIS Media Partners still retaining oversight and responsibility. IP was WIS's only vendor.

To get us up to speed, Mark Burnett suggested IP hire talent producer Suzanne Bender, known for *America's Got Talent*, *Dancing with the Stars*, *Showtime at the Apollo*, and *American Idol*, to name a few.

"I love Suzanne," Jon said. "We worked together on AGT!"

The first order of business was to establish Suzanne's fee. She seemed reluctant to join, but when the rest of the group agreed to double her fee, she was on board. The talent-scouting team was quickly in place and responsible for allocating a portion of IP's budget for performers. Jon and Mel worked directly with Chris Wagner, and Suzanne Bender with PIC CEO Sara Armstrong.

Everything seemed under control, but that feeling was short-lived.

Like a broken record, I kept expressing my concerns about budgets. Also like a broken record, I became everyone's problem.

Jon emailed me. "Rick and Sara were given budget yesterday. . . . Frankly, the pressure to reduce the budget is internal, mainly from you, Stephanie, so that's why we're analyzing each line item diligently. If we are to deliver the show DJT wants and in line with the creative we've proposed, then PIC already knows this will be $20M to $28M."

As if there weren't enough cooks in the kitchen, Rick introduced us to a talent producer from Texas, Walter Kinzie, the CEO of Encore Live. Jon Reynaga and I had no idea who Kinzie was. Rick seemed to know him and bent over backward to praise him when he talked about the talent he'd bring in, acts like Josh Weathers, the Green River Ordinance, the Band Perry, and Chris Janson. (Honestly, I'd never heard of any of them. Sorry, guys!)

"I smell a scam," texted Reynaga. "Walter is not known by ANYONE in the industry."

C. J. said, "You may know [Walter] from such events as . . . Blue Apron's employee appreciation lunch and Mattress Firm's regional bus tour."

C. J. wasn't joking around. He sent us a link. Who was this guy?

Kinzie went on and on about a concert at the Verizon Center, or maybe at the convention center, scheduled depending on what was available. He was planning a concert for the night *after* the swearing-in. I had not heard a thing about this event, but once Rick told us it wasn't under WIS's purview and the PIC was handling it, we wanted to know why we were wasting all of this time with people and events "we didn't have anything to do with."

"Walter is going to pay all this money to talent and then take a cut for an event we don't know about," texted Jon. "Something dodgy is going on."

Melania was clueless about this concert, too, nor had she heard of Walter Kinzie.

As we discovered, Rick had hired Walter Kinzie, a school friend of Don Jr.'s, to produce a concert separate from the concert on the Mall at the Lincoln Memorial and the Freedom and Liberty Balls at the convention center, ones IP was doing. The concert Kinzie was working on for Don Jr. and Eric was the evolution of Camouflage and Cuff-links. "Bald Eagle" ticket buyers (for $1 million) would get to meet the new president. "Grizzly Bear" buyers (for $500,000) would get to go on a hunting/fishing trip with Don Jr. and Eric. (How fun!) One of the affiliated sponsors of the event was the National Rifle Association. All the music acts were red-state faves. The Trump boys created a nonprofit for the event called the Opening Day Foundation, with two directors, Gentry Beach and Thomas O. Hicks Jr.

I wrote to Jon, "It's like the Country Music [Association] Awards, only with people you've never heard of." He sent back an LOL. "I'm not laughing!" I replied.

Was there really a gun-lover event planned on Trump's first day in office? Planned behind his and Melania's backs? "I'm furious," I wrote to Jon. "We have to stop this." After a supposed "peaceful transition of power," the phrase I'd inked into memory, Trump was kicking off his presidency with guns and saddles ablazing? Note to self: Follow up with Melania.

Burnett was official. On December 7, Maggie Haberman and

Nicholas Fandos of the *New York Times* reported that Donald, Tom Barrack, and Burnett had "kicked around ideas for his inauguration in his office at Trump Tower."

They wrote, "Mr. Barrack said Mr. Burnett was actively involved in producing the inauguration week festivities. He will have a large team to work with, as the committee's staff in Washington is expected to swell to more than 300 people by Inauguration Day. . . . 'Mark is a genius, and the president-elect loves him,' Mr. Barrack said."

Tom wrote, "Mark [Burnett] had the greatest idea for a ticker-tape parade in New York City, and then Trump traverses to the top of Trump Tower and helicopters off to Washington!"

My response: "The city is going to LOVE cleaning that up. LOL."

Forty-Three Days Until the Swearing-In

Things were getting a bit tense with Jon. He'd started to call me a micromanager because I insisted on reading every email that came to me, from C. J., Wagner, our lawyers, my lawyers, Lindsay Reynolds and Ramsey Ratcliffe, Hargrove, and Tom and his assistants. I read and reread all correspondence so no one could say to me what I was saying to them: You're not giving me what I need. So, yes, I micromanaged. Guilty as charged!

Jon wrote, "If you want to review all emails you can. You will go crazy."

He got that right.

Mitch Davis was following up with the band Kiss for the outdoor concert on the National Mall, and if they fell through, the boss gave Tom and Mark Burnett the green light to go with Mark's idea to do a "With the People"–themed event and invite unknown bands and acts to perform.

Jon and C. J. were racing ahead with the infrastructure of the broadcast for the concert. I was focusing on the creative and programming.

Plus, something bad was going on with my neck. The pain was

indescribable. It ached and cramped all the time. I was taking tons of OTC pain meds just to function.

I perked up whenever Mark Burnett emailed me. "How are you?" he wrote. "See [in the recent article in] *Variety* that I made sure they mentioned you!! You are the General. I am your soldier. I will come back next week again. [Music executive] Irving Azoff is calling all his clients from us for [the concert on] the Mall."

I replied, "I will take you up on that! Thank you."

"YOU ARE THE BEST! Your vision and insight are priceless!!" His emails were priceless. For the Candlelight Dinner, I pushed for a full orchestra. Burnett texted, "Yes yes yes!!!!!! An orchestra is so much more elegant, like you!!"

You see what I mean? Butter.

Rick Gates, on the other hand, barraged me with emails about ticket design, entertainment, production, the website, as if I weren't laboring twenty hours a day on the creative.

Forty-Two Days Until the Swearing-In

Rick Gates reached out to let us know he was working on a budget with Production Resource Group [PRG], who'd be providing the event technology for Steve Wynn's Showstoppers at one of the balls. Rick said, "Our head of production assembled a budget of potential costs for transferring the show to a Ball. He's quite familiar with Showstoppers, as the company he owns was responsible for creating the design, technology, and AV for the show at the Wynn."

If Showstoppers was coming to DC, it would be a crime for them not to perform at one of the inaugural balls, to be broadcast for all to see. Rick Gates presented what he called a "30,000-foot level take on what it would look and feel like at an Inaugural Ball, and a production budget range estimate for discussion/review." *So far, so good*, I thought. The email continued: "This budget keeps in mind the level of standards of the original, along with new approaches to the main background scenic (LED with video set changes), all designed for a convention center hall and this scale of an event. If the final direction/intent is to completely re-create the entire show, exactly as seen in Vegas now, the budget below would increase. If this direction/intent is for the performers to perform a selection of acts/numbers on a simpler static side stage, the budget below would decrease. Budget Implications $3,900,000–$5,000,000 Total Budget Estimate Range." Wynn's Showstoppers performed only at the Chairman's Global Dinner.

Forty-One Days Until the Swearing-In

On December 10, I was cc'ed on an email between Lindsay Reynolds, Ramsey Ratcliffe, and Patricia Tang, the Trump International Hotel Washington's director of sales and marketing. It said, "For eight days, Sunday through Sunday, for all space including room rental and minimum [food and beverage], the price is $3,600,000."

The buyout amount, before the costs of the events, would cost the PIC $3.6 million. That figure couldn't be right. I thought to myself, *Surely there's a mistake here—wouldn't Donald be donating the space or charging a steep discount?* There was no way this was the going rate. This amount appeared to be quadruple the standard price. Besides the problematic optics, it seemed ethically wrong.

Forty Days Until the Swearing-In

Melania and I were meeting again at Trump Tower, deciding on her inauguration looks, when Burnett texted me. I mentioned that I was with Melania right then. "Please give my love to her," he wrote. "Roma [Downey, his wife] and I adore her. Cameron [his son and Melania's ring bearer] says hello. I am here for you . . . 24/7. Regarding music. Unless it's a huge performer. We don't want it, right?"

Melania nodded. Only the tippy top for Donald!

He said he'd had a conference call with the set designer of *The Voice* and his "video screen team" to talk about the Candlelight Dinner.

"I explained theme is SWW ELEGANT. THINK OSCARS. THEY GOT IT. I ALSO GOT INTEL HEAD OF GOVT RELATIONS FOR DRONES IF DESIRED [caps his]. I think the drones would add [to the experience]. And it would be free."

Drones for the concert on the Mall and/or the swearing-in ceremony? Burnett thought big and bold.

On December 11, there was a very bizarre meeting about entertainment. No A-listers wanted to be associated with Trump. "What happened to Steven Tyler?" we asked. "What about Kiss?" They just disappeared.

There was one bright spot that made me bounce in my chair. Jon Voight was on the call. Mitch recruited Voight, and he in turn tried to recruit others. "Jon just saw Andrea Bocelli in Manhattan and had an idea with GOP friendly Katharine McPhee," said Mitch.

I said to Voight, "Very much looking forward to connecting," and I genuinely was. Finally! Someone who *wanted* to be a part of the inauguration.

Thirty-Six Days Until the Swearing-In

We had one more A-lister on board: Andrea Bocelli, the opera superstar, was a friend of Donald's and he'd vaguely agreed to perform at an inaugural event. Boris Epshteyn, the PIC director of communications, thought we should announce it to the world. "TMZ, *Page Six*," he wrote. "We go wide." But Bocelli was not yet confirmed. If he released that, it would make us all look bad.

A little after seven thirty in the evening, he sent me a draft of the announcement that included this: "Top-line entertainers from all over the world are reaching out in order to perform at events related to the inauguration. The president-elect, however, is hesitant to invite any performers who supported Hillary Clinton and helped artificially inflate crowds at her events."

Why would Clinton supporters like Beyoncé or Bruce Springsteen have any interest in performing at Donald's events? They wouldn't. It made no sense. And the media already knew we couldn't get top-line entertainers.

He emailed, "[Donald] wants to push on this."

I convinced Boris to hold off until Bocelli was official.

Ivanka texted me that evening. "Random question. Is the Candle-light Dinner on Thursday night black tie? A ball? Press will be there?" This couldn't wait? It was over a month away.

I told her I'd have someone get back to her.

Mark Burnett reached out. "Is there a party on Jan 21? Alabama performing?? TMZ just asked me to confirm. Hunting trip with Don Jr. sponsored by McIntosh [a political fund-raising firm]?? It's nonsense. Right??"

TMZ broke the story about Eric and Don Jr.'s (canceled) Camou-flage and Cufflinks event. It looked horrible that the boys were trying to sell face time with the newly elected president.

I told Mark, "We just found out Steve Wynn wants Alabama performing at the Chairman's Dinner before Showstoppers," but "as for Don Jr., I have no idea about the party on January 21?!"

Mark was outraged. "Someone is back channeling press. It's apparently 16 people who pay one million $ to go on hunting trip with Don Jr. and Eric?? And it's on Jan 21, the same day as million-woman march??? You're not producing this. Right?"

I wrote, "We have NOTHING to do with this. This is all Don Jr."

"Well, I don't want us lumped in," Mark said. "I think you need to make this very clear. Imagine your friends asking you about the HUNTING DINNER??" He was so right!

Thirty-Five Days Until the Swearing-In

Back in New York, I attended a meeting with President-Elect Trump in his office. The space was packed with boxes, trinkets, and piles of paper. And I thought *I* was a hoarder! His office looked like a garage sale. Andrea Bocelli; his wife, Veronica Berti; his son; and their security guard were already there. I sat in back. Bocelli dropped the bomb: his wife and family had been receiving death threats about the possibility of his upcoming performance, and for that reason, he was going to have to back out. He and his wife couldn't have been more friendly, and no one could blame them for canceling.

Thank God I'd stopped Boris from sending that statement!

It was a huge blow to Donald, though. We all agreed to put forward the story that Bocelli had offered to perform because of their friendship, but Donald had told him that he wasn't needed, "thanks but no thanks." After handshakes and kisses, the door closed behind them.

"Stephanie," Donald said, "tell me what's going on with the inauguration planning."

Tom had told me not to present anything—not a tablecloth or a color theme or a table chart—directly to the boss, but he couldn't be angry at me for following Donald's orders, could he? My objective was to make Donald and Melania happy. Rick, perhaps, had other objectives—for starters, at times he seemed more concerned about making the Trump children happy. If I told Donald and Melania about the inauguration plans, it could prevent others from pushing their own agendas.

Ivanka joined Donald and me for the meeting, and I presented to the two of them.

I grabbed my binder, went over to Donald's side of his desk, and sat with my knees on the floor. He sat in his red leather chair, leaning back, clasping his hands, ready for me to proceed. Ivanka hovered over me.

I went through hundreds of pages, covering all eighteen events. Ivanka made comments and asked questions. "Will there be a red carpet?" "Where do we walk during the parade?" "What about seating at the swearing-in?" "After-party?"

About the parade on Pennsylvania Avenue, Donald said, "I don't want floats."

"Okay," I said.

"I want *tanks* and *choppers*. Make it look like North Korea." There was no way . . . He really wanted goose-stepping troops and armored tanks? That would break tradition and terrify half the country.

When Ivanka heard North Korea, she didn't bat an eye.

About our lack of securing a top performer, she said, "My father is the biggest celebrity!" He smiled at her.

But we had to have *someone*. Was Donald going to sing the national anthem himself?

I walked out of the meeting ruffled and worried. I texted Jon Reynaga, "North Korea–style military parade. Bad idea?!"

I hit send and my phone rang. Rick. "A little birdie told me you attended the Bocelli meeting," he said.

Huh? Who had told him I was in there?

Donald came out of his office and said, "Stephanie, come with me." I hung up on Rick and followed Donald down the hall. He said, "Great job, really great job." I was thrilled that the president-elect was flashing me the classic double-thumbs-up pose. (I'm easy to please.)

PEOTUS walked me to a nearby conference room that was cluttered with MAGA and *Apprentice* paraphernalia. He introduced me to the woman at the table. "Stephanie, this is Monique Breaux. She's working on the Oval Office. Monique, Stephanie is a pro. She did the Met Gala and has a great eye. I want you to run her through what you have here," he said, made an about-face, and left.

Melania had mentioned Monique to me. Apparently, she did a lot of decorating for the Trump Organization and worked very closely with Ivanka.

The evening before, I had asked Melania, "Don't you want to decorate the Oval Office?"

Of course she did, but she told me, "If Donald wants Ivanka to do it, then let her, I don't care."

"Don't you think you should?!" I asked. "You're the first lady." Does Ivanka have any boundaries?

"Yes," she finally admitted. "I want to decorate the Oval Office."

Monique showed me her vision boards, swatches, and samples. She was keeping it Trump traditional with silks, velvets, and lots of tassels. The golden/yellow/slightly greenish hues of the colors reminded me of the off-color surprises in my babies' diapers when I was breastfeeding them.

"I'd really like to see how this photographs," I said. "Do you mind if I take a few pictures?"

"Not at all!" she said, smiling proudly. "I'm also designing a custom carpet for the Oval Office."

"I'd love to see it," I said as I snapped away.

Once I'd seen enough, I left the conference room, went to Rhona Graff's office, and gently knocked on her door. "Come in, Stephanie," she said. "What did you think about Monique's designs?" she asked me.

"I'm not sure I should get in the middle of this," I told her. *But since* you're *asking* . . . Sure, I wanted the job of decorating the Oval Office to fall upon the First Lady, but I also knew TV and I knew Donald. "Monique's not thinking big-picture," I told Rhona. "It's the Oval but it's also going to be Mr. Trump's set for at least the next four years.

"The shimmering threads she has for wall coverings just don't work," I said ever so gently. "It's gold mixed with green, and we all know Donald hates green!" I said. "No matter how tan he looks, he'll look drained out."

Rhona nodded and said she would speak to Donald, but I knew that was it. Monique was out, and my girl was in.

Within minutes, I told Melania about Monique's gold braids and she said, "Are you kidding me?"

Ivanka and I spoke later that day. I told her, "Rick called me right after the Bocelli meeting. He said a 'birdie' told him I was there. I want you to know that I would never disclose to anyone what was said in the room between your dad and Bocelli."

She sharply replied, "Stephanie, you better figure out how to make things work with Rick [Gates]."

My heart stopped beating for a minute. She had actually shown her hand. Rick's "little birdie" was definitely Ivanka. They told each other *everything*, just like I told Melania everything. Rick was, in effect, Ivanka's spy and protector. No wonder Gates had an all-access security badge for Trump Tower. I needed to be very, very careful around him and assume that talking to him was like speaking directly to Ivanka.

If Ivanka controlled Rick, and Rick had allegedly written Melania's convention speech, did that mean Ivanka was behind that major faux pas/sabotage? If she felt threatened by Melania, she'd make her look bad in the press and block her efforts—and the efforts of others, like me, made on Melania's behalf.

Still, later than night, Monique emailed, "Lovely meeting you today. I have sourced more gold fabrics and spoken to [White House operations people] regarding the quality, timelines and gold yarn colors in the rug. Let me know when we can connect in the next week to finalize golds and wall finishes." I didn't have the heart to reply. Rhona had to do the dirty work the next day.

Thirty-Four Days Until the Swearing-In

I thought that Melania should wear and showcase the extraordinary talents of American designers *only*, and ideally those who were also immigrants. As one of America's most famous immigrants, she could use her visibility to celebrate and endorse the creativity and accomplishments of others like her who came to America and made their mark.

When I laid out my sartorial vision and excitedly explained to Melania how it could send a unifying message to balance out her husband's anti-immigration rhetoric, she said, "But I want to wear Lagerfeld!"

Thirty-Three Days Until the Swearing-In

Hallelujah, we had talent. Jackie Evancho, then sixteen, who rose to fame on—wait for it—a Mark Burnett Production, *America's Got Talent*, signed on to sing the national anthem at the swearing-in ceremony. All other music that day would be from Donald's approved song list, the same one he used at rallies, heavy on senior white dudes like the Rolling Stones, Creedence Clearwater Revival, Elton John, and Luciano Pavarotti.

Thirty-Two Days Until the Swearing-In

"My team has asked to get their contracts signed. Can you please facilitate?" I asked Rick. He replied, "Can you guys please provide a breakdown of the $1.62m in the proposed contract." We'd done that already. WIS Media Partners was paid $1.62 million with the financial responsibility to pay WIS's and IP's executive teams' supervisory fees. WIS retained $1.195 million of the fee to pay Jon, Mel, C. J., me, and eleven other employees. PIC authorized WIS to pay $425,000 to the three executive producers, Chris and Jim from IP, and Carol Donovan, a TV producer, for their broadcast production fee. WIS was also tasked with overseeing and paying IP's $25,000,000.00 preapproved broadcast budget.

Part of the problem with signing up talent was we didn't yet have an approved budget and we'd been chasing down the PIC CEO Sara Armstrong to generate contracts and approve advance payments. But it was impossible to get anywhere with her. She had no authority to make decisions, but she was great at following them. The PIC made getting paid a huge hurdle, not just for the talent, but for us, too!

Rick wrote an email to Tom and me confirming that "we are removing the public concert on Friday night. We will reflect the changes in the new schedule." He was referring to the Camouflage and Cufflinks event that was to have been hosted by Don Jr., Eric, Gentry Beach, and Thomas O. Hicks Jr., and produced by Walter Kinzie. The Trump boys must have been looking to put my head on a stick, but Mark Burnett also wanted that event axed.

Thirty-One Days Until the Swearing-In

Melania had a meeting scheduled with David Monn, an event planner and interior designer, "to talk about potentially working with her in the White house at some point, somehow," she told me. Jamie Burke, the director of presidential transition personnel in 2016, organized for them to get together. (Jamie Burke is currently the commissioner at the President's Commission on White House Fellowships and president of the 45 Alliance.)

Melania and David's meeting had nothing to do with the inauguration or me. But I have to admit, when she told me about the upcoming meeting with David, I was elated. "Do you think I should ask David for help with the inauguration?"

Melania paused and said, "Great idea."

Music to my ears. I sent him an email but he was unavailable "doing a wedding in South Africa." Of course he was! Too good to be true.

Melania sent me a draft of her holiday letter that she hoped to release to the press that ended with "Wishing you a Merry Christmas and prosperous New Year!" It was signed, "First Lady Elect, Mrs. Melania Trump."

Face palm. Here we go again.

I texted, "Honey, I love you, but you were not elected."

"Protocol office says it's fine!" she told me.

I went back to look at previous administrations' wording. None of them said "First Lady–Elect Michelle Obama" or "First Lady–Elect Laura Bush." Melania did. Not. Care.

On December 20, Ivanka set up a "family logistics" telecom meeting with Tom and Rick (and me and Jon) to run down a set agenda and invited Don Jr., Eric, and Tiffany Trump, and copied Rhona and Lindsay Santoro, former Trump family chief of staff. It was a huge time suck, but whatever. It had to happen eventually. Ivanka wanted to know the nitty-gritty. We ran through an overview of the inaugural activities and schedule, logistics and transportation, the swearing-in ceremony, broadcast rights, and digital "behind the scenes."

A couple of hours after the family conference call, Tiffany Trump wrote to Rick to ask about her transportation to DC, and if her boyfriend could sit with her and stay at Blair House with her. She also asked how many outfits she'd need and if hair/makeup stylists would be available to her, and then signed off, "Thank you so much!" Tiffany seemed genuine and humble. A very different style than her sister . . .

Rick was on it. He responded to Tiffany right away, assuring her that she could bring her boyfriend and a small entourage. He even gave her packing and style tips. "You might want to throw in an extra daytime ensemble in case you want to change after the Wreath Laying Ceremony and the Welcome Concert on Thursday," he wrote. "If you have some specific needs [for hair and makeup] let us know and we will see what can be arranged. Hope this information helps." When it came to the Trump kids, Rick was like the concierge at the Four Seasons.

Thirty Days Until the Swearing-In

Rick emailed Ivanka the seating chart, and she was assured by Rhona that her mother, Ivana Trump; her grandmother Marie Zelníčková; and her childhood nanny Dorothy Curry were in the VIP section and very well taken care of. Ivanka asked me, "Are these good seats? Any suggested changes?"

I wasn't sure which seats she was referencing—hers and Jared's, or her mom's.

Ivanka was very focused on *Ivanka*. Seating position and photo ops were of paramount importance, especially during the swearing-in ceremony, "the most iconic moment of the inauguration," she told me. If she could have swapped spots with Melania, you bet she would have!

Thanks to Ivanka's concerns, I got my hands on a seating chart. Up until that point, I had not been involved in the seating, nor had I seen a seating chart. With diagram in hand, I told Melania about our meeting. Melania specifically requested that I find out for her where on a drawing she, Barron, and her parents were placed, and she wanted to approve the seating order, and she did.

Ivanka was the least of my worries, though. I was increasingly frustrated by Hargrove's lack of urgency and compliance. I wrote to Vice President Ron Bracco, cc'ing president Carla Hargrove McGill, "I am concerned. I have not seen anything [but creative] for these events. We need to see the outdoor and indoor setups. The tenting, the entrance, lighting, the check-in area. I need to see samples of everything as we discussed! I need line by line, which includes the item, unit price, extended price, and description. I hadn't seen any of that, in spite of being promised so many times." They seemed allergic to transparency, which was infuriating and troubling. I drove Tom and everyone else nuts with my ceaseless and unanswered requests for help. Then I was told my presence was no longer needed in any future budget meetings.

Twenty-Nine Days Until the Swearing-In

On December 22, Matthew Hiltzik, PR crisis manager, once the head of corporate communications and government relations at Miramax, reached out to Ivanka to say, "The narrative surrounding the inauguration is going awry. Mark [Burnett] and I were talking, and he specifically suggested/requested that I raise this issue with you after he and I discussed the situation. Basically, in order to better control the narrative, you should have Stephanie be front and center on this and there needs to be a clear direction expressed publicly about what the inauguration plan IS (celebration of talent of lesser known but incredibly gifted Americans) as opposed to being defined by what it is NOT (no—or few—Hollywood and top mainstream musical talent). Always best to be defined by what you are, vs what you are not. An approach which served your father quite well during the campaign."

Awry?! It was more like a national disaster.

Hiltzik is like a Michael Clayton image "fixer." He was warning Ivanka to distance herself from the bad inauguration press and pushing me to the top of Shit Mountain.

Twenty-Eight Days Until the Swearing-In

Chris Wagner, of Inaugural Productions (IP), wanted assurances from WIS Media's budget director, Melanie Johnson (Mel), that he'd have enough money to satisfy Donald's vision. He wrote, "DJT wants it to be bigger/better and outside of the box than any other inauguration."

Yeah, we knew, Donald and Mark wanted what they wanted, but there were limits. Mel replied, "The more modern, innovative design and décor that DJT has approved includes more union labor, scenic build, and install costs involved in a short time span. Vendors are charging premium prices for holiday turnaround." In addition, "New pavement at Lincoln Memorial has a very expensive workaround because no heavy machinery is allowed."

Fireworks? *Boring.* Mark Burnett wanted to light the sky up with drones, and Donald and Melania loved the idea. Mel explained, "Aerial Light Show and logistics around that is a new expense never been done before. Any further detailed explanations around Staging, Lighting, Art Direction, Talent, and Travel would be beneficial since those are the high numbered items."

Wagner also needed to transport the stage itself from New York to DC. Why couldn't Hargrove build it in DC? Johnson described his requests as "like creating the pyramids all over again!"

Trying to get real numbers from Hargrove about past inaugurations was a tragicomedy. They estimated $30,000 for a decorative tree, but market rate for a similar one was $7,000. So many hours of my life were lost yelling over the price of plants. And did a stage *really* cost $6 million? Why was IP subcontracting to Hargrove now, too? The PIC was already contracted directly with Hargrove and paying them, too. These kinds of questions kept me up at night.

While it seemed some people were burning through cash, I was trying to bring some in. During our broadcast meeting regarding the underwriting and sponsorship, I learned that Barack Obama raised $5 million for his inauguration by selling exclusive broadcast rights. My competitive inner beast emerged. I thought, *I'm going to sell the broadcast rights to the ball's first dance*. And then I did! CNN verbally committed to me to sponsor it for $2 million.

I called Tom and said, "This should cover a lot of expenses, including my entire team's salary!"

"That's great!" he replied. "The boss is going to be happy about that!" But then he continued. "We have to be careful here, because Donald and Rupert Murdoch are best friends, and CNN has been very difficult for DJT, so I have to clear all this politically first." Tom tried.

The boss was not happy about anything having to do with CNN. That deal was off.

Twenty-Seven Days Until the Swearing-In

Ivanka was weighing in on talent, and Sara Armstrong was not having it. Sara sent an email to Jon and me that said, "I'm worried [a certain performer] gets into the lower level that Ivanka didn't want. My opinion is that we need to decide if DJT is the final sign off on all entertainment (which I think he has to be) and then present to him the full plan of entertainment for each and all events before we pull the trigger. What I don't want to do is invite entertainment and then DJT not like it. We can't please everyone in the family. The decision maker has to be DJT. I think we need to have a plan that we present to Tom who then presents to DJT. That's my 2 cents."

It was Donald's inauguration, not Ivanka's. But no one was brave enough to tell her that.

Twenty-Six Days Until the Swearing-In

Tom reached out to say, "Merry Holidays! Hope you're getting a little rest. DJT just called me and asked if we still have the Rockettes. I said yes. I hope that's true!"

"So do I!" I said. "That has been arranged by Rick so we are waiting for the next steps on that. I will follow up with him. Have a wonderful holiday!"

Twenty-Five Days Until the Swearing-In

To reinforce my American-only policy, I turned to one of my dear colleagues, interior and events designer David Monn, whom Melania trusted as well. He agreed with me. "I asked around with a few friends," he texted, and he said they agreed with us, but "interestingly for different reasonings." The first reason he mentioned was the business aspect. Jobs. Commerce. Similar to US politicians driving American cars, it's just a good policy. The other reason was to show that Melania did have *some* support in the New York fashion world.

Melania and I were still going back and forth about which designer she should wear to the swearing-in. Although her heart was set on wearing Lagerfeld, I told her to think big, and she finally got it. There is *no one* like American icon Ralph Lauren.

I'd known Ralph Lauren for over twenty years and had almost worked for his charitable foundation. I had no idea when I asked him if he'd consider my proposal to dress the incoming First Lady for the swearing-in ceremony, much less if he'd agree. When Ralph gave the green light, I teared up.

"I'm grateful, thankful, and hopeful," I replied. What a historic moment for all of us.

"They got lucky with you," he said. Insert lump, throat.

Ralph, along with his senior design team, got to work and produced beautiful sketches of a cropped double-faced cashmere jacket and mock-turtleneck dress in the same fabric. For the color, he proposed camel or baby blue since it would be January. (The secret service call her "Muse," but my nickname for Melania was Bella Blue [BB].) With her Manolo Blahnik BBs, BB wanted baby blue, a color that would set off her eyes. Whatever Melania wants . . .

Twenty-Four Days Until the Swearing-In

On December 27, 2016, I reached out to Ron Bracco. "Just arriving in DC. I am looking at this budget and I was hoping to see the edits based on our two-hour call. Many of the revisions we discussed are not represented here?" I let him know that "We will need to spend all afternoon at the Hargrove office and will review this line by line."

Rick was perplexed. "What is up with these guys? I am really getting concerned about their lack of focus and accuracy!"

There was constant flak, conveyed through Tom's assistants, about the details of the Chairman's Global Dinner. The guest list, which I was never allowed to see, had ballooned to six hundred. Tom wanted to hire ballerinas, dressed in sexy Elie Saab dresses, to escort the guests from cocktails into dinner. He suggested we bring in his personal décor guy from Los Angeles.

"Have him send a vision board," I said.

I should have just let Tom do what he wanted. But I was so worried about how this opulent event would reflect on Donald and Melania. I tried to step out of the event several times but was always pulled back in. I sent photos and info about the venue to David Monn. We'd fix it together.

Melania and I talked about Tom's dinner, including the playlist from Mrs. Wynn's fiftieth birthday party (personally curated by Mr. and Mrs. Wynn) to be played throughout the evening, and Steve Wynn's Showstoppers from Vegas. "Tom, Donald, and Steve, the three of them have this love triangle dynamic, and I don't want to get in the middle of it," I said.

"No," she said. "It doesn't sound very fun."

Silence.

Twenty-Three Days Until the Swearing-In

On December 28, Hargrove invited WIS and IP for a meeting at their warehouse facility. We were ready to see where the magic took place. Carla, Ron, and other senior staff met inside their spacious conference room. About ten of us had a seat at the table, and another five people sat on the periphery. They handed out an updated proposed budget for the inauguration, to the tune of $29,501,798. (This was the last Hargrove budget ever shared with me.) Their management fee was $1,538,510.00.

I almost fell off my chair. I asked for a tour.

In the warehouse, there was not one table on-site, only the tools and machinery to construct them. They didn't have any finished product to show us. No words could explain the shock we were in.

I asked a very reasonable question: "Where's your stockroom?" I wanted to see items from past inaugurals, from past administrations.

Didn't exist. No storage room.

Two and a half weeks before showtime, and Hargrove had nothing to show us?

"Not to worry," Ron said. "We've been doing this since the 1940s."

What a relief. *Not.*

After we regrouped and caught our breath, we had to figure out who we knew with available assets and could get them to Washington in two weeks.

Chris Wagner of IP, WIS's only subcontractor, wasn't concerned: he was set and had vendors lined up for everything broadcast related, including lighting and staging. Since IP and the PIC said they had that and other events covered, I believed them—I didn't have the bandwidth to question this. I needed to take care of the original events I'd been brought in to produce. I wasn't about to take any chances with Hargrove, so again I reached out to David Monn.

Unfortunately, he was still in South Africa. Texting him, I gave a brief summary of how screwed we were and begged him for his help, knowing he could whip this together in his sleep. Whether he'd be available or not, I explained, still furious about the lack of transparency and helpfulness from the PIC, "I only want to be with people who are kind, honest, and loyal!"

He replied, "Kind, honest, and loyal. Those would be the three principles that I too believe in and actually live by! It's actually a very strange thing that I kept the calendar open for the first part of January, as I wanted to 'feed my soul' in some way. To celebrate our democracy, our process, our people would 'feed the soul' for sure!" This was a godsend.

I almost collapsed with relief, and prayed the PIC would sign off and maybe even reallocate some of Hargrove's budget to David. He would be back in New York on January 4, just several days away. The team, including Melania and Ivanka, were happy to hear that David was on board.

Twenty-Two Days Until the Swearing-In

Hargrove was the PIC's main vendor and general contractor. We had a shared responsibility to make sure the inauguration was a success, so I needed to stay on top of them and tried to make nice with Carla Hargrove McGill, the company president. I explained in a long email about our communication issues with their staff, the undelivered renderings and floor plans, the lack of available assets, and the pricing, or, more specifically, the lack therof!

She replied, "In the spirit of moving forward as you suggest, we would like to offer you the following for consideration. Hargrove will provide ten bars at your approved design at no charge. We will also offset the costs of your linens in our budget."

It seemed they were charging a fortune for items that didn't seem to exist, but they'd throw in ten bars and linen for free? Could they throw in a few cases of tequila, too? And maybe some Xanax?

The best part . . . my day was just getting started.

Rick called me that afternoon and said, "I need to see you ASAP!" Hopefully he realized how screwed we all were.

I walked into a room and saw the staffer in charge of the parade and outdoor programs, Ryan Price. He nodded hello. "Hello, Ryan, lovely to see you," I said.

Rick chimed in, "We need you to come up with an event to hold at the Ellipse for the preshow," he said. "We have nothing to put in it." He paused. "Maybe an event having to do with children." Just another request to add to my overflowing load of responsibilities.

So let me get this straight: the PIC agreed to pay Hargrove millions to get the Ellipse (the park next to the White House) built out for an event, but they had no entertainment planned and wondered if I had any suggestions? Someone in the room suggested a blood drive. I said, "Give me an hour."

I walked out in a daze and ended up in my PIC office, where I plopped down in my chair. On top of everything else that was going on, they needed me to come up with another act? Nothing came to mind as I stared out into space and devoured a stale cookie, which tasted incredible. *Nothing made sense.*

I thought, *What about the Girl Scouts?*

Since Melania's initiative was going to be about the overall well-being of children, the Girl Scouts were perfect. Their anti-bullying program protected kids from cyberbullying and promoted STEM (Science, Technology, Engineering, and Math) education for girls. I'd already been working with them on a nut-free cookie idea as part of my (pre-Trump) food allergy initiative with the Sean N. Parker Center for Allergy & Asthma Research at Stanford, in collaboration with the Safe + Fair Food Company. I'd created the partnership, so I had the relationships in place. It was a wholesome, easy ask.

I checked in to see what Melania thought of the idea of hosting an event welcoming the Girl Scouts and highlighting their program. Without missing a beat, she said, "Of course."

I told Rick and Ryan the great news. "Melania suggested we invite the Girl Scouts to participate in a welcome event, followed by walking in the parade and giving out Girl Scout cookies," I said.

Disaster averted.

But there was another one sneaking *right* around the corner. I asked Rick for a follow-up on my contract and he told me, "We had a breakthrough (subject to final approval from our attorney) in regards to the broadcasting and production elements in conjunction with the WIS contract. We will discuss during our meeting today. Thanks."

This sounded complicated. I just wanted my "simple" contract.

Twenty-One Days Until the Swearing-In

Lindsay Reynolds, the deputy director of the PIC's special events team, was aware I was interviewing candidates for the East Wing staff and offered to set up a couple of meetings. I met with Lea Berman, former White House social secretary during the George W. Bush administration, in my room at the hotel so no one would see us together. She also suggested I meet with former White House chief usher Gary Walters, who had served seven presidents and could help me go through protocol and operations. I acknowledged that it was a good idea and was really appreciative that they'd offered. When we all met at the Trump International Hotel in DC, Lindsay had to leave early and accidentally left behind a paper bag, which I took up to my room.

The following morning, I rested Lindsay's bag on top of my suitcase. The bag ripped and fell over . . . and out came a DC Events binder full of renderings, schedules, and the run-of-shows from the two previous inaugurals that I'd been asking for since November. She'd kept it from us all this time.

The power struggle between the PIC and WIS never let up. I'd had enough. I wrote to Tom's assistant, "WIS is out." The PIC, including Lindsay Reynolds and Ramsey Ratcliffe, did everything in their power to keep us out of the loop by not inviting us to meetings, dropping calls, and making blanket decisions.

I went to see Jon. We were enraged and called Rick and Tom. If we were to stay, something had to change!

Rick did the dirty work and fired Lindsay and Ramsey.

Ramsey got herself hired right back through Colony Capital (just like Rick Gates). Lindsay stayed in the background to help the PIC for a bit, but then she was sent home to her husband and kids in Cincinnati.

I sent a fiery email to Heather about the stonewalling we'd been dealing with. "I am DISGUSTED by the lack of transparency about the PIC's funding," I wrote. "I asked Hargrove last night for the millionth time to send me PAST renderings. I can't approve any budget if I don't have something to compare it to! This is unacceptable and a pure lack of any ethical standards."

I wasn't asking to compare apples and oranges. It was apples to apples. Same venues. Same events. I could not get an inch with these people.

Finally, a bid from Hargrove came in. Chris Wagner, used to dealing with very big budgets, was knocked off his feet by Hargrove's bid for one of the inaugural balls. He sent an email to our team saying, "We just received Hargrove's bid. It came in at $2.95M ($193K for their on-site labor). We have $650K budgeted for this set build. For reference, this bid is literally five times anywhere else would be. We've accounted for some premium increase, but this is exceptionally high. We have concurrently reached out to additional vendors and will keep you updated."

I wasn't the only one who was outraged by the overpricing.

Hargrove, PIC's largest vendor, also entered into a Master Service Agreement directly with IP, WIS's largest subcontractor, and was paid over $2 million for a section of the stage at the Lincoln Memorial.

On New Year's Eve, I was reeling about the invitations and tickets the PIC had outsourced to Ted Jarrett's Cavalier Communications. Ted emailed Ramsey the designs, and we noticed that the attire was listed incorrectly on multiple invites. Ted said, "Rick and Sara approved all of these." The tickets had been printed, and now they had to be redone. There was no time!

The only power Sara Armstrong had was the power of the pen. She signed off on all budgets after they were reviewed by Tom and

Rick and approved by the PIC treasurer, Douglas Ammerman, and Jeff Larson, Sara's advisor, her boss at the RNC. She wasn't counting every penny, but I was, and they all wanted me to just shut up.

That was how 2016 ended for me: furious, burned out, and feeling very much alone. I had no time for celebrating, only more mountains to climb.

Maybe it would all change in 2017, with less than three weeks to go.

— 5 —

Showtime

I hoped that a miracle would happen and all the factions involved with planning the inauguration would come together in patriotic spirit. If we didn't, the big weekend would be a disaster, an embarrassment to the Trumps and a humiliation seen around the world. I would not let that happen. Melania, for one, did not deserve that. Our nation, however divided, needed to at least feel proud of the celebration of a new leader. I dug deep and kept going, one frustrating day at a time.

Nineteen Days Until the Swearing-In

As for the gifts for guests at inaugural events, Lindsay Reynolds and Ramsey Ratcliffe had been in charge. I'd expected that they'd follow protocol from previous administrations.

And then thousands of dollars of goods showed up at my door in New York, all from the White House Historical Association. Books, mugs, fleece blankets, scarves, coasters, and tote bags. I'd never seen or approved any of this stuff. And why was it in New York? The events were in DC. The PIC wanted my approval, which I never gave. I couldn't find room in my apartment for the samples and sent them back to Lindsay at the PIC office in DC.

A hundred emails later, I learned that Heather Martin had approved the gifts for PIC staffers, "family and friends," donors, and elected officials. Lindsay and Ramsey blew the entire gift budget of $500,000 on tourist junk to give to "family and friends."

At one point, Heather asked Ramsey, "Is Stephanie going to source additional gifts?"

Ramsey replied, "I do not believe so."

She could have asked! Melania Trump was not about to give travel mugs to million-dollar donors at the Candlelight Dinner. Heather told us Michelle Obama gave crystal bowls from Tiffany & Co. at hers.

"We have to return it all," I wrote to the brain trust at the PIC at one in the morning.

Heather Martin's bright idea: "For ninety-nine cents apiece, we can make sparkling wine bottle favors and put the PIC logo on them!"

The next morning, I called Melania and said, "Guess what? There's no budget for you and Donald to buy a gift for your guests."

"Are you serious?"

Dead serious.

Melania would not hear of it. We priced those same Tiffany bowls and made the decision to give one to every couple. We had to beg for extra money for Melania and Donald's gifts!

In the end, we still came up short. Some couples took two; other couples went home empty-handed.

Eighteen Days Until the Swearing-In

Hargrove was in, then out, then in . . . We didn't know what was happening.

Regarding the Chairman's Global Dinner, Rick told us, "My discussion with Hargrove last night was to indicate that they would be involved in *certain* aspects based on our previous conversations but that PRG was running point based on the call with PRG from Friday.

Unless something has changed between PRG and Hargrove that I am not aware of, nothing has changed. I will reach out to Jim [at PRG] right now and confirm."

Seventeen Days Until the Swearing-In

Ralph Lauren's team reached out to make sure the First Son was taken care of, too. (Barron already had his suit, however.)

Ralph had discussed every tiny detail of Melania's dress design with his team. Was it floor length or knee length? Pencil shaped? Was the jacket belted? Should it be cropped? Go over the hips? How much volume around the neck? Should the hat be the same fabric? Veiled? They constructed the outfit to Melania's specs and proceeded with fittings.

Ralph created a couture ensemble of multiple pieces—a dress, a jacket, a hat, gloves, and a clutch—for Melania to wear to multiple daytime events on January 20, including the St. John's Episcopal Church prayer service; a White House tea with the Obamas, Bidens, and Pences; the swearing-in ceremony; the Joint Congressional Committee on Inaugural Ceremonies luncheon; and the Inaugural Parade on Pennsylvania Avenue.

Sixteen Days Until the Swearing-In

Hargrove was not a dependable vendor, to say the least. I'd spent the last four days banging my head against a wall dealing with them, their ridiculously high budgets, and ulcer-inducing execution strategy. Regarding the floor plan for the Candlelight Dinner, our Emmy-winning production designer wrote to Carla Hargrove McGill, "There is too much wrong with this plan for me to go into without literally sitting next to someone at a computer and school them on some design basics. I'm actually shaking my head at how badly arranged this is." Everything they touched or sourced had to be redone, at huge expense.

But Rick Gates was elated. The PIC raised "too much money," he said. I wasn't sure what that meant, and I didn't have time to find out.

I thanked God that David Monn was back in town. We'd had a great meeting the afternoon before about the two events I needed help with, the Candlelight Dinner and the Chairman's Global Dinner. The Candlelight was high-end. Melania wanted to capture a Camelot moment at the beginning of the Trump presidency. Barrack's dinner was, as Tom said, "like the weaving of a tapestry" of ambassadors and VIPs from around the world. It would be a very extravagant affair and attention to detail was paramount. I told David about the ballerina escorts and asked, "If this doesn't go away, maybe we should hire male models, too?" Tom was quite anxious to see some samples of David's vision.

David volunteered to load up a U-Haul truck with 120 uphol-stered tables, chairs, candelabras, place settings, and more from his warehouse. He said he was "thinking the driver could leave New York around 5:00 a.m." to drive it all down to DC instead of battling with Hargrove and other vendors for the assets, and I accepted the offer. It shouldn't have been necessary. You'd think we could rent everything we needed in Washington. I didn't know if PIC was reallocating part of Hargrove's budget to David, although we believed they'd already been paid some, and the budget Heather sent was like smoke-and-mirrors math, with placeholder numbers where the real ones should be. We were two weeks out.

Perhaps you've planned a wedding—venue, food, alcohol, tables, place cards, invites, custom floral arrangements, entertainment, an AV system, parking, gifts—for a couple hundred people. How long does that usually take? Six months? We had to organize all the basics, along with security, road clearance, a motorcade entrance, building a stage and media platform, signage, custom carpeting, and a VIP pre-party, in a fucking train station, for fifteen hundred VIP donors, *in fifteen days, while we were also planning seventeen other events!* And I thought the Met Gala was stressful! Compared to the inauguration, that was like planning a kid's birthday party.

I got really upset that afternoon about how crazy all this was, the pressure, the increasing pain in my neck. I was on the verge of saying "Fuck it" and walking out. David Monn calmed me down. He said, "Breathe. Inhale lavender, exhale pink, and the world will be prettier!"

And you know, it really was.

Fifteen Days Until the Swearing-In

Hervé Pierre, a French-born naturalized American designer with stellar credentials, had been recommended to Melania and met with her at Trump Tower. Coincidentally, I arrived just as he was leaving. Seeing each other, we squealed, hugged, and did the classic, "Oh my God, how *are* you?" I was so happy to see a familiar face. Hervé and I had worked together for eleven years.

As soon as he left, I told Melania that she had to bring him in. "He's an incredible talent. Snap. Him. Up." She did, as her personal stylist.

Melania and I had been talking about who would be designing the gown she would wear to the inaugural balls—the Liberty Ball, the Freedom Ball, and the Salute to Our Armed Services Ball—and for Donald and Melania's "first dance" as the First Couple to "My Way." This was a major decision. It was going to be a part of a two-hour live broadcast, and her look had to be perfect.

It was a historically important look, too. Melania's choice would be displayed in the Smithsonian National Museum of American History's *The First Ladies* exhibit. Melania's counterparts have been donating their inaugural gowns since Lady Bird Johnson.

Everyone presumed it would be Karl Lagerfeld.

I had a better idea. "It would be incredible if you and Hervé Pierre designed a gown together," I suggested. "He has the qualifications, and the story would be great!" I wanted to highlight the magnitude of two immigrants making something together, but I didn't bring it up because she would have probably decided against it. Melania loved the idea of getting to play designer for a day, but highlighting to the press that she and Hervé were both immigrants was out of the question. Her take was to let the clothing speak for itself and not to bother with the backstory. I was just thrilled that Hervé would get his moment to shine.

For her "collaboration" with Hervé, Melania gathered inspirational looks of tailored dresses with sharp lines. He described them as "no-fuss" style. Once they had a clear aesthetic, he began sketching.

Although Hervé and Melania spoke a common language of design, they spoke to each other in English. Not once did I hear or see either of them speak or write in French. It seemed odd to me: Melania claims to be fluent in Hervé's native language. (Come to think of it, I have *never* heard her speak a single word of any language besides English and Slovenian with her parents and Barron. Not that I'm saying that there's anything wrong with speaking only two languages— that's one more than I can! But *I've* never claimed otherwise.)

Hervé texted me, "I'm putting the dress to work on Monday. I am so honored. She's really fabulous. I love her. I can't hide it. We started to speak about money, but I told her that the priority at the moment was her gown and we shall speak about fee after the inauguration."

His first mistake. Never try to get money from a Trump after the fact.

Hervé updated me at every step of the process as he had muslin fittings, sewed on the embellishments, and made petite sketchbooks of her outfits. But he still hadn't pushed Melania about payment. I asked him why, and he admitted, "I'm afraid."

I knew exactly how he felt. There's an imperiousness, a *grandeur*, about the Trumps that makes one scared to mention something as trifling as fair compensation. People tend to tiptoe around the subject. The Trumps treat people as if being in their orbit is its own reward.

Fourteen Days Until the Swearing-In

Soon after the election, Anna Wintour had visited Trump Tower to congratulate Donald and invited him to meet with the editors of each Condé Nast magazine at their One World Trade Center offices in the coming days.

Per Melania, I heard that Ivanka was playing matchmaker between Anna and Donald behind the scenes. Melania said Donald told her to "come down from the penthouse and join the meeting in his office." It sounded more like an afterthought. She didn't go. I could hear in her voice that her feelings were hurt. She thought of Anna as a kind of friend.

As he and Anna had discussed, Donald took an off-the-record trip on January 6 to meet with the Condé Nast editors, some of whom had raked him over the coals for decades, like Graydon Carter of *Vanity Fair*, who'd dubbed Donald the "short-fingered vulgarian" at his previous gig as the founding editor of *Spy* magazine. David Remnick of the *New Yorker* was no Trump fan, either. And yet they all sat at a conference room table together and talked about Vladimir Putin, women's rights, and climate change.

Tom Barrack went with Donald to the hour-long morning meeting. Although Tom and I had had some tense exchanges, we got along well. I spoke my mind, which he seemed to like—I wondered if anyone else talked to him the way I did. Since Condé Nast was my "haunt," as he said, it was cool that he kept me updated on the meeting by text. He sent me a photo of Anna smiling charmingly and described her as the meeting's host. Another photo showed the entire table and all the editors. "Graydon looks like he saw a ghost," Tom texted.

Of Anna he wrote, "Elegant ice queen."

Thirteen Days Until the Swearing-In

On January 7, I was in New York and Jon was in DC when he texted "Trouble!" Hargrove had sent him samples of the "lock-up," a.k.a. the

Presidential Seal—"The Inauguration of Donald J. Trump, the 45th President of the United States of America"—that was printed on all graphics, scenic backdrops, and stage sets for the Trump inauguration. "Please note that Tom himself has approved option 4 of the attached— but waiting on you, SWW, for approval on rest ASAP!!!!!!" he said.

Trump is a branding machine, and maintaining a visually consistent "TRUMP" on all of his collateral was paramount. This included every color palette, inaugural seal adaptation, and font, along with the Presidential Seal. Much to our disbelief, the designs included both Donald J. Trump's and Mike Pence's names. Historically, it should have only the president's name.

"Tom and Rick approved the Trump-Pence lock-up," Jon said after he had researched it, and told me no previous inaugural lock-ups had both names. I was picturing Melania and Donald's first dance with POTUS and VP splashed across the screen.

Why give Pence's name such prominence and defy tradition? Was this a positioning of Pence as Trump's equal in standing in the administration? I'd heard rumors from all kinds of sources about Mike Pence being owned—lock, stock, and Bible—by billionaire corporate overlords who intended to elevate him to president as soon as possible.

I marched right over to Trump Tower and showed the lock-up to Melania and Donald. Jon, who was with Rick and Tom the same time I was with the Trumps, later told me that Tom took a call from Donald, hung up, and said, "That fucking bitch!"

The new lock-up design hit my inbox within the hour with Mike Pence's name removed.

Later that night after I got home, I had second thoughts about what I'd done. I'd really pissed off Tom and I really didn't want to be on his bad side. But I was just watching out for Melania and Donald.

I called Melania in such a panic that she put Donald on the call. "Am I going to end up on the bottom of the Potomac River?" I asked them.

"Don't worry, Stephanie," said Donald. "You're fine."

Twelve Days Until the Swearing-In

We were less than two weeks out. Rick said, "We need to finalize all budgets today to the extent possible and lock down the numbers. In addition, we need to review the budget line items for each event, particularly the Hargrove pieces." He directed Heather to "take the lead and circulate the latest budgets for each of the events to everyone. We need to see as much budget detail as possible. I will find a time today that we can all meet to review the events and corresponding budgets. As we schedule the meeting if you need to bring in others to support this exercise then please let us know."

The PIC still didn't have a budget? How is that possible?

Some things were solidifying. We had a talent roster for the concert on the Mall: Toby Keith, Jon Voight, the Piano Guys, Lee Greenwood, DJ RaviDrums, and 3 Doors Down, among others.

Clearly we needed more performers. The broadcast on the Lincoln Memorial was shaping up, but we still had a two-hour live broadcast at the convention center for approximately forty thousand people (though that number was highly contested). Executive Producer Carol Donovan came up with the genius idea to ping-pong the broadcast from stage ABC in the convention center to DE, keeping the performance pace moving for live broadcast. We had the Rockettes confirmed, but we needed more talent. I called my friend and goodwill ambassador of peace, Lord of the Dance Michael Flatley, and asked him if he would consider hopping on a plane with his troupers and performing at the inaugural. Without missing a beat, they took DC by storm. He was a savior, God bless him!

Then Donald went on a rampage about seeing a tablecloth for the Candlelight Dinner, and I had to run to the PIC office to get it to Tom so he could show it to him. Every detail and decision required dozens of emails, texts, and calls, and Donald and Melania's input and approval.

That night, Jon reached out to WIS partners Mel Johnson, Owen Leimbach, Kyle Young, and me, saying, "Meet in my room, ASAP!"

Our anxiety and stress skyrocketed, and we were all a little paranoid. We emptied the minibar, swearing our rooms were tapped and we were being followed, by whom we could only surmise.

Jon didn't mince words. "WTF is going on here?!" Real or imagined, we had our suspicions.

Around 2:00 a.m., Mel walked me to my room. I hugged her good night, feeling my heart thumping and my mind racing.

Since early January, Ivanka had been agitating about the family portrait, a traditional photo of the new First Family, usually shot in the Blue Room of the White House. She'd been sending me emails she'd received from famous photographers Max Vadukul and Mark Seliger asking to shoot it. Melania turned them all down. Ivanka could have risen Richard Avedon from the dead for that family portrait, and Melania would have said, "Nope."

The only photographer Melania would work with was Régine Mahaux, who flew in from Paris for the big day with a team of five to capture Melania's every second.

The scheduling of the portrait was up for debate. Rick Gates sent Ivanka some options and she went back to him asking for *specific* times, along with when sunset would occur, so the timing didn't interfere with Shabbat.

Melania was not thrilled about Ivanka's steering the schedule and would not allow it. Neither was she happy to hear that Ivanka insisted on walking in the Pennsylvania Avenue parade with her children.

After I'd met with the Homeland Security and Emergency Management Agency, District of Columbia, Melania and I discussed pending security issues. She was cautious, and rightfully so. She did not want to put Barron in harm's way and told me, "We're not walking at all." We'd heard rumors about snipers and death threats.

I was so scared about the rumors, I called off the Girl Scouts from walking the parade route, too. Melania, however, decided to take a few steps, at least.

Eleven Days Until the Swearing-In

Tom traveled the globe making sure the most powerful people in the world would be at the Chairman's Global Dinner to formalize inroads with the new administration. The dinner wasn't one of the three events WIS had signed on for so my partners desperately wanted out, but I just couldn't leave him in the lurch.

Tom emailed me. "No one is returning our calls, and we need to finalize design and numbers today on Chairman Dinner and Candlelight! If your event team is withdrawing it is okay and we will wrap it up appropriately! Of course this process is frustrating for all! We just need to drive forward one way or the other tonight!"

I couldn't walk away from Tom for such a historic assembling during the inauguration, and I told him so.

"Thanks," he said, and at this point, "we can bask in simplicity that we could just execute perfectly."

If only.

There was no shortage of drama brewing on other fronts. Rhona Graff forwarded me an invoice from Monique Breaux, the woman whom we'd fired from redecorating the Oval Office. The total amount: $22,000! (Monique kindly waived $12,000 in design time, so her bill ended up being only $10,000.) Rhona asked me if the bill would be covered by the PIC, even though the Oval Office redesign had nothing to do with the inauguration. I said, "No!" and she took care of it.

It seemed like every person was trying to run off with money from the PIC.

I'd tried to block all inaugural events from being held at the Trump Hotel, but Ivanka, Don Jr., and Eric had figured out a way to do it after all. Rick sent Ivanka an email that I was (mistakenly?) cc'ed on: "There will be an after party at the [Trump International Hotel] following the inaugural balls on Friday. DJT is not expected to attend but it was more for you, Don and Eric."

Rick had previously told me that he had spoken with Ivanka and they had decided not to have the after-party, but this email was proof the party was on after all. Ivanka wouldn't lose a second's sleep about using PIC donations to pay for a party for herself and her brothers at her family's property to honor her father, who wasn't even going to be there.

The Trump Hotel was also booked for the "leadership luncheon," with each kid hosting a table. This family was not pulling any punches.

Ten Days Until the Swearing-In

David had magnificent tables that he'd brought from his storage in New York that were upholstered with studs, but we told Tom, "David and I want DJT to be happy and he wants tablecloths, so cloths he will have!"

Eight Days Until the Swearing-In

Ivanka texted me a photo of Barack Obama's swearing-in, his hand on the Bible, Michelle, Malia, and Sasha standing to his left. She wrote, "FYI regarding the swearing in. It is nice to have family with him for this special moment."

Why send this to me? She wanted to make sure I knew how badly she wanted to be in the iconic photo, the one people would remember, of her father's hand on the Bibles, taking the oath of office. I can understand that she wanted to be by her father's side for this historic moment, of course. But why was she coming to me for this? Did she think I would persuade Melania to step aside? That wasn't happening.

Five Days Until the Swearing-In

Melania and I launched Operation Block Ivanka to keep her face out of that iconic "special moment." To plan this, I needed to know exactly where the family would be seated and the camera angles. Tiny Horse executive Brandon Arolfo, who managed all the budgets with Mel Johnson, sent me notes from the walk-through. He had been prohibited from taking pictures; instead he'd drawn a sketch to give me a decent overview of the Trump section and where the chairs would be positioned in a semicircle around the dais. We knew where the cameras would be located because the platforms were already in place.

Using Brandon's sketch, we were able to figure out whose face would be visible when Donald and Melania sat in their seats, and then when the family stood with Chief Justice John Roberts for Donald to take the oath of office. If Ivanka was not on the aisle, her face would be hidden while she was seated. For the standing part, we put Barron between Donald and Melania and made sure that Don Jr. stood next to Melania, not Ivanka.

We were all exhausted and stressed out. Yes, Operation Block Ivanka was petty. Melania was in on this mission. But in our minds, Ivanka shouldn't have made herself the center of attention in her father's inauguration.

This sentiment was confirmed when Ivanka wrote to Rick yet again about the family portrait. "It would be really helpful to me if we could do the earlier time," she said. "Do you think that you can make that happen? Looping in Stephanie."

Loop me out, *please*. Melania said, "No, we cannot make it happen."

In all fairness, whose scheduling needs were more important? The president-elect and the soon-to-be First Lady's, or Ivanka's? She should have been accommodating *them*!

Later that day, I received an email from her office. "I notice that Ivanka's car is not part of the family motorcade. Is there any way to add that?" It. Never. Ended.

Rachel reached out. "I still have not received any invitations [for the inauguration]. Should I book cars??" Melania's guest list included a couple dozen people. We weren't surprised by the lack of respect for Melania. "Arm's distance," Rachel said. "Don't trust anyone but your family, and just protect our girl, MK!!"

Four Days Until the Swearing-In

The networks still hadn't gotten the transmission and satellite coordinates from the PIC. Without the proper codes, there would be no broadcast! Jon reached out to the PIC's communications department: "As you know, the objective is to get as many eyeballs on the Welcome Celebration, and Inaugural Balls. Right? Would PIC like to provide [the transmission and satellite info] to anyone who'd want access to it?"

We couldn't understand why the PIC would sabotage the viewership of Trump's inauguration. I pushed Jon to call them out on their bullshit. He said, "I need them to send the information—only they have the press database!"

Could you imagine if the viewership of the inauguration was *zero*?! Donald would have likely said, "Off with their heads!"

Three Days Until the Swearing-In

January 17, 2017, curtain call! It was go time. It was the first night of the official 58th Presidential Inaguration Committee events, opening with Tom Barrack's Chairman's Global Dinner beginning at 6:30 p.m. at the Andrew W. Mellon Auditorium. PEOTUS flew into town without Melania. Tom was pleased, and it made all of the inroads worth battling.

We had our morning walk-through at the convention center, two balls coming right up. The site supervisor raised some concerns and expressed his frustration to me, and much to his relief, I wasn't in disbelief. It was alarming but not surprising. I looped Rick in to let him know that "most of the constituents hadn't received their tickets to the balls" and "there is confusion regarding digital ticketing versus hard copy."

Rick had the answer at his fingertips. "Tickets are being distributed at several locations depending on which group you are part of. For example, tickets are being distributed at Trump Hotel and the Fairmont. Additionally, other tickets have been sent via email, and we have several thousands of people that have received them. As a backup we have paper tickets, should the need arise to use them."

I had no idea what he was talking about. Guests would have to go pick up their tickets?

The press release for the two inaugural balls went out and announced that there were $50 tickets for the general public to purchase at the PIC website. Too bad the website didn't work. That same day, Melania forwarded me an email from Lynne Patton, Eric Trump's personal assistant (who is now head of Region II in the Department of Housing and Urban Development), addressed to the main office at the Trump Organization. It said that the physical tickets were to be trashed. "If you have already received email or physical tickets to ANY events, please disregard. They are no longer valid," wrote Patton. Reprinted valid tickets would have to be picked up at certain hotels in the area, Trump's and Barrack's. I had a walk-through at a few venues that day and the event managers were afraid no one was going to show up! No one would explain the ticket snafu to us. We wondered, had the tickets ever gotten printed? That was a question for Ted Jarrett of Cavalier Communications, who, as I found out later, per the PIC IRS Form 990, was paid $3,999,585.00 to design and print all the tickets and invitations. We never saw them.

The incompetence and mishandling of information never stopped, and neither did the fake outrage. Rhona forwarded an email from Hope Hicks, written by a woman named Stephanie Grisham from PIC's communications team, who was known to be an Ivanka favorite.

"SWW Production company has been tasked with a made for TV broadcast of some kind and are refusing to allow any still photographers in the head-on shot at one of the memorials for inauguration day," wrote Grisham. "This was a spot that was pre-arranged and approved by PIC, allowing members of the major outlets (AP, Getty, AFP, Reuters, NYT, etc.) to be there, and now that access has been rescinded. Suffice it to say, the outlets are all very upset. I bring this up because I fear this could become a story OR that the major outlets could boycott things altogether."

Notice how she just said "SWW Productions"! We were WIS Media Partners. She only used my initials because this wasn't about access for photographers. It was about making trouble for me.

I copied Jon and Rhona on a reply: "We are doing EVERY-THING collaboratively with PIC, so I am not sure what she is talking about."

Jon sent out an email to explain what was *really* going on. "Stephanie Grisham and Hope Hicks are working with Boris Epshteyn's PIC Comms teams. All press positioning, accreditation and access is handled by that team, not us. For the three broadcast stages we are producing, we have worked with PIC Comms team to ensure press risers are in place for both TV and still photography. We presented to Mr. Trump last week. [Our setup] ensures maximum viewership for the 2-hour show to beat Obama's audience. Let me know if Hope or you have any remaining questions." (Beating Obama's numbers was the directive from above.)

Rhona said, "Thank you, Stephanie and Jon, for clarifying this. One less thing to worry about now!"

I had to do an on-camera press interview from the convention center, the location of the two inaugural balls, and I was a nervous wreck, completely exhausted. Jon handed me a bottle of tequila and said, "Drink this." If I hadn't had a swig, I wouldn't have made it through that interview.

Two Days Until the Swearing-In

January 18, 2017, we were on a roll. Ivanka emailed, "Will there be a step-and-repeat [at the Candlelight Dinner]? Where will it be?" I assured her there would indeed be photographers from Getty Images and *Women's Wear Daily* and that the step-and-repeat was in the reception area. She could pose alone, with Jared, with friends, and make pouty faces until rictus set in.

"As an aside," she wrote, "I was chatting with dad about how amazing he thought the event was yesterday [the Chairman's Global

Dinner]. He was blown away by how beautifully everything was done. I mentioned that initially there was going to be limited press and he told me to make sure you had 'tons' of press at the Candlelight Dinner and Balls. He thinks that they will be beautiful and wants it well documented. Major red carpet."

Ivanka and Grisham were on the same page: need more press. I replied, "We have provided every opportunity to make all the inaugural events as open to press as possible."

Why did I feel like I had to justify myself to her? By this point, she had to realize that the PIC tried to keep every event *closed* to the press, which made no sense to Jon and me. I was caught in the middle.

Ralph Lauren's team emailed to confirm that Melania was going to wear all five items at all the planned events. She replied to me that she wasn't going to wear the bag or the hat. "Won't wear it. Don't tell RL team!" After all the work that went into that hat, I was sad it wouldn't see the light of day. I wish I'd known earlier to give them a heads-up, but at least her elegant updo made up for the tragic loss.

Melania lands in DC.

One Day Until the Swearing-In

Finally, the day I was most excited for, Thursday, January 19, 2017. Melania's unveiling to the world, her first appearance at the inauguration of her husband, the forty-fifth president of the United States.

David texted me that he and the kids had arrived in Washington. I was so excited to see them but so overwhelmed and stressed out. The streets were packed with protesters, and David and the kids got blocked by barricades and couldn't make their way to the hotel. My hands were tied. I called Rick, who thankfully took care of it.

I spent much of the day backstage at the dress rehearsal for the Lincoln Memorial concert, meeting with the crew, reviewing and revising the run-of-show based on Melania and Donald's timing, and making sure *Women's Wear Daily* was ready to go with its embargoed exclusives on Melania's fashion. The clock was ticking when Melania texted me, "On way to Arlington." Her first appearance during inauguration weekend was a visit to Arlington National Cemetery, where more than four hundred thousand American veterans are buried, for the ceremonial traditional laying of a wreath at the Tomb of the Unknown Soldier by the president-elect and vice president–elect to pay tribute to the US armed forces and the veterans who made the ultimate sacrifice for our freedom.

Melania did not want "the kids" at Arlington. I tried my best, but after I sent Ivanka a schedule that left Arlington off, she texted, "Has the wreath-laying ceremony been canceled? I am pretty confused as I had always planned to attend and was going to bring [her daughter] Arabella as well. Can you please give me a call to discuss? This is very different from what was confirmed." She didn't miss a trick.

I wanted to reply, "Melania doesn't want you there!" It was her first appearance of inauguration week. She wanted the event to be with *her* family, Barron and her parents. I almost wrote to Ivanka, "Out of respect for our fallen heroes, this isn't a photo op and should be handled with dignity and humility." But Ivanka got her way. Don Jr. and Eric also came with their spouses.

After Arlington, the president-elect and "the family" made their way over to the Make America Great Again! Welcome Celebration at the Lincoln Memorial, which was broadcast live for all to see.

We were going to be LIVE on TV and we were running late. While they were in the car on their way over, I was standing in the wings with Mark Burnett and Jon Voight, the MC of the concert, waiting. Jon Reynaga texted, "Where are they? Once they arrive, get 'the family' seated in the box." The VIP box was the family seating area, a bulletproof-glass-enclosed cube with chairs at stage right for the Trumps. Tom Barrack joined them.

I texted Melania at 3:23 p.m., "What's your ETA?" and sent her a video of me walking in my heels down the twenty-one steps from the top of the Lincoln Memorial to the VIP box with my arm on PIC staffer Tim Tripepi and added, "Are you okay walking down these stairs? Donald must hold your arm!"

"Do you want to take my job 😊?" she asked.

At 3:51 p.m. she reached out to say, "Just leaving Arlington." Two minutes later, I told her, "They are holding the show for you," and she replied, "3 minutes away. Should we come in or wait?" With a palm to my forehead, I said, "Go into holding green room."

Enter the Trumps (twenty minutes later).

Melania and Donald appeared at the top of the Lincoln Memorial, standing in front of the nineteen-foot-tall Georgia-marble statue of Abraham Lincoln.

I will never forget the sight of Donald and Melania standing there, crowds applauding, then walking down those long, steep steps to make their grand entrance, her arm perfectly wrapped around his, just the way I'd told her. She didn't falter.

Following the president-elect's first planned remarks in Washington, DC, fireworks by Grucci—kindly discounted—lit up the National Mall. It was a triumph. And Melania looked magnificent, indeed, in her black military-inspired jacket and dark sunglasses. The next big event that night was the Candlelight Dinner in Union Station, the elegant black-tie sit-down dinner Melania and Donald were hosting for 1,500 guests on the eve of the swearing-in ceremony. The inspiration for the event was Camelot; Melania had told me she was a great admirer of Jacqueline Kennedy. (On a June 24, 2019, phone interview with *Fox & Friends*, President Trump likened that former iconic First Lady to his wife, saying, "We have our own Jackie O today, it's called Melania. Melania. We'll call it Melania T. Okay?")

Yes, he called his wife "it."

Kennedy worship might be one of the few things Melania and Ivanka have in common. Ivanka and Jared are big Camelot fans, too. It's no coincidence that all three of their children—Arabella, Joseph, and Theodore—share names with Kennedy family members. Edward "Ted" Kennedy and Joseph Kennedy you know; Arabella Kennedy was JFK and Jackie's stillborn daughter.

Between the MAGA concert and the formal Camelot-themed Candlelight Dinner, I had no time to get to a private room to change, so I went into one of the production tents behind the Lincoln Memorial, asked the staffers to give me a moment, and tugged on my dress in relative privacy.

Melania looked glamorous that evening in a glimmering gold floor-length gown that was designed by Reem Acra, a Lebanese-born, New York–based American designer.

The Jim Gray Orchestra, whose compositions and arrangements have been featured on NBC's *The Sing-Off*, *America's Got Talent*, and *Big Brother Australia*, did a magnificent job entertaining the guests. They played classics by George Gershwin, Leonard Bernstein, and Aaron Copland, and ended the evening with "Mona Lisa," "Days of Wine and Roses," and "New York, New York."

The Candlelight Dinner itself was a huge success, and I did get some love that night from the Trumps. When Donald gave his speech to the crowd, he said, "Stephanie, where's Stephanie? What a job! Are you okay now?" That last part referred to all the times I had cried hysterically to him, saying I was afraid I was going to be thrown into the Potomac River. When he said, "Are you okay now?" no one else could possibly have understood what he meant, and I couldn't quite believe he'd say it in a room full of people. But then again, how could I be surprised by anything that came out of his mouth?

At the end of the evening, I crossed through the barrier of Secret Service men to get to the Trumps' table and squatted between Donald and Melania to say hello. Melania stood up, pulled me into a big hug, and said for only me to hear, "Thank you for everything." Her eyes shone and I felt a real zing, a hit of love energy passing between us. In that moment, just for that moment, my eight weeks in hell felt worth it.

The next day, I got a lovely note from Mark Burnett about the concert on the National Mall. "Congratulations on such a successful concert! I wanted to reach out to say how impressed I was by the entire production team. I can't imagine the countless hours and dedication that went into making this show, and I hope you know that your hard work truly paid off."

"No," I replied, "Thank *you!*" It was *his* vision, *his* broadcast team, and *his* relationship with Donald that made it all possible.

The Production Service Agreement between WIS Media Partners and The Roush-Wagner Company (IP) was NOT signed until that day.

The Day Of

January 20, 2017, arrived too quickly, and not a moment too soon.

The 58th Presidential Inauguration, of the 45th President of the United States, Donald J. Trump was upon us.

The Trumps kept to tradition and spent the night at Blair House. Melania assigned rooms. The First Family was awake early and waiting for Donald and Melania to start this historic day.

Donald signed the Blair House Guest Book by eight fifteen a.m., and then they made their way to the service at St. John's Episcopal Church.

At nine thirty a.m., the president-elect and Mrs. Trump arrived at the North Portico of the White House and were then hosted inside by the Obamas and Bidens for tea, along with the Pences.

She wore the Ralph Lauren ensemble as planned. I couldn't believe *I* was responsible for what *this* woman would be wearing in the procession to the Capitol and the swearing-in ceremony at the 58th Presidential Inauguration of the United States of America.

The first peek most Americans got at the much-loved and labored-over ensemble was when the Trumps arrived at the White House to be greeted by President Barack Obama and First Lady Michelle Obama. Donald, ever the gentleman (*not*), rushed up the steps without waiting for Melania or taking her arm. Melania gifted Michelle a blue box from Tiffany & Co. that contained a silver picture frame.

Meanwhile, the risers at the Capitol began to fill up with former presidents, senators, and members of Congress. Tom, Rick, and the family stacked the rows. Melania's guests were not seated up there. Donald's opponent, Hillary Clinton, stood within rows of Melania's seat. On a day that must have been excruciating for her, Clinton wore a suffragette-white cashmere coat and pantsuit . . . by Ralph Lauren.

If Melania had known Hillary would also be dressed in Ralph Lauren, she would have been angry and might have decided not to wear the outfit. To me, his designing both women's outfits proved Lauren was truly an American icon.

Around 10:00 a.m., the outgoing president and vice president and their families walked their incoming counterparts to the Capitol. Melania walked gracefully down the steps. She took her seat next to Barron, in front of Tiffany; Ivanka; Jared; Don Jr.; Don's (then) wife, Vanessa; Eric; and Eric's wife, Lara. The gang was all there.

By eleven a.m., my family arrived at the Capitol, and I was informed my tickets were for the standing area only. Forget about sitting on the riser; we didn't have a seat anywhere. We'd have to sit on the grass. The explanation from the PIC for this oversight came from Cassidy Dumbauld, who said, "We didn't think she needed passes because she'd be working."

My husband knew the work I'd put in, the months I'd been away from him and the kids to make this happen. Being told to go sit on the grass was more than an insult. It was a massive "fuck you very much."

Fortunately, as David, the kids, and I were heading toward the spectator area, I ran into a Trump insider named Frank Mermoud. He said, "Where are you going, Stephanie?"

"Our tickets are for way back there," I said.

"Come over here." He brought us to a VIP area about three hundred feet away from the stage that had seats but not much of a view, unfortunately, but still way better than nothing. We watched the swearing-in on the two massive screens from there. It was only good luck that Frank saw us in the crowd and let us in.

At eleven thirty a.m., the big moment finally arrived.

Once we were settled and the ceremony started, I focused on witnessing history with my family. Later, when Melania asked, "How were your seats?" I told her we didn't have seats. Her response was,

"We were told the same by many of our guests." If the shoe had been on the other foot, I would have been apoplectic.

Rachel Roy was watching on TV from her hotel room in Washington. She texted a photo she'd taken of the screen showing Melania's head *completely blocking Ivanka's*. "Happy MT blocked IT! 😂😂😂"

I started laughing so hard, David thought something was wrong with me.

The Mormon Tabernacle Choir sang "America the Beautiful," followed by Jackie Evancho, who performed the national anthem.

Right after the swearing-in, I walked back to the Trump International Hotel with my family and David Monn. We didn't stay around for the parade. We had too much to do for the balls at the convention center. Melania was taking her stroll down Pennyslvania Avenue, and she looked imperial in her baby-blue Ralph Lauren suit.

Jon was already at the convention center. "Meet me in the broadcast production trailer," he said.

Tom was leaving the hotel in an armed escort car that would get me to the convention center hassle free. I couldn't say the same for my family, and I felt awful. Protests were taking place on the street as well as in my head, and I told David, "I don't want the kids and you to be out there trying to get to the convention center. Maybe watch it on TV." They weren't about to do that after all I'd sacrificed to make this happen, and besides, they were excited. I got them a placard for the car window that enabled them to pass through security checkpoints. David told me, "Not to worry. I love you." I kissed them all goodbye and said, "I love you guys."

Tom and I hopped in the car. We were sort of . . . speechless. With SO much going on, both of our fingers were doing all the talking into our cell phones. I was picturing the Trumps in the White House, taking their family portrait.

Liberty and Freedom: The Official Presidential Inaugural Balls were open to the public and broadcast live far and wide by the Roush Wagner Company (a.k.a. IP). Those balls were followed by the Salute to Our Armed Services Ball, open to invited guests who serve our country in our communities, at home, and abroad. This event was produced by Walter Kinzie of Encore Live.

The President of the United States of America and First Lady Melania Trump (late again!) danced to "My Way" at the Liberty Ball (then were joined on stage by the family, and the Pence family as well), and then went downstairs to halls D and E in the convention center and did it all over again.

For the portrait, Melania debuted her collaboration with Hervé Pierre. The floor-length dress was off the shoulder, with six layers of vanilla silk crepe, matching vanilla silk gazar details, and a red silk faille ribbon to accentuate her waist.

Hervé's gown was a smash among the guests at the inaugural balls and the breathless press. In the coming days, Hervé was inundated with media requests from all over the world, and he seemed excited about being part of something this big. But he still didn't have the confidence to ask FLOTUS for feedback, or payment.

Meanwhile, I received an email with the subject line "OPO Inaugural Celebration Invitation." "OPO" stood for "Old Post Office," the location of the Trump International Hotel.

"The First Family invites you to attend a very intimate inaugural celebration after the official Inaugural Balls. This email is intended only for you as an individual and does not include a guest unless otherwise indicated," it said. The after-party. It was happening and the PIC was paying for it. We didn't attend.

The Day After

Ralph Lauren's team reached out to let me know that "Ralph says 'good work, Lady W!' Coverage is great. Hillary in Ralph Lauren too!" I loved them.

I forwarded to Melania a news item that reported Ralph Lauren company stock had soared after the inauguration, despite calls on Twitter for a boycott. She replied with a snippy "They must be happy."

That was it. No "I'm happy for them" or "Thank Ralph so much, and Charles and Kimball, for all their hard work." Or "Thank *you* for leveraging relationships you'd built over two decades to help me look my best." I wasn't expecting a round of applause, but an acknowledgment of their graciousness would have been nice, even if she was bitter about sharing a designer with Hillary.

Although Frank had gone out of his way to give us better seats for the swearing-in, from where I had been in the VIP area, I hadn't been able to see the moment that captivated the nation the day after. Toward the end of the ceremony, with the family and VIPs assembled on the riser, Barron, on Melania's right, started fidgeting. Ivanka and Tiffany were standing behind them.

Donald turned around to smile at his wife. She smiled back at him. As soon as he turned away, she frowned aggressively. Twitter went nuts, and the hashtag #FreeMelania was born. Viewers of the footage assumed that she only smiled when Donald was watching, and as soon as his eyes were off her, she let her true contempt show.

It wasn't at all what had happened. Melania suddenly frowned and looked down and to her right because Barron had kicked her in the ankle by accident, she explained to me later. It hurt, and her annoyed face reflected that.

As her advisor, I suggested she set the record straight about the #FreeMelania frown. She said, "Who cares what they think? It's my private business. I don't owe them an explanation."

"They" happened to be the American people.

In the aftermath, I received an email from Rick. "What an epic experience we shared together. Nothing will ever change that. At least now you will be better prepared in 4 years when we do it again, right?"

Nope!

— 6 —

White House–keeping

*M*y forty-sixth birthday was the day after the swearing-in. Melania sent a beautiful white floral arrangement to my hotel room, and I was touched she had remembered with all that had been going on. I celebrated in DC with my family, mostly lying in bed; I could barely move.

The following morning, I gave them all giant hugs and kisses goodbye before they drove back to New York. I was staying in DC for the day. I headed over to the White House to meet with Melania. My life had been far from normal for months, and that wasn't going to change in the foreseeable future.

Walk-Through

On Sunday, January 22, 2017, Melania and I walked through the deserted East Wing of the White House to see the First Lady's offices and the Executive Residence, where Melania, Donald, and Barron—along with her parents and Daga, her loyal housekeeper from New York—were going to live. Donald would have to be alone there for a while yet. Much to the consternation of New Yorkers—they weren't thrilled to foot the additional police bills—Melania wasn't leaving Trump Tower in a hurry.

She was adamant that she wasn't going to disrupt Barron's life by uprooting him in the middle of a school year. For so many reasons, I couldn't comprehend how she thought it was okay to stay in New York just because she wanted to. I said, "You're going to have to move here as soon as possible. This isn't about *you* anymore. It's about our country."

She looked at me and said, "I get it."

The reality was, she understood just fine, but, as she explained to me, "I don't care what people think. I will do what is right for me and Barron."

I was pretty sure Melania had to put her hand under my chin and close my jaw. She was going to do right by herself, as expected. That was Melania's way.

On the ground floor, we walked into the main White House kitchen. "So, this is where the magic happens," I said.

The executive chef looked shocked to see us poking around by ourselves, but as soon as Melania said, "Hello, everybody," a calm spread through the room, and everyone there smiled back.

I was in awe just being in the White House. I'd been in there before, on October 26, 1999, when I was the director of special events at *Vogue*. In the East Room, President Bill Clinton, First Lady Hillary Rodham Clinton, and Anna Wintour hosted photographer Annie Leibovitz and writer Susan Sontag in honor of their collaboration of essays and photographs in *Annie Leibovitz: Women*, a companion catalog to an exhibition opening the next day at the Corcoran Gallery of Art. David and I, and my brothers, Gordon and Randall, posed for photos with the Clintons and had a wonderful time.

I hope the ghosts of presidents past don't strike me down for saying it, but when Melania and I toured the place, my first thought was, *What a dump!* It looked shabby, tired. Everything was old and sad, from the furniture to the carpeting to the paint job. The rooms themselves were a mess. Mostly what the past administration had left us were a few dozen broken computers and keypads piled high at the entrance to Melania's office. I was shocked.

I said, "Here we go again." We'd have to start from scratch with no time and a limited budget, under intense scrutiny, to make it shine. Luckily, having worked hand in hand with Melania during the inauguration, David Monn and I were well prepared to transform her vision into a reality.

When we got to the Residence, Melania took one look at her bedroom off the West Sitting Hall and said, "I'm not moving to DC until the Residence has been renovated and redecorated, starting with a new shower and toilet."

Gold plated?

She did not go so far as to say that she would not sit on the same throne as Michelle Obama or whoever had used this bathroom. It could have been the queen of England's. But Melania did not conduct her most personal business on a previously used john.

On my ongoing mental list of housekeeping items, I added, *Melania's bedroom. New paint, new furniture, new everything.* I knew Melania's decorator, Tham Kannalikham, was in charge but until she arrived, Melania asked me to keep an eye on everything and report back.

After spending the day in the East Wing, taking notes on all that was required to get Melania's office up and running, I walked over to the Executive Residence and ascended a winding staircase to the State Floor, where I joined the First Family for dinner in the Old Family Dining Room. At its center loomed a magnificent table, around which sat the Trump dynasty: Don Jr. and his wife, Vanessa; Eric and his wife, Lara; and Melania. Tiffany wasn't there. Ivanka and Jared's absence was noticeable, but I didn't ask about their whereabouts. The president of the United States extended his arms when he saw me, as he always did, and said, "Hello, Stephanie! Isn't this great? Look at this!" He gestured around the room with his hands. He was excited to be there and so was I. He said, "You did a great job on the inauguration!"

"Thank you, Mr. President," I said.

I turned bright red. I'd known Donald forever, but seeing him felt different now. I mean, he was the president. After giving him a hug hello, I zigzagged around the table to Melania. We kiss-kissed, and I sat in the seat next to her she'd saved for me. On my other side was Lara, clutching her still-flat belly as she shared the news that she was pregnant. The dinner had a celebratory feel. I remember easy laughter, family unity, and feeling honored to be included in its intimacy.

The flight back to New York for the family—minus Donald, Ivanka, and Jared—was scheduled to leave in an hour. I was joining them. After dinner, we motorcaded to the plane and flew home along with Hervé, who was still riding the high of seeing his gown on the First Lady at the inaugural balls. He was bursting with ideas about what Melania could wear next. I felt the same excitement and sense of wonder and possibility.

Priority Number One

I reported for duty at Trump Tower early the next morning, ready to go over my housekeeping list with Melania, starting with the top item: hiring a highly qualified and experienced staff. I needed candidates for so many of the jobs I needed to fill—I'd been doing everything for her during the transition for months now, but Melania said, "Even you can't do it alone." You think?

Anna Wintour has always said that I'm a hard worker but not the best delegator, and that I need to learn how to trust other people to do their job so that I can do mine even better. I had a clear vision for the First Lady's office, a Lincolnian team of rivals, a bipartisan group of smart, creative women who believed in transparency with the media and hard work.

Go big or go home. Melania's initiative would have to be multipronged and nationwide. She kept saying, "Cyberbullying," and I agreed that it had to be part of the program. But it was a symptom of a larger problem. You had to ask why such behaviors like cyberbullying were so prevalent in the first place. If kids were taught to deal with

their emotions and express themselves freely from a young age, bullying in all forms would diminish. I'd read the evidence-based research
on the subject. Our focus was on prevention instead of intervention.
Plus, there was the obvious problem that a cyberbullying platform
would be mocked and attacked because of Melania's husband's nonstop slinging of hostility and aggression on Twitter.

I didn't harp on the initiative goals that first day. We were still
on the basics: staff, roles, renovations, logistics, and how she envisioned things working.

During the inauguration, Melania had sent me an organizational chart for the First Lady's office with dozens of slots to fill with
important-sounding titles. She needed directors of policy and projects,
communications, correspondence, scheduling, and advance, along with
a social secretary, and deputies and assistants under each directorship.
Michelle Obama's staffers had received high five- to low six-figure
salaries, enough money to keep them happily and gainfully employed.

During the transition, Melania gave me the go-ahead to start
meeting people semi-secretly to try to get a staff ready for day one.
The only person the RNC had assigned to Melania during that period,
Marcia Lee Kelly, had practically begged to be Melania's chief of staff.
Melania forwarded Kelly's overly flattering email, proving the point.
We agreed Marcia wasn't the right fit for her. During the inauguration,
she didn't seem to be good with follow-up, failed to send requested
information, spelled names wrong, and made mistakes on guest lists.
I couldn't figure out if Marcia was not great with follow-through or if
she was keeping information from me. Besides that, the Trumps are
all about image, and Marcia's attitude was a bit too rough to represent
Melania. (Kelly is currently the president of the Republican National
Committee.)

I didn't mind being the acting chief of staff (COS) until we found
the right person. Melania asked me on several occasions if I would
consider taking the top job, but the COS was required to live in DC,
and I wouldn't leave my children and husband. Melania and I reviewed
lists of candidates I'd already interviewed during the inauguration in

my room at the Trump International Hotel. I started to jot down a list of names to fill the spots. I sent it back over to Katie Walsh, deputy to Chief of Staff Reince Priebus in the West Wing, and she said, "Ignore that chart [the one Melania had sent]. I'm sending an updated one."

The updated chart had a handful of positions, and only several of them came with a six-figure salary that would attract qualified people. The eliminated spots were deputies and assistants. Melania's staff allotments were for directors only, at low salaries.

Walsh informed me that the West Wing had already used up the staffing budget and coveted titles by hiring an unprecedented number of assistants to the president (APs), special assistants to the president (SAPs), and deputy assistants to the president (DAPs). In other words, those that should have gone to the First Lady's staff had already been allotted.

Melania wrote to and called Reince Priebus, requesting more information about her staffing budget and organizational chart, but answers were slow in coming. We didn't know the extent of the protocol for hiring. East Wing candidates would have to go through a rigorous vetting process by the FBI, along with being approved by the West Wing. I couldn't tell you which would take longer.

How was Melania supposed to pay salaries? Host events? Order stationery? Do the redecorating? With Melania ensconced in Trump Tower, it was up to me to get answers to these questions. She asked me to meet with Angella Reid, the chief usher. The chief usher is responsible for the care and maintenance of the Executive Residence, overseeing all of the White House's support staff including the ushers, butlers, executive chefs, pastry chefs, stewards, curators, calligraphers, and floral designers—the people with whom Melania was going to share her home, "The People's House," in due time.

I'd first met Angella on January 22, when she kindly reached out to let me know she'd added my name to the WAVE (White House Worker and Visitor Entry System list), which granted me access to enter the White House for my meeting with Melania. She'd met me with a smile, and I was looking forward to working with her. Hired by the Obamas in 2011, she was the first woman to ever hold the position.

The next time we met, our meeting didn't go as I'd expected. She said she "sensed a bit of frustration" when we chatted about budgets for the events. She got that right! I was hoping she'd share information from past administrations, but instead she wanted to give me a class in "record management," telling me, "all administration records leave with the outgoing administration, so we don't have copies of detailed event costs on hand." I J.U.S.T. wanted someone to share the most basic information with me, like what I should be budgeting for any of the First Lady's upcoming events.

The vibe I got from Reid was that we shouldn't look to her to make things any easier on us. I could tell she was going to be a tough nut to crack. Melania said, "We can't fire her yet. It's too soon." In other words, *Make it work, for now.*

I wanted to hire Jessica Boulanger as our press secretary/ spokesperson. She was qualified, dignified, and respected, and we'd worked very well together during the inauguration. Melania agreed, and we put in a request to the West Wing's Walsh and Priebus to offer her a competitive salary. Jessica already had a big communications job (executive vice president of public affairs at Business Roundtable), and patriotic duty might not be enough to lure her to the East Wing full-time. Diddly was left for the First Lady's office, and there was no way we could come close to offering Jessica what she deserved. I offered her the most we had available, and she politely declined. I felt defeated that day; Melania was none too pleased either. With no budget, how were we going to assemble our dream team?

Still, I wasn't going to let Jessica's loss, my increasingly brutal neck pain, and my ignorance about protocol dishearten me. Ivanka had quickly hired her staff, including Goldman Sachs's Dina Powell. We were off to a slow start. Previous administrations had shown up with full staffs, raring to go. We had me.

Full of piss and vinegar—and a bottle of migraine meds—I showed up the next morning in "tippy-top" shape, as Melania loved to say, sleeves rolled up, ready to make the East Wing a beautiful, inspirational space in which to do great things with qualified and decent people.

On our paltry organizational chart, my name filled the top box as chief strategist and senior advisor. The COS would be below me. It was widely known inside and outside the White House that I was Melania's go-to girl. On January 20, *Women's Wear Daily* (WWD) reported that I'd helped Melania with her inaugural wardrobe and called me the "senior adviser to the First Lady." On January 26, *The Washington Post* referred to me as her "adviser." Rachel Roy reached out to me: "Yay!!! MK told me about your position!!! Best news EVER!!!! You & MK will make the best team and change the course of history!!!"

Melania trusted me to choose her COS and said, "You'll hire the right person," but technically, *I* wasn't really hiring anyone. Only Melania had the power to pick up the phone and say, "I want *that* one." I was responsible for finding *that* person. Although I was allowed to sleep on the third floor, right above the president's and Melania's rooms, and walk around the Executive Residence unescorted, I didn't have an access pass to get my work done for the First Lady, and had to be checked in every time I entered the building. I also didn't have the clearance to meet potential candidates in the East Wing. If that's not maddeningly counterproductive, then I don't know what is.

So, I would pack up my bags, order an Uber, and ride over to the Trump International Hotel. I'd meet the candidate in the lobby bar, where I paid for the beverages and food. Many times, when I needed to be covert, I'd invite them into my room at the hotel, which I also paid for (at a friends and family discounted rate), and offer them something from the minibar, a box of gummy bears or M&M's. Between the hotel room and the snacks, it added up to thousands of dollars in out-of-pocket expenses.

For Melania's chief of staff, I brought back Lindsay Reynolds, the same woman who'd been canned from the PIC by Rick and Tom after I accidentally unearthed her three-ring binder containing critical information from past inaugurals that we'd been requesting, which could have saved us hundreds of hours and probably thousands of dollars, as we had had to start from scratch trying to re-create them. So why did I recommend her to Melania for this important post? Our options were severely limited; and frankly, we were desperate. No one—and I mean no one—I'd ever worked with in New York would even pick up the phone.

Lindsay made mistakes on the PIC but she did have White House experience, having run the Visitors Office for the George W. Bush administration, under the purview of the East Wing. How was I supposed to arrange tours? I didn't even know where the bathrooms were.

Since Lindsay had been a third-grade teacher, I thought she'd be a valuable resource when it was time to launch Melania's initiative about children. From her RNC days, Lindsay knew Katie Walsh and Reince Priebus, but she didn't seem to have a deep connection to them. In fact, when my email about bringing Lindsay to the East Wing went around, Katie Walsh was taken aback. If Katie didn't like her, then I *loved* her.

Unlike me, politics ran through Lindsay's veins. Her husband's father was an ambassador, and I could imagine the embarrassment brought upon her family after she'd been fired from the PIC. But during the planning of the inauguration, she too had been outraged by Ivanka's requests, as if she'd just become First Lady. I was willing to take my chances. She seemed like the perfect mother hen, which resonated with me, and that's all I really thought Melania needed at the time. Someone to watch over the roost. So, I was willing to turn a blind eye to her lack of judgment and give her the benefit of the doubt.

When I called her to see if she'd consider the role, she was so taken aback, she had to place her Target shopping bags down curbside and register our conversation. Lindsay was willing to commute to DC from Cincinnati and see her husband and kids only on the weekends. That showed a sense of duty that I admired. Lindsay was on board with reporting to me, even though she would be COS. It was an unorthodox arrangement, but so was the entire Trump administration. She'd witnessed my relationship with Melania and knew all the work I'd done for her. We offered her a salary of $179,000, which she accepted. (This was the salary initially offered to me.)

I'd been given an AP title, higher than an SAP or DAP. All three categories came with salaries and access parameters. Since the East Wing was granted only one AP title—with a salary of $179,000.00 because the West Wing had taken all the others—and Lindsay needed access, what was I supposed to do?

Katie Walsh suggested to me, "Well, we can make your AP an honorary one, and when someone leaves or gets fired from the West Wing, we can move it over to you."

I gave my AP title to Lindsay. Without it, she wouldn't have been able to attend daily senior staff briefings. We'd have to make do with SAP and DAP titles for whoever else came in. Apparently, possessing quality, experience, and expertise were not a consideration to represent the First Lady's office. The focus was on quantity—the fewer the better.

Lindsay told me she almost didn't answer her phone that day when I called. I was happy when she got there. I wasn't *totally* alone.

Space Wars

Those Obama pranksters. When Lindsay arrived and hung her coat on the hook on the back of her office door, it fell to the floor. The screws had been loosened. The next day, the head of security and a deputy came to the East Wing to see us and to apologize for the fact that they couldn't replace the red high-security phone in Lindsay's office with a pink one. Lindsay and I had no idea what they were talking about. He said, "We got a call that Mrs. Trump requested a pink phone."

It would have been a more clever prank if they'd said Mrs. Trump wanted a gold phone. *Duh.*

The only East Wing offices that were currently occupied and functioning were the Calligraphy Office and the Military Office. Patricia
"Pat" Blair, the White House chief calligrapher, was the first person
to welcome me in the building. I was grateful to her for helping us
with the transition by providing us with some key information on past
events that no one else seemed to know anything about or be willing
to share information on.

Office supplies? Apart from the pile of broken computers? Zilch.
There wasn't a piece of paper, a schedule, a pen, a paper clip, a stapler, a
notepad, or a contact sheet to be found. Since I happen to carry a por-
table office in my shoulder bag—it weighs twenty pounds and had to
be one of the reasons my neck pain was so debilitating—I was a walking office supply store. I had pens and notebooks on me at all times.

Media reports that the East Wing was a dark, lonely, sad, cob-
webbed place started popping up in the press. We suspected Ivanka
immediately. According to Vicky Ward's book *Kushner, Inc.*, Ivanka
had said during the transition that the First Lady's office would
become, under Daddy's administration, the "Trump Family Office."
In late January, when only Lindsay and I occupied Melania's space,
Lindsay got an alert that members of Jared's staff were coming to the
East Wing to look over our offices. The West Wing wasn't big enough
for the Kushners. They wanted the East Wing as well.

I called Melania to tell her what was going on and she said, "This
is ridiculous! You have to do something!"

I dug into my bag; pulled out my red Sharpie and yellow Post-it
notes; scribbled "conference room," "chief of staff," "deputy of advance,"
etc., on them; and slapped them on the office doors.

By putting our mark on each office, Jared's people couldn't very
well say, "Well, if no one's using it . . . we'll take it."

I blocked those offices with my body. Although I didn't yet have
a contract to serve as Melania's advisor, I was pretty sure "linebacker"
would not be in my job description.

People to Meet, Slots to Fill

About that contract . . . it was in the hands of lawyers, where it would remain for months. Journalists I'd known and worked with for decades asked constantly about my title and duties. Their guesses were as good as mine. I'd been her eyes and ears throughout, and now I'd agreed to be her as-yet-uncontracted, unpaid senior advisor and chief strategist. Privately, these reporters told me they disapproved of my loyalty to the Trumps, but they respected the work I was doing. I didn't tell Melania every time a reporter asked me, "But why in the living hell are you working for the Trumps?" She never doubted my loyalty for a minute. And why would she? I'd given up my career to work on the PIC and given up all partnerships. I stuck around despite what I'd seen from Trump cronies on the PIC, despite friends urging me to run (not walk) away from Trump World. But if I left, Melania would have no one looking out for her. Ivanka would steamroll her. Donald would probably prefer his wife to do nothing but inflate his ego and raise their son. The number of people who could see the possibilities about Melania's potential as First Lady could be counted on one hand: Melania, me, our friends Pamela Gross and Rachel Roy, and Lindsay, maybe.

We needed more people on our side.

I'd corralled Vanessa Schneider, who not only worked with me during the inauguration but also in New York during Fashion Week, with a mid-five-figures offer, as well as my cousin Devon Weiss. The only way I was able to beef up salaries was by giving up my own.

Devon, a graduate of Georgetown University with an MBA and a Master of Science in Foreign Science, was bright and ambitious and had worked for me during the PIC. During our weeks together on the PIC, I had been up to my neck in the ineptitude and frenetic activity that had been swirling around us. Devon had tried hard to problem-solve, but I was so frustrated, and I lashed out at her because I could; she was family. Throughout, she held her head up high.

Somehow, I convinced her to stay on in the First Lady's office. Even though I'd been really tough on her, she said yes, feeling a sense of patriotism. (It must run in the family.) We needed Devon. I trusted her and so could Melania. With her experience and education, she was qualified for the director of policy and projects position, with an SAP title. Understanding Melania's dire situation, she also agreed to have a dual role, as personal aide to the First Lady.

Tim Tripepi, RNCer, PIC's deputy director to Ryan Price for the outdoor events, and formerly lead advance for DJT, had become my inside guy during the inauguration and shared information with me and WIS that we'd otherwise not have been privy to, giving us the big picture. He was well aware I was interviewing candidates for the East Wing, so he approached me about being lead advance and operations for the First Lady. I didn't even know what that meant, so I listened to him. It meant that when Melania was traveling, he'd be in charge of setting things up for her in advance of her arrival.

I was suspicious of everyone from the PIC and the RNC, and Tim fell into both categories. But Tim flat-out worshipped Melania, which went a long way with me. He convinced me he would do right by her. As I said, we were desperate, and he had experience in operations and as an advance man. In retrospect, I would have preferred to hire Mary-Kate Fisher, who served as an event manager at the PIC, but I didn't get to know her until after the inauguration, after Tim suggested I meet with her to hire her as his deputy. He was spot-on about her! I was thrilled when she accepted to be deputy director of advance in the office of First Lady Melania Trump.

Tim had been a valuable part of the PIC team, but he got off on the wrong foot at the East Wing by being demanding about his title, and agitating for more money and more staff. He said, "The White House manual states that FLOTUS is allowed three [advance staff] at each stop, a lead, a site, and a press lead."

I told him, "I will need to meet, and Mrs. Trump will need to approve, all the candidates. We are also reviewing the number of staff required." He agreed to the title deputy chief of staff for operations for the First Lady. There was no budget for me to receive a salary, but it still wasn't enough. To pay Tim what he needed, and to hire another staff person, I asked Devon to give back a portion of her salary, as well as her SAP title. It was robbing Peter to pay Paul. It wasn't fair, but Melania was only given three senior level positions (SAP titles).

Melania told me to meet with Katie Walsh to request a couple more senior-level positions. Katie had the audacity to tell me she was "working seamlessly to ensure that the president and first lady have the support they need." Was she kidding me? The West Wing's ego-centered self-serving attitude and disrespect for the First Lady was astounding.

Basically, the First Lady got what she got, and she'd have to wait until April for the new budget to even think about hiring anyone else.

She then told me, "We'll be able to reimburse you through the RNC for all of your expenses." I had spent thousands in Ubers, meals, and hotel charges. I wasn't sure if that was legit, and the RNC was the last group that I wanted to take anything from, so I told Melania, "I'd rather take nothing from them." She asked, "Are you sure?" I ate those expenses.

After my meeting with Katie, I told Devon that Walsh had promised to bump her back up when we had a new budget in a couple of months. Devon quit instead, and I didn't blame her. In hindsight, it was a brilliant move.

One of our support staffers, a woman I'll call Abby—the only pseudonym in this book, by the way—hit a snag during the FBI background checks process. I'd been through it, and it felt like a full-body flossing. The FBI asked her if she'd ever smoked pot. Abby said, "Yes. Just once." Security came and took her away. So then everyone started asking whether they should lie on the background checks. Apparently, if you want a White House job and the FBI asks if you ever got high in college twenty years ago, your answer should be no. Abby came to my hotel room that evening in tears. I had no words! Another one bites the dust.

I continued to meet candidates in secret for other high-level spots. Lindsay was out of the loop. Just trying to help, she sent a long list of candidates to Melania and me. But FLOTUS was in circle-the-wagons mode and said, "Don't let Lindsay hire anyone. Until it is approved by you and then me, no one can get a position in the office."

I sent Lindsay an email on January 27 that said, "As I have expressed, we have a few other people in mind that Mrs. Trump and I have already interviewed and that she likes. We must handle this very carefully and not have any sidebar conversations with possible staff as no one should be considered until you and I have spoken. Mrs. Trump cares very much that her messaging is kept internal and we do not want staff discussing possible positions that do not even exist or ones that they would not be considered for. I must meet and approve everyone considered and then we can see if it's appropriate to meet with Mrs. Trump."

Lindsay probably read my email and said, "Fuck you, Stephanie!" to the screen. But I'd been given instructions by the First Lady, and I followed through. How could Lindsay possibly know what Melania wanted? And why would Melania trust her judgment? They *hadn't even met* yet.

Meanwhile, those highly qualified candidates I was meeting in secret? We had so little to offer them, they turned us down. Or the West Wing's vetting process dragged on so long, they lost interest. Or they were rejected outright. Or they went to work in the West Wing.

Melania told Priebus it was unacceptable that she'd lost out due to budgetary issues and West Wing politicking. To create a bipartisan "no policy, no politics" staff and create her initiative, we needed more money and faster approval.

"Write what I should send to Reince today?" Melania requested.

I drafted a short message. We really weren't asking for the moon. Just enough to bring in one or two excellent, experienced people. Was that too much to ask for the First Lady of the United States? It felt like they wanted to keep the East Wing offices empty, as if the budget and vetting process was being used like a weapon to prevent Melania from filling them. They seemed to enjoy disenfranchising the East Wing so they could totally control Melania. Ivanka was relentless and was determined to be the First Daughter Lady and to usurp office space out from under Melania; she wanted to be the only visible female Trump on the premises, and she was actively using her influence with Katie Walsh, Reince Priebus, and Hope Hicks to thwart our efforts.

Ivanka wasn't playing by the rules, but she never, ever got in trouble. On January 24, Suzie Mills, Ivanka's assistant at the Trump Organization, sent an email to her entire mailing list that said, "Hi Everyone, Hope you all are well. On behalf of Ivanka Trump, I will like to share her new email address. Effective immediately Ivanka will no longer be using her Trump Organization email address." The new email used a family domain. Not a government one.

Can you say "private server"?

Ivanka was asking her work contacts at the White House to write to her at her private email—the exact offense the Trumps had lambasted Hillary Clinton for during the general election. Would anyone chant "Lock her up!" about Ivanka's private server? Doubtful. The email thing was hypocritical, to say the least. But the Trumps made their own rules.

Paint the Wall

Vogue reached out to Melania, hoping to schedule an Annie Leibovitz photo shoot of the First Lady in the White House, with writer Rob Haskell shadowing her for a few days to write a profile. All that sounded great, but the magazine could not guarantee that Melania would appear on the cover.

For the record, not all First Ladies are put on the cover of *Vogue*. Michelle Obama and Hillary Clinton, yes. Laura and Barbara Bush, no. Melania wasn't going to do anything for *Vogue* or any other magazine if she wasn't going to be on the cover. "Give me a break!" she texted. "Forget it."

To add insult to injury, Melania told me, "Ivanka is trying to get the White House photo shoot and profile."

I'd heard as much from my sources and told Melania, "She's angling for the cover!"

It never happened.

Interior decorator Tham Kannalikham was on her way to DC with colors and swatches that Melania had approved. I couldn't wait for her to arrive and whip this place into shape. She wouldn't have much to work with from the existing materials. We'd received a list from the General Services Administration (GSA) of the furniture inventory to choose from, excluding what was currently being used:

Large wingback chairs (not matching), 2
Small wingback chairs, 2
Fabric-back chairs, 2 sets of 2
Settee, 1

If we were lucky, we might be able to pull a three-seater sofa with the settee's fabric from another office.

But that was the least of our worries. Since Tham wasn't yet in DC, I tried to hold down the fort until she arrived. Talk about things going awry! One day Lindsay popped into my office and said, "They painted Melania's office; it's so beautiful. Come and see."

When I opened the door I felt like I'd been sucked inside a cotton candy machine. "It's so pink!" I said. "Was this another joke?" Nope!

I FaceTimed Melania so she could see it for herself. "That's the color Tham and I chose," she said. "Farrow & Ball, Dorset, England, Middleton Pink."

"It really doesn't work, Melania," I told her. "You won't be able to host meetings in here." But she wasn't planning on bringing any of her guests to the East Wing offices very often. She told me she'd use the Map Room, Red Room or Blue Room, or any of the other Executive Residence Rooms instead; "So much nicer," she said.

That wasn't the only issue. The GSA was busy and had no budget to spare for the First Lady at the time, and the Stark carpet they'd installed had a seam running right down the middle. Tham would have to spin straw into gold—or a nice shade of ivory—but if anyone could do it, she could.

Fortunately, the FLOTUS suite of offices wasn't huge. Melania wanted my office right next to hers, and the chief of staff at the other end of the hallway, "So you can keep an eye on all the staff," she said. Lindsay on one end, and me on the other.

Housekeeping item #47: Check the ivory paint in Melania's bedroom now that it was dry.

I reeled back and gasped. "Chief Usher Angella Reid!" I yelled. "Someone splattered two patches of paint on Melania's bedroom walls."

Much to my disbelief, she replied, "I was told the president wanted to see some deeper tones." *Oh my,* I thought to myself, and texted Tham. "Please hold off on the curtains for MT bedroom," I wrote. "Will need to redo all."

This wasn't Donald's bedroom, though. It was Melania's, and she liked the color she had chosen. The paint job was finished! And now the whole bedroom needed to be redone. This job was like bashing my head into a wall. Why was I doing this?

I texted Melania a photo of the wall with the two dark splotches on it.

She wrote back, "What is that? Call me."

I was far more upset than she was. She was like the Buddha, completely composed while I was freaking out. I tried to channel some of her inexplicable calm . . . and succeeded.

I had to choose my battles, and this wasn't one of them. Her bedroom had to be repainted with a darker hue, but at least she was thrilled with her Middleton Pink dressing room and the built-ins going inside of her dressing room doors. Disaster averted.

Rachel checked in, and when she heard this story, she was livid. She said, "What are these reports of MT & DT sleeping in separate rooms? ALL PRESIDENTS have separate rooms, why wasn't this a story then? Such bull!!!"

I agreed.

Housekeeping item #48: Get someone to test the soil in the

White House gardens. Someone told Melania there might be "something wrong with it."

Housekeeping item #87: Per Melania, put her glam squad—Nicole Bryl (makeup), Mordechai Alvow (hair), and Hervé Pierre (wardrobe)—on notice about not speaking to the press without her prior approval. The week before, Bryl, Melania's makeup artist of ten years, had told *Us Weekly*, "There will absolutely be a room [in the White House] designated for hair, makeup and wardrobe. Melania wants a room with the most perfect lighting scenario, which will make our jobs as a creative team that much more efficient, since great lighting can make or break any look. [It takes] about one hour and fifteen minutes of uninterrupted focus. If you want the look to be flawless and have it last [throughout the day], you do have to take a little extra time to make that happen."

Gerald Ford had built an outdoor swimming pool for the White House. Nixon had put in a bowling alley. Obama had installed a basketball hoop. In March 2020, the Trumps started building a tennis pavilion. Melania wanted a glam room. Was that so far-fetched? The trouble was, it played into the narrative of her being a beautiful empty vessel. Even her husband reinforced the impression every time he said, "Isn't she beautiful?!"

She wanted a glam room; she got one. And she made good use of it. I watched her from a neighboring chair get her hair blown out and styled. She never varied from the same style. Not long after she became First Lady, André Leon Talley told *New York Times* columnist Maureen Dowd, "I am so tired of the long hair falling on both sides of her face. She has to upgrade her coiffure. She's very much like a high, super, superglamorous Stepford Wife."

Her hair had taken a beating over the last couple of years, with her appearing in public more than ever. She told me, "My hair is getting really dry." It did look brittle and alarmingly thin.

Melania had to control her image in the press, of course, and Bryl's blabbing about the glam room was a misstep. But forbidding her makeup, hair, and wardrobe people from speaking publicly about their work didn't feel right. Nonetheless, I sent a letter to each of them. "On behalf of the First Lady's Office, we wish to inform you that all services rendered are private and confidential," it said. "The Office of the First Lady kindly asks for your respect in maintaining complete privacy and not divulging any information about her, the First Family or the work you have performed. Any press requests must be formally submitted to and approved by the Office of the First Lady."

So, in Melania's first week as First Lady, she and I dealt with the photographer, makeup artist, hairstylist, fashion stylist, wrapping paper, stationery, and decorator. My housekeeping items list was getting shorter, but it was still a mile long, and I continued to be hamstrung by protocol.

No Way In

I still didn't have a contract or an access badge to get into the East Wing, where I was working, or the Residence, where I sometimes slept in room number 326, but I did have a tremendous amount of the responsibility.

I needed access to do my job! Every day, I had to check in and go through the security process before I could enter the East Wing. In my most resentful moments, I imagined Ivanka and Katie Walsh gathering around the live feed of my daily bag searches and laughing their asses off.

Melania wrote to Reince Priebus about my contract and badge, but he wouldn't get back to her for hours. Can you imagine someone ignoring any other First Lady like that? It was so disrespectful. Apparently, they didn't care that this was a priority for her. I watched and listened to her do her best to fast-track approval for my badge, and yet, it didn't materialize. Was it paranoid to think that the West Wingers did not want me physically in the building? I think not.

All week, Lindsay and Tim tried to schedule a sit-down with members of the White House Management Office to be briefed about planes, vehicles, computers, phones, and additional assets they would be providing. They finally met, and Lindsay was given her assets the very next day. I couldn't get them to slot me in, which was frustrating. I didn't even know how to communicate with them. How was I supposed to correspond on behalf of the First Lady without using government email or a secure phone? More items to add to the list.

Late on Friday of our first week, Melania told me, "I'm not going to DC tomorrow." *Heavy sigh.* Really? Was it such a good idea to leave Donald all alone during his very first weekend as president? Who knew what he'd get up to without her grounding force. (That Friday, Trump signed Executive Order 13769, a.k.a. the Muslim Ban, the first wildly controversial EO of his presidency.) If only Melania had changed her mind, perhaps this ill-advised decision may never have occurred. Doubtful, but you never know. That one extra opinion might have swayed him.

For a fleeting, insane moment, I thought, *Maybe it's a good thing that Jared and Ivanka will be around to keep him company.* I'd barely seen *my* kids in weeks. Clearly, I was thinking about needing family around for myself; I shook it off. I didn't have time to think about me.

A text came in from the First Lady, instructing me to advise the West Wingers that she would not be attending the National Prayer Breakfast on Thursday. They needed to know ASAP so they didn't reserve a seat for her. This was the same National Prayer Breakfast where part of the president's address mentioned how much Arnold Schwarzenegger sucked as the host of *The New Celebrity Apprentice.*

Why was she backing out of it? "They told me two days ago," she wrote. This was becoming the West Wing's modus operandi, to ask Melania to drop everything at the last minute—for her, that means four days' warning—and jump *this high* whenever they called. She was not given access to her husband's schedule and was always the last to know about where he was and what he was doing.

It had been going on since the campaign, and she was sick and tired of it.

"I am going to let them know how it needs to be moving forward,"

I promised, not sure what I could do other than make requests. It was chaos over there. I had no control. Any power she could generate was muffled by her being in New York, so I had to fight her battles by myself, without a phone, email, contract, or badge.

Melania *did* intend to leave Trump Tower the following weekend, February 3 to 5, to go to what the press was calling the "Winter White House," Mar-a-Lago, in Palm Beach, for the Sixtieth International Red Cross Ball. "Find out if Donald is going?" she asked. She was so out of the loop, she didn't know what Donald was doing. She couldn't ask him because he didn't control his schedule either.

She said, "I'm traveling alone. Want to come?"

Er, no, thanks. I wanted to go home to my family.

Then I heard from Rachel. "Morning! I want to plan a tea at the WH celebrating MK our FLOTUS, her sister, her mother/father, only like 10 people or less, a true intimate party to toast the historical moment she is living in! I thought I would hire a children's choir and have a tea since she does not drink, just simple and sweet??? Thoughts?"

Was she kidding me? Nope! So I told her, "I would love to plan, but we should wait. I'll explain when we talk."

Social Anxiety

My last meeting of my first grueling, awesome, panic-filled week in the White House was with Katie Walsh to discuss our anemic organization and salary limitations. From Walsh's email summons, I got the idea that I was supposed to feel a sense of privilege that the doors of the West Wing were being flung open to me. I'd been granted permission to walk the hallowed halls, to tread on the same carpets as luminaries like Ivanka and Jared, to breathe the same rarefied oxygen as Hope Hicks and Sean Spicer.

I'd have to mark my calendar: this was a super-special day.

Look, interviewing staff and setting up Melania's office was my job. To do it, I had to walk from one place to the other, so I needed a pass. I absolutely considered it a privilege to work in the White House, but Katie's condescension sucked the joy out of it. At the meeting, which was delayed (I kept checking my watch repeatedly because I had a flight to New York to catch), Katie explained in detail why we were so limited and that, at this point, the only big slot we could still fill was social secretary. I walked out of there shell-shocked. How in the world would we be able to do anything with so little support?

(PS: I missed my plane.)

Melania's emoji finger must have blistered from all the 😴 😴 😴 😴 😴 😴 😴 😴 😴 😴.

My top choice for social secretary was Natalie Jones, former deputy chief of protocol for the Obama administration, once the finance director at the Democratic National Committee and a high-level staffer on Hillary Clinton's 2008 presidential campaign. I met with her for the first time on January 26, 2017, at six p.m. at the Trump International Hotel.

The only reason she'd agreed to meet with me in the first place was because of our shared friendship with David Monn. The job was to plan and coordinate all official and social events for the president and the First Lady, including state dinners, the Easter Egg Roll, the White House Christmas Party, and many, many (so many) more.

David told me I'd love Natalie, and she was *perfect*! As soon as she left my hotel room that evening, I called Melania and said, "We hit the jackpot!"

Natalie and Melania met face-to-face the following day, and their mutual appreciation was obvious. "I had a very nice meeting with Mrs. Trump," wrote Natalie. "She is everything you described."

I told Melania, "We must hire her!!!"

Melania and I had a quick confab and then offered Natalie the job.

"I need a day," said Natalie. After she slept on it, she accepted, with a few requests. *Finally*, someone worthy of the job! I began lobbying the West Wing for a fast vetting, more money, and an AP title. Our budget and the title available to us at that point would have been inappropriate and downright insulting for a woman with her experience.

On January 29, 2017, I emailed Melania in the morning with the subject "Social Secretary note for Reince Priebus from you." I wrote out exactly what she should send to Priebus: "I offered the Social Secretary job to Natalie Jones. She comes highly qualified and would be a great asset to my team. She needs a DAP title and Social Secretary salary of $150,000. Résumé attached. Thank you, Melania."

I added, "PLEASE LET ME KNOW WHEN YOU SEND. THEY ARE GOING TO TELL YOU THAT YOU DON'T HAVE THAT BUDGET! You will need to explain that they must find the budgets for your top people."

Jones was a Democrat, so, in my mind, she would bring balance to the First Lady's office. Party politics didn't really come into play in the position anyway. Plus, she was eminently qualified. I was beyond thrilled, imagining our working together, doing our country proud.

On January 30, 2017, Sarah Huckabee Sanders, then the White House deputy press secretary, sent a press release over to the East Wing to be approved by Melania announcing Lindsay, and cc'ing Katie Walsh and Reince Priebus.

First Lady Melania Trump Announces White House Staff: WASHINGTON—First Lady Melania Trump today made the following announcement in regard to White House Staff additions at the Office of the First Lady:

"It has been *humbling* to take on the responsibility of the position of First Lady, with its long history as an important representative of the President, his family, and the traditions of our nation around the world," said First Lady Trump. "I am honored to be bringing on such a professional and highly experienced team, and I look forward to joining with them as we work together to make our country better for everyone."

The additions to White House Staff are as follows:

- Stephanie Winston Wolkoff, Assistant to the President and Chief Strategist and Senior Advisor to the First Lady
- Lindsay Reynolds, Assistant to the President and Chief of Staff to the First Lady

Melania zoomed right into the word *humbling* and told me, "Humbling? I would say *honor*."

Katie held it back.

On February 1, 2017, in the late afternoon, Natalie texted, "Please call me ASAP."

"I'm slammed," I replied. I didn't tell her that I was busy begging for money for her.

"I just want to make sure you are aware of the *Washington Post* article," she said. I found it online. The piece went on for several paragraphs about Jones's Democratic credentials and how liberal DC was shocked she'd even consider the job. David Monn was mentioned. My name was mentioned, too, in the context of my efforts to staff the First Lady's office.

Melania texted me, "Donald said Reince asked him if I am sure I want to hire a Democrat."

"What did you say?" I asked.

"I told him I need expertise and if she is okay to work for us, I am okay."

Yes! Melania had put her stiletto down! A qualified and dignified human being would be joining the East Wing. I did a small happy dance.

Reince's response six hours later was, "Hire your person within reason," and he told Melania, "I do have a slight concern about a Hillary Clinton and DNC employee being on the list."

Melania and I were exasperated.

"If you are getting pressure to look at other candidates, I understand," Natalie texted. "But it may be foreshadowing that this is not meant to be."

The White House wanted "the best people," but not the most qualified or intelligent? In order to be best (hmmm, that phrase had a nice ring to it), our candidates only needed to be one thing: Donald Trump loyalists.

I was a *Melania* Trump loyalist. I wondered how long I'd last in this environment. It wasn't like anyone was trying to lock me down; my contract languished in red tape.

Emily Heil with the *Washington Post* contacted our office for a confirmation or comment about Natalie Jones's declining the social secretary job. Natalie saying that she had declined protected Melania from further embarrassment.

Natalie Jones is a class act. If we'd been allowed to hire her, she would have done incredible things in the role. But the West Wing wouldn't allow it.

Now that we'd publicly stated that we had several qualified, enthusiastic candidates for social secretary, we had to scramble to fill the spot. The truth: there was no pool of candidates. But I'd had Anna Cristina "Rickie" Niceta Lloyd in the back of my mind from the beginning. I'd gotten to know Rickie on the PIC; she was one of the few people I respected and trusted. She'd worked for Design Cuisine, the DC catering and design company, and labored alongside David Monn on the Candlelight Dinner and the Chairman's Global Dinner and every other event, along with her assistant, Emily Biddle. I knew them both to be hard workers with good attitudes. They could do the job. Rickie would need a deputy and they made a great duo working on the inauguration. They both appreciated that I'd thought it through to consider them both.

Rickie was married to the grandson of the late Bunny Mellon. Bunny had been a friend and mentor to Jacqueline Kennedy; they had designed the White House Rose Garden together. The connection checked the "central casting" box.

We were really under the gun to hire someone. The Governors' Dinner was a couple of weeks away. I knew it wouldn't look good for Melania to not have her social secretary position officially staffed before her coming-out.

The White House florist, Hedieh Ghaffarian, gave me an envelope with two fabric swatches and pictures of floral arrangements. I showed them to Melania in Trump Tower when I went back to New York.

I just knew what Melania was going to say, but I wanted her to see for herself.

She looked at the swatches, looked at me, and said, "Nope!"

I heard that David Monn signed a contractor agreement with the East Wing to work on specific projects for an allotted amount of time, and I was pleased for him. I was working on everything with no "event" parameters, so a contract like his—one with access and a proper salary—wasn't an option for me. That's the excuse I was given.

Working together, David and I prepared two vision boards with two different sets of color schemes, table linens, floral arrangements, and china. Two days later, I was back at the penthouse, showing them to Melania. "This one or that one?" I asked. David had the yarn spinning, and later that day we flew back to DC.

David wanted the White House to represent Melania in every way, to touch all five senses with Melania's colors, scent, music, fabrics, and flavors. There was a ton to do and we needed help ASAP. He agreed that Rickie was a great option.

I sent Melania Rickie's résumé and some photos of her, telling her, "Feels so right!!! She is the perfect person. Her background is ideal. I loved working with her. You will love her!"

Melania liked what she saw. She said, "Let's move with Rickie."

Another hire of hers based on my recommendation, sight unseen. Rickie sailed through approval with the West Wing, and we announced officially soon after. And with that, our meager slots were full, except for a communications director.

Pink Cookies

Lindsay, Vanessa Schneider, and I called a meeting with the White House staff. I remember walking into the East Wing dining room and finding the butler, ushers, chefs, and florists seated on one side of a long table. The head butler, William "Buddy" Carter, had been at the White House since the first Bush administration, and it was obvious from his frown that he wasn't a Trump enthusiast. From the look of it, they all distrusted us. Many of them had been hired by the Clintons, Bushes, or Obamas, all enemies of the Trumps. They probably assumed that anyone associated with the family had to be as offensive as Donald.

We sat down at the other side of the table and introduced ourselves. They followed in turn, barely getting their names out. We just wanted to meet them and understand how things worked. But this wasn't going to be easy. We didn't know anything and started asking questions. How many events did they typically do per week? How many people were available? What were their individual roles? When we were planning the Governors' Dinner, how did we coordinate the menu?

They answered our questions tersely, coldly. It was a tough room. On our request, the kitchen staff brought out some cookies for us to sample, and as delicious as they were, they weren't exactly the kind of desserts that Melania would go for.

I walked out of there worried for Melania having to live in a house where everyone in it despised her by proxy. Since I was spending more time there than Melania was, I felt the chill up close and personal.

Housekeeping item #208: Hire a food taster for Melania?

On January 28, FLOTUS texted to ask me how my day went.

Now, mind you, it was ten o'clock in the evening. I was finally in my own bed in New York. I'd climbed figurative mountains for Melania all week and my neck had been in throbbing pain all day. I couldn't allow myself to even think about an honest reply or I would have burst into tears. Instead, I asked back, "How was yours?"

"Unpacking from last week," she said. "A lot to do."

Unpacking? I thought. *A lot to do?*

She wanted to know how the kids and David were doing and urged me to get some rest and to have some "peaceful time" with them.

I sent her a long string of 😆 and 😎 and wrote, "Hope that answers it! I am laughing at myself!"

She signed off with "Love you ♥"

And I replied "Love you too ♥"

We exchanged 😉s, 😋s, and 😊s all day every day, and it felt intimate and close. The sentiments were real. But how could she tell me to have peaceful time with my family—her self-care mantra was "Schedule it!"—when she knew I was running myself ragged for her and there was too much to deal with to drop everything and relax? Was she just not thinking, or didn't she notice? Or maybe she just didn't care?

I'd been hauling myself between the Trump International Hotel in DC, the White House, and New York on repeat, lugging heavy bags wherever I went, for more than two months now. I was getting analgesic shots and sleeping pills because the pain in my neck was so severe, it was impossible to nod off otherwise.

The opportunity cost to me for working on the inauguration and in the White House was that I had to give up all the partnerships and investments I was working on so there would be no perception that I might be trying to profit from my relationships.

My press release at the White House continued to be delayed. I was notified on February 7 that the lawyers also wanted my husband to disclose his full financial statements. David said no and explained, "I don't want my financial information to be public record," and I understood. The president won't even make his tax returns public. This sent the lawyers back to square one with my contract. With the background checks, unreasonable demands, lack of access, and West Wing's disapproval about pretty much everything, the East Wing was both disturbingly empty and suffocating.

With no salary or acknowledgment of a definitive position, I had to wonder if I should continue. David wanted me to quit. But if I did, Melania would be at the mercy of the West Wing. She'd become a laughingstock or irrelevant, and I'd waste the greatest opportunity I'd ever had to help her. I had to psych myself up and remember that with Melania's enthusiasm and participation, her platform and the right initiative, we could effect real, positive change. Look at what Michelle Obama had done with Let's Move! She'd motivated a generation of kids to be healthier and more active. We could do the same on the emotional-wellness front with an initiative to teach kids how to express themselves and develop the coping skills to deal with difficult feelings. Melania was still on board with the goal.

I woke up in New York that Sunday and checked my phone. Melania had texted that she'd called Reince *again* about my badge and contract. No answer.

We got on the phone. She said, "I want to tell Reince to take care of you too."

"I'm sure they realize that they shouldn't have given out so much budgetary money to the West Wing," I said.

"And you should be reimbursed for your expenses from the RNC."

"Thank you . . . we will figure it out," I said.

I wanted to be reimbursed, don't get me wrong. I would have loved to draw a salary, too! But if I'd kept the six-figure salary offered to me as chief advisor, I'd have had little or no support staff. Dividing it up solved a problem for me, and for Melania. So essentially, I was paying to serve my country—physically, mentally, and financially. I was being depleted on all fronts.

We didn't have a press person yet, our only open slot. Tim spent most of his afternoons in the West Wing and always came back with the same request: "Will you consider meeting with Stephanie Grisham?" She was the West Wing deputy communications director.

Left to right: David Wolkoff and Stephanie Winston Wolkoff with President Bill Clinton and the author's brothers, Randall Batinkoff and Gordon Winston, at the White House reception for *Portraits, Profiles, and Progress: Celebrating Women of the Twentieth Century,* Washington, DC, October 26, 1999.

Guests at the wedding of Stephanie Winston and David Entratter Wolkoff at The Pierre Hotel, New York City, March 18, 2000: *Top row, left to right:* Gordon Winston, Dr. Martin Weiss, Roz Weiss, David Wolkoff, Stephanie Winston Wolkoff, Bruce Winston (father of the bride), Randall Batinkoff, and Barbara Winston (mother of the bride); *seated:* Joel and Ethel Carnel, the bride's grandparents.

Stephanie Winston Wolkoff and Anna Wintour at the Wolkoffs' wedding.

Melania Trump and the author attend New York-Presbyterian Hospital/Weill Cornell Medical Center 2006 Bottega Veneta Fashion Show and Luncheon at Cipriani 42nd Street, New York, NY, May 9, 2006.

Wintour and Winston Wolkoff at the Metropolitan Museum of Art's Met Gala, New York, NY, May 7, 2007.

Left to right: Wintour, Winston Wolkoff, and Diane von Furstenberg attend DVF & CFDA Celebrate Lincoln Center & Stephanie Winston Wolkoff at DVF Studio, New York, NY, January 19, 2010.

Donald and Melania Trump with David Wolkoff at the Met Gala in honor of Poiret, May 7, 2007.

André Leon Talley and Stephanie Winston Wolkoff attend Dennis Basso Fall/Winter 2010 Collection, New York City, February 16, 2010.

The Wolkoff family, *left to right:* Alexi, Stephanie, Zachary, David, and Tyler, New York City, August 2008.

TOP: *Left to right:* Melania and Donald Trump with the author at the Met Gala in honor of the *Alexander McQueen: Savage Beauty* exhibition, New York, NY, May 2, 2011.

LEFT: Stephanie and Melania at the author's Fortieth Birthday Luncheon at The Modern at the Museum of Modern Art, New York City, 2011.

Stephanie Winston Wolkoff and Melania Trump at Aspen Snowmass Ski Resort, Aspen, CO, March 3, 2012.

Stephanie and Melania at the Columbia Grammar & Preparatory School Street Fair, New York, NY, May 14, 2016.

Left to right: Rachel Roy, Melania Trump, and Stephanie Winston Wolkoff at Jean-Georges restaurant in the Trump International Hotel & Tower, New York, NY, September 8, 2016.

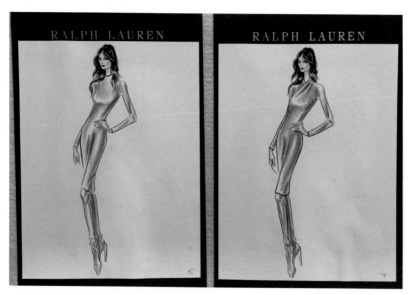

Sketches of the powder-blue Ralph Lauren outfit and accessories Melania Trump wore to her husband's swearing-in. "The presidential inauguration is a time for the United States to look our best to the world," a corporate spokesperson from Ralph Lauren said. "It was important to us to uphold and celebrate the tradition of creating iconic American style for this moment." December 2016.

Left to right: Stephanie Winston Wolkoff with her WIS team: Brandon Arolfo, Jon Reynaga, Melanie Capacia Johnson, and C. J. Yu at the dress rehearsal for the Make America Great Again! Welcome Celebration at the Lincoln Memorial, Washington, DC, January 16, 2017.

Winston Wolkoff and Tom Barrack Jr. at the Chairman's Global Dinner, Andrew W. Mellon Auditorium, Washington, DC, January 17, 2017.

Stephanie Winston Wolkoff and Mark Burnett at the Make America Great Again! Welcome Celebration at the Lincoln Memorial, Washington, DC, January 19, 2017.

Stephanie and Melania at the Candlelight Dinner at Union Station, Washington, DC, January 19, 2017.

Stephanie Winston Wolkoff and Ivanka Trump at the Candlelight Dinner at Union Station, Washington, DC, January 19, 2017.

BELOW: Melania Trump sent her customary all-white floral arrangement to the author for her forty-sixth birthday at the Trump International Hotel, Washington, DC, January 21, 2017.

TRUMP
HOTELS

Dear Stephanie,
Happy Birthday. We love you.

Love,
Melania, Donald, and Barron

Hervé Pierre and Stephanie Winston Wolkoff on Melania Trump's airplane back to New York City the Sunday after the swearing-in ceremony, Washington, DC, February 22, 2017.

Left to right: Lindsay Reynolds (Melania Trump's chief of staff), Stephanie Winston Wolkoff, Anna Cristina "Rickie" Niceta Lloyd (Melania's social secretary), and David Monn at the Governors' Dinner in the East Room of the White House, Washington, DC, February 26, 2017.

Stephanie and Melania in the waiting room for Trump's first public address before a joint session of the United States Congress, Washington, DC, February 28, 2017.

Left to right: Jared Kushner, Melania Trump, and Ivanka Trump in the waiting room for Trump's first public address before a joint session of the United States Congress, Washington, DC, February 28, 2017.

RIGHT: The author and her daughter, Alexi, board Air Force One to attend a campaign rally in Melbourne, Florida, with Donald Trump and Melania Trump, Palm Beach, FL, February 18, 2017.

BELOW: *Front row, left to right:* Melania and Donald Trump; *back row, left to right:* David, Tyler, Alexi, Stephanie, and Zachary Wolkoff at the Mar-a-Lago Club, Palm Beach, FL, February 18, 2017.

ABOVE: The First Lady on her airplane en route to New York City, accompanied by the author, to read Dr. Seuss to children at NewYork-Presbyterian/Weill Cornell Medical Center, March 3, 2017.

LEFT: *Left to right:* Rachel Roy, Stephanie Winston Wolkoff, and Pamela Gross at the United Nations General Assembly luncheon hosted by Melania Trump, New York, NY, September 20, 2017.

Donald and Melania Trump with the Wolkoff family—Alexi, Stephanie, David, Tyler, and Zachary—at the White House family Christmas party, Washington, DC, December 3, 2017.

Left to right: Tyler, Alexi, Zachary, David, and Stephanie Wolkoff in the author's White House East Wing office, Washington, DC, December 4, 2017.

The office of the First Lady of the United States, White House East Wing, Washington, DC, January 10, 2018.

Left to right: Dr. Robin Stern, Stephanie Winston Wolkoff, and Dr. Marc Brackett attend the UN Women for Peace Association 2019 Awards Luncheon at United Nations Headquarters, New York, NY, March 1, 2019.

Nope!

I suspected it wouldn't be long before Ivanka and Jared tried to install their handpicked stooge in the East Wing. All of a sudden she was cc'ed on emails from Hope Hicks to Lindsay. Grisham was being presented as a fait accompli.

A Fish Tale

On Monday, January 30, Ian Drew, entertainment director of *Us Weekly*, contacted Hope Hicks to do an accuracy check with someone in the White House for his next story about the First Couple, in particular their leading separate lives in different cities. (The piece was never published.)

News flash: that wasn't going to change any time soon!

"*Us Weekly* [which would soon be bought by Trump BFF David Pecker] has been doing several positive cover stories on the First Family so would like to continue working with you moving forward," Drew wrote to Hicks, as if that would sway her one way or the other.

Hicks and Grisham forwarded the most time-sensitive and highly damaging story line queries to Lindsay, who forwarded them to me. Why not cc me on the queries and save everyone a step? Why exclude the First Lady's top advisor from potentially damaging information? Didn't they realize they were just hurting Melania? Then again, it seemed like the West Wing's calling the shots for the East Wing was *the whole point*. They wanted to contain her, and I was in the way.

Ian's email included a list of statements about the Trumps' sleeping arrangements and other bits of gossip. For example, "Donald doted on Melania all Inauguration weekend until she returned to NYC on January 22," and "[Melania] enjoys time to herself when she can get it." The nuggets had been divulged by a close "source," per the reporter. This statement made me bark: "[Melania] is leaving a lot of the traditional First Lady duties to Ivanka and Jared so she can focus on being a mom. She feels her role is to be a mom first and also support Donald so he can do his job." Ian asked that we merely confirm or deny the statements. If we didn't reply, he'd consider it tacit confirmation. The magazine needed our response by the end of the day.

I could only guess the identity of Ian's source.

Ivanka had garnered a reputation as being one of the biggest leakers of stories that made Jared and her look good—and, perhaps equally important, made everyone else look bad.

My response to the fake news about Melania gleefully handing over her role to Ivanka: "A source close to the First Lady said, 'Mrs. Trump is actively building her team with her Senior Advisor, Stephanie Winston Wolkoff, including hiring a Chief of Staff and a Social Secretary, among other key positions, to assist with the implementation of the First Lady's key initiatives. While she is a mom first and her child is her number one priority, she is very much embracing the role and responsibilities of First Lady and will have a complete team to help her with her platform.'"

Ian asked one final question that seemed innocent enough: "[Did] Melania and Barron spend this past weekend with the President in DC?"

Short answer: nope.

Long answer: it's quite a tale.

The reporter was on a fishing expedition, and the fish in question was a Pacific blue tang named Dory.

Someone had organized a movie night in the Family Theater in the White House Residence over the weekend. The film screened was *Finding Dory*, an animated feature starring Ellen DeGeneres about a young fish's desperate journey to reunite with her long-lost parents in another country. The choice was particularly tone-deaf, because the president had just signed the travel ban, which effectively tore families from different countries apart.

Minutes after the *Us Weekly* email, I texted Melania that I was looking into the movie screening in the Residence. Melania told me that she'd asked Hope about it the night before and she'd told Melania, "I'm not sure, but I did warn the President it was a bad idea and wouldn't be taken well." Melania talked to Donald too, who said, "he didn't have any idea what the movie was about." So neither Donald nor Hope knew it was Ivanka who had requested the screening? That seemed odd.

I promised Melania, "This will never happen again."

"Stephanie, you need to make sure that the press knows Barron and I were not there this weekend!"

A second later, she said, "Ask Angela whose idea was it."

A second after that, she asked if I knew a great personal assistant. "Maybe someone from *Vogue.*"

What? The sudden change in direction gave me whiplash. Were we in crisis about the *Finding Dory* fiasco, or were we finding her an assistant, as if anyone in the fashion and magazine world would want to work for her (besides me)?

Before I could even start to reply, she said, "Now they think I was involved." She attached a link to a breaking news story from *Express,* a British tabloid, titled "Donald Trump 'watches FINDING DORY with family' as protesters gather outside White House."

Aha! Now we knew for sure who had organized the screening *and* leaked it to the press. Ivanka's fingerprints were all over it. She knew the story was about to get out because of press queries to Hicks. Instead of reporters writing that it'd been Ivanka or Donald's idea, she jumped ahead with "the family" to dilute the blame and rope in Melania. Whenever she needed to deflect the harsh media eye away from herself, she would use the phrase "the family" to cover her ass. It wasn't Ivanka and Jared who had set up that offensive screening. It was "the family."

Melania's next tirade of texts asked who approved Ivanka Trump—a White House staffer—to use the screening room, which was part of the Residence, a.k.a. Melania's domain? All things pertaining to the Executive Residence had to be approved and hosted by the president or First Lady.

It didn't matter if Princess was the First Daughter. She wasn't allowed to invade the Executive Residence whenever she liked. But she knew as long as a Principal (Donald or Melania) was present at the event, she was allowed to host one. Donald stopped by.

That afternoon, DeGeneres talked about the White House screening on her TV show *Ellen*. "A lot of protests going on at the airports all over the country because of the president's travel ban . . . I don't get political, but I will say I am against one of those two things. Like I said I don't get political, so I'm not going to talk about the travel ban. I'm just going to talk about the very nonpolitical, family-friendly, People's Choice Award–winning *Finding Dory*. Now, of course, *Finding Dory* is about a fish named Dory. And Dory lives in Australia. And these are her parents and they live in America. And I don't know what religion they are, but her dad sounds a little Jewish. Doesn't matter. Dory arrives in America with her friends Marlin and Nemo, and she ends up at the Marine Life Institute behind a large wall, and they all have to get over the wall. And, you won't believe it, but that wall has almost no effect in keeping them out," she said. "Even though Dory gets into America, she gets separated from her family. But the other animals help Dory. Animals that don't even need her, animals that don't even have anything in common with her. They help her even though they're a completely different color. Because that's what you do when you see someone in need. You help them."

Because of "the family" headlines, Melania would be included in the (righteous) ridicule about the screening, despite her having nothing to do with it.

That tore it. Melania decided to draw a line in the sand. No one would be allowed to enter the Residence, her home (eventually), without prior approval of the First Lady, including Ivanka and Jared. "This is my home," she said to me. "Do they come walking into my apartment in New York whenever they want?" No!

In White House politics, you take your small victories when and where you can.

All this had happened during *the first week* in the White House. I could only imagine what the next four years would bring.

Trial by February

Our first full month in the White House was like living inside an emotional washing machine that only made you feel dirtier with every rinse. Even though I believed we'd come out ahead, it felt like I was being dragged down. I missed my family. I missed my old life.

AWOL FLOTUS

I had never been a secret special advisor in the White House before. Melania had never been First Lady before. Since Melania was still living in New York, she wasn't even a full-time First Lady yet. Our team of Lindsay, Rickie, Tim, Emily, Vanessa, Stephanie [Grisham], Mary-Kate, David Monn, and I was a motley crew. Every single thing we did or didn't do was under the media microscope.

Even if Melania didn't do anything, it made news. On January 30, 2017, the front page of the *Washington Post* "Style" section dubbed her "the AWOL First Lady." After speaking with Melania, I emailed Reince Priebus and Katie Walsh, attaching the article, and said, "I understand that we have hiring restrictions but when it comes at the detriment of the First Lady (see below) it is not something we can ignore. We have an incredibly qualified Communications Director [Jessica Boulanger,] who is eager to begin but we need budget approval. We do not need a lot of staff, but we do need qualified staff."

Two days later, February 1, brought a blistering article by CNN's Kate Bennett and Betsy Klein, called "Whither Melania Trump: 12 days without a public sighting." The gist of it was, while the president was making news with his executive orders and the travel ban, Melania was missing in action. Where had Melania been since the inauguration? It wasn't exactly a mystery. She was home at Trump Tower with Barron.

I was endeavoring to solidify the staff, do the renovations, and field press queries. Not a minute went by that we weren't scrambling to get things done. But the frenzy behind the scenes didn't matter if nothing was going on in the public eye.

The CNN piece said that Melania's "20-30" staff slots (I WISH!) remained wide open and that she hadn't announced an initiative or a social schedule of events. The tone mocked her as a do-nothing First Lady who was so uninterested in her role that she refused to visit DC, let alone move there.

The official reason Melania had decided to stay in New York was so that she could be with Barron while he finished the school year, at a total cost of $150,000 per day for added security and traffic control around Trump Tower. In an interview with the *New York Times*, Donald said that Melania and Barron would move to Washington "very soon" and would visit on the weekends.

The truth? She really did want Barron to finish off the school year in New York. But also, renovations to the White House Residence weren't finished yet, and she wasn't going to move into a construction site.

Every day, as her spokesperson, I had to defend her decision and swear that the First Lady would, one day, be THRILLED to move to DC and was ECSTATIC to be FLOTUS. I was quoted in the CNN "whither" article: "Mrs. Trump is honored to serve this country and is taking the role and responsibilities of first lady very seriously. It has only been a short time since the inauguration and the first lady is going to go about her role in a pragmatic and thoughtful way that is unique and authentic to her."

The line in that article that got under my skin: "[When] Trump boarded Marine One to pay his respects to a fallen service member's family in Delaware, he was accompanied by first daughter, Ivanka—a reminder that she is his closest family in Washington."

As irritating as they were, AWOL FLOTUS articles were only presenting the evidence. Melania lived in New York. She didn't appear in public or release statements to the press. Her social media was quiet. Ivanka rushed in to fill the void as the "acting" First Lady, issuing constant social media posts and press releases galore about her involvement with women's issues, lobbying Daddy about climate change (alas, unsuccessfully), and attending every meeting she could slink her way into.

To prove to the press that we were filling slots, I sent a draft of yet another press statement to Hope Hicks for approval so we could finally announce Lindsay as chief of staff and myself as senior advisor. Four hours later, Hicks emailed, "Looks fine. I assume you have connected with Reince, Katie, counsel? Adding needed parties here!"

Katie Walsh confirmed at eight p.m. that she'd sent out the press release.

I texted Melania, "It's out!"

Except . . . my name wasn't mentioned. It was only about Lindsay, her experience in political fundraising, event management, and logistics; her previous service for President George W. Bush; a quote from her about reopening the White House Visitors Office.

My name, title, bio, and quote had to be removed. It was a gut punch to be deleted from the statement I had written.

In a series of emails to Reince, Hope, and Katie, we got to the bottom of my erasure. Apparently, the protocol office in the West Wing didn't know what to call me and what type of contract to give me. The press had been referring to me as a "senior" or "special" advisor to the First Lady, but my official role was yet to be named or announced because I was waiting for counsel to get me a contract. The White House lawyers Don McGahn—the very same Don McGahn whom Donald had railed about the night he "fired" Rick Gates from the PIC—and Stefan Passantino, the White House deputy counsel in charge of ethics policy, were trying to figure out what to call me, given the unorthodox nature of my role, unpaid and under the radar. And only once they cracked that mystery would an announcement be made. (It never was.)

Melania was hopping mad and reached out to me to say she wanted my press release to go out, and Reince needed to "get it and move on it." Then she wanted to know if I had secured my phone. Can you imagine Barbara Bush or Hillary Clinton being ignored or denied by West Wing bureaucrats the freedom to send out a press release to announce her choice for senior advisor? It was like Priebus, Walsh, Hicks, and Joe Hagin, deputy chief of staff for operations, put all of Melania's emails, texts, memos, and phone transcripts into a paper shredder.

In our private discussions, Melania and I talked about why the delays and runarounds were happening. We circled around it again and again, asking, "Who gains from an impotent, invisible First Lady?"

Our list was short. Very short.

Seeing Red

Lindsay, Tim, and I were preparing Melania's schedule for the week ahead. We had everything under control. She'd be leaving Trump Tower on Friday with her father to meet Donald in Palm Beach. I read the flight manifest—a description of the trip that included specific instructions about food and beverage preferences. The manifest had a warning: "As an FYI, Muse [Melania's Secret Service name] has an Almond Allergy to which we do not know the extent yet. The approved meal on the flight today has nuts and wanted to make you aware for future flight meal plan reviews."

Wait, WHAT? Melania was allergic to nuts?

She knew what we'd been through over the years with Zach. She'd heard me sobbing over his scares and cheered him on during his desensitizing therapy and had given me sympathy and emotional support. All this time, she'd had a nut allergy and never once mentioned it to me? It seemed unthinkable, considering how many dozens of hours we'd spent talking about Zach. She knew I had put SWW Creative on the shelf for two years to enroll Zachary in a life-changing oral immunotherapy (OIT) food trial, under the oversight of Dr. Kari Nadeau, the director of the Sean N. Parker Center for Allergy & Asthma Research at Stanford University. I'd invited Melania to every fundraiser I'd organized for this cause over the years, but she'd always said she was unavailable for those particular events. To the best of my recollection, she'd never once written a check for them, either.

I should have confronted her and said, "Almond allergy? What gives?" But I let it go, as I always did. I had every intention of picking it up later, when we had five minutes to breathe and I had an inkling of what I'd say. I never did.

On February 3, while Ivanka was spending the weekend in DC, Melania joined her husband at Mar-a-Lago for the Sixtieth International Red Cross Ball. Naively, I thought this trip would be well received. She would be seen in public, spending quality time with her husband.

But the media found a way to trash her anyway.

When Melania arrived in Palm Beach that day, she stepped off Air Force One in a red Givenchy cape dress. I'd kept hammering the "American designers only" rule, but what Melania wants, Melania gets.

Kate Bennett tweeted, "looks to me like @FLOTUS is wearing this $2,000 @givenchy. 🤚, it's me again #fashiondetective," with a link to the dress's page on Net-a-Porter.

Vanessa Friedman, the *New York Times* fashion director and chief fashion critic, requested a comment about why Mrs. Trump wore a French designer, and I said, "It was in honor of National Wear Red

Day, which is to highlight the importance and raise awareness about heart disease. . . . Mrs. Trump is a proud and longtime supporter of American fashion. She appreciates fashion as art. As a former model, she has always been a patron of the world's most distinguished designers both here and abroad. Mrs. Trump buys from an international mix of brands because that is what reflects her uniquely American life experience and style."

At the Red Cross Ball, Melania wore a hot-pink Dior gown. She did wear garments by American designers—the Row and Derek Lam—at the Super Bowl party at the Trump International Golf Club on February 5, but the media didn't care. They only reported Melania's slipups.

I was incensed. We tried so hard to get it right, and they roasted her anyway. She said to me, "Why do you care? You can't win."

But I *wanted* to win them over. I knew the media and the whole world could be convinced to love Melania, too. If only she'd stick with the plan! And if only I had more help to do it!

Once in a Lifetime

Melania was not content with an apology and retraction from that Maryland blogger Tarpley and the *Daily Mail* about writing in the summer of 2016 that she'd once been an escort. She re-sued the British tabloid in New York for defamation to the tune of $150 million. The language of the complaint raised eyebrows. It said that the plaintiff (Melania) "had the unique, once-in-a-lifetime opportunity, as an extremely famous and well-known person, as well as a former professional model, brand spokesperson and successful businesswoman, to launch a broad-based commercial brand in multiple product categories"—apparel, accessories, makeup, hair care, jewelry, fragrance—"each of which could have garnered multi-million dollar business relationships for a multi-year term during which plaintiff is one of the most photographed women in the world."

Immediately, we got a query from journalist Julie Bykowicz, then a reporter at the Associated Press, who said, "That has been interpreted to mean she intends to make money from her exposure as FLOTUS. Is this the case? Is that appropriate? Do you have any other comments on this issue?"

Melania instructed me to shut down Jessica from commenting on the multiple press inquiries about the lawsuit. Charles Harder, her attorney, replied to the AP himself. "The first lady has no intention of using her position for profit and will not do so," he said. "It is not a possibility. Any statements to the contrary are being misinterpreted."

Two weeks later, Harder refiled the claim, taking out the phrase "once in a lifetime" and shifting the impact of the "escort" slur toward Melania's feelings. Per the revised complaint, "Defendant's false and inflammatory statements about Plaintiff have caused tremendous harm to Plaintiff's personal and professional reputation and prospective economic opportunities, as well as causing her significant humiliation and emotional distress."

Unless you haven't been paying attention, you know by now that Melania doesn't register humiliation or distress. She *was* angry that complete strangers had used her story for their own profit and notoriety. She would tell Donald to stop talking about people. Every time he does it, he only makes them more famous, and that's what they want. As far as Melania's suffering great anguish about being misunderstood by the public, it did not happen. Ever the pragmatist, she reasoned that since she had no control over people's thoughts, why should she care what they believed? Pretty incredible wisdom, if you can actually pull that off. Mere mortals cannot, but our superwoman First Lady could and did!

Melania settled with Tarpley, who, per Harder, "agreed to pay a substantial sum as a settlement." She also settled with the *Daily Mail*, which agreed to pay her legal fees and damages, believed to be about $3 million. Melania was pleased about winning. But I wouldn't describe her reaction as celebratory or even victorious. In her mind, justice had been done.

Journalists who knew me personally would contact me directly with press requests for Melania, but many requests went to the West Wing. The vexing trend of Stephanie Grisham sending the inquiries to Lindsay without cc'ing me continued.

Hajimemashite

On the same day as the "once in a lifetime" debacle, the First Lady's office received our instructions from the West Wing about the upcoming White House state visit with the prime minister of Japan, Shinzō Abe, and his wife, Akie Abe, kicking off on February 10.

The State Department's Office of the Chief of Protocol sent a briefing memo with background about Mrs. Abe ("She is a fan of South Korean soap operas," "She opened a pub that serves only organic food," etc.) and Japanese etiquette. For example, when meeting people for the very first time, the Japanese say "*hajimemashite*," which translates to "it is the first time," and not "*konnichiwa*" (hello). I found that to be particularly relevant, since this was not only Abe and Donald's first meeting but the first state visit for the Trumps and Melania's first diplomatic mission. We really wanted it to go well and took the reassurance from the State Department that, as the schedule solidified, they'd continue to provide protocol guidance for every aspect of the visit.

There would be an exchange of diplomatic gifts, and the item itself was for us to choose. Lindsay told me, "The gift can be up to two thousand dollars and it *must* be made in the USA." She said, "What about a pashmina?"

Did she think that Mrs. Abe needed to be swaddled?

"No problem," I said. "We'll think of something else."

Ideally, the gift would have cultural or historical significance and relate to Melania's big-picture mission about the health and well-being of children and families or American design and creativity.

After Lindsay prattled about how pretty the newly painted cotton-candy-pink walls were in Melania's office, which I had to have repainted, I didn't trust her to wrap a gift, much less choose one. As for her track record with gift spending, she was the one, along with Ramsey Ratcliffe, who'd blown the whole $500,000 PIC gift budget on trinkets from the White House Historical Association.

I turned to my consigliere and arbiter of art and taste, David Monn, and he suggested a porcelain "Rose in Bloom" flower by Ukraine-born American artist Vladimir Kanevsky. Melania loved it. We tried to arrange for the artist to add Mrs. Abe's initials to the gift, but there wasn't time.

Gift done. On to scheduling. Tim Tripepi attended daily schedule briefings in the West Wing, where he learned that Mrs. Abe had plans on Friday afternoon to visit Gallaudet University and the Japanese embassy for a meeting with the National Cherry Blossom Festival committee. Via emails with the West Wing, we confirmed that Melania's official duties would begin when she and Donald accompanied the Abes to Palm Beach on Air Force One Friday evening. They would have dinner that night at Mar-a-Lago. The next day, Mrs. Trump and Mrs. Abe would tour the Morikami Museum and Japanese Gardens in Delray Beach, followed by lunch and maybe a spa treatment to be named later. "I'll let you know which service I'll have, and which Mrs. Abe would like," Melania texted me. She probably would want to book a Tammy Fender facial for herself.

We arranged for Melania to fly in from New York. We were all set and felt pretty good about our efforts. And then, a bomb dropped with Kate Bennett's name on it. Her article "Without Melania Trump, Mrs. Abe rolls solo in Washington" came out on Friday afternoon. The big scoop was that Melania had broken long-standing tradition by not entertaining the spouse of a visiting dignitary while he was in a meeting with the president. Michelle Obama and Laura Bush had shown Mrs. Abe a good time in DC in years past. But Melania, the piece implied, couldn't be bothered to show up.

Melania was outraged when she sent me the link. My response: "OMG! WTF?!!!!!"

"The West Wing did this," said Melania. "This is unacceptable!" She reminded me that she *had* suggested a lunch with Mrs. Abe, but we were told that she already had plans.

I emailed Lindsay, "Read the CNN piece. This is horrible! MT is so angry! What can she do?"

Lindsay came back with some intel from Bennett's office. "Kate said she called and emailed Jessica [Boulanger, who volunteered to handle Melania's press during the inauguration and we tried to hire but didn't have the budget for], but she never responded, and [CNN] ran with the story. We need to hire press people today. They are writing bad stories because we have been silent."

"I need those emails. Jessica didn't tell me because Jessica wasn't working with us anymore! Why did Bennett go to Jessica and not reach out to me? Besides that, if she didn't get a response, why didn't she next ask me?"

Lindsay said, "I don't have them, and Katie Walsh at the request/demand of POTUS and FLOTUS, who are both really upset, is on the phone with [Bennett] who wrote the story."

I hunted down the emails that Kate Bennett and her colleague Betsy Klein had sent to Jessica the day before. Klein had written, "Checking back to see if you can provide any scheduling guidance for the First Lady tomorrow—will she be in Washington to greet Mrs. Abe? We heard a rumor to the contrary but let me know if you have anything reportable for us."

Kate Bennett's February 9 email to Jessica: "Hey. Any comment on this? Spicer from the gaggle a bit ago: 'I'm not sure . . . I think that they're waiting until Barron gets out of school. I would have a hard time thinking that they're going to land [in DC] . . . I would guess she would fly from NY straight to Florida.' So, will Mrs. Trump be in Washington? Or will Ivanka Trump? Are either of them going to spend time with Mrs. Abe tomorrow in DC?"

Sean Spicer's alternative facts strike again.

Bennett covered her ass by writing in the article, "Requests for clarification about Mrs. Trump's whereabouts earlier in the day on

Friday went unanswered by the White House. Mrs. Trump has not yet named her own spokesperson." Bennett knew they should have reached out directly to me for comment, but that wouldn't have been in their best interest.

Lindsay said, "State Department was told Mrs. Abe had her own schedule and would meet at the airport. We never declined an invitation or were asked to participate in anything. West Wing press shop has offered to push back on it if we want and respond."

Was she kidding? Let the "West Wing press shop" do *what*, exactly? So far, they'd done nothing for FLOTUS except jam us up.

Melania texted the group to ask who was in charge of state visits. Was it Reince Priebus?

Tim Tripepi reported, "Everything goes through Reince Priebus, then through State, and then lastly through Jared."

What? Jared?

Jared Kushner was organizing state visits? The Secret Service and State Department knew what Mrs. Abe's plans were because they organized her schedule hand-in-hand *with Jared*.

As we were sorting all this out, Melania was sitting on Air Force One with the Abes and Donald and dozens of others. With people all around her, I knew she'd keep her game face on. Behind the mask, though, she was seething.

Her texts came fast and furious:

Send Reince the story.

We need to contact CNN to make a retraction.

Need to send them a statement. To fight back.

Getting killed on social media.

I told her to take a moment. Breathe. How could we handle this? Did we want to tell the world that the State Department and Jared had set up the First Lady to look bad? Melania was ready to have someone fired, and no one could blame her one tiny bit.

I drafted a statement with Melania that she forwarded to Hicks and Spicer, hoping we could release it within the hour.

I felt played by the State Department and was livid at Bennett.

My first line of defense was to email her, lodging my complaint about her failure to confirm and clarify her information with the First Lady's office, and for writing a story with a predetermined narrative—that Melania was disregarding tradition—before she had all the facts. She'd embarrassed the First Ladies of two countries so she could get her bogus scoop.

To make matters worse, she tweeted, "Japan's First Lady, Akie Abe, attends tour of @GallaudetU solo, w/out @FLOTUS or @IvankaTrump to host, accompany. Very unusual."

Two hours after Melania sent my statement to Hicks and Spicer, they hadn't approved or released it. It seemed like blatant sabotage. Finally, it came out, and Bennett updated her story:

"Hours after this story was published Friday afternoon, Mrs. Trump's office released a statement explaining her whereabouts: 'The First Lady was very much looking forward to welcoming Mrs. Abe to the White House upon her arrival in Washington; however, she was informed that Mrs. Abe had previous commitments during her stay in DC,' the statement said."

Throughout the evening, I updated Melania and kept one eye on the social media reaction to the story. Kate Bennett posted a few pictures of Jacqueline Kennedy in white pants and a navy top on Twitter. While flying to Palm Beach with the Abes, Melania wore a Michael Kors navy top and white slacks. Was Bennett implying that Melania paled in comparison to Jackie Kennedy?

Enough was enough. The First Lady needed her *entire* statement made public, so I reached out to some of my major media contacts, relationships I'd built over the years based on hard work, respect, and integrity. I told them I needed to fix the misinformation Kate had disseminated to the world.

By 10:19 p.m., eight hours after Bennett's article was published, I had written to Melania, "Done! Confirmed. Online. On Don Lemon."

It aired exclusively on *CNN Tonight* with Don Lemon: "The First Lady was very much looking forward to welcoming Mrs. Abe to the White House upon her arrival in Washington; however, she was informed that Mrs. Abe had previous commitments during her stay in DC. The First Lady flew to AAFB to meet the President, Prime Minister Abe and Mrs. Abe to be able to fly with them on AF1 as it was Mrs. Abe's first opportunity to spend time with the First Lady. They will all be together for the weekend at Mar-a-Lago and have a full itinerary. Mrs. Trump is delighted to be able to welcome the Prime Minister and Mrs. Abe to the First Family's winter home, which is a very special place to her and to the entire Trump family. We remain eager to work with the media to inform the American people truthfully, with transparency and integrity, while adhering to the highest journalistic standards. We are only too happy to confirm the facts of a story prior to its publication when given the opportunity."

It took me twelve hours to make this happen. But it had taken decades to build relationships with colleagues who respected and trusted me first. It was a crash course in crisis management for Lindsay. I schooled her on our policy going forward: (1) I would handle all false information that was published about the First Lady; (2) general inquiries and follow-ups could wait; (3) everything went through us, *not the West Wing*.

It was a rough day, but it ended well. Lindsay thanked me for handling this disaster. She texted, "We are out on a lifeboat alone and it's beyond what I thought and I'm realizing what you have been telling me all along is true."

She'd missed the final weeks on the PIC, after all. I replied, "Stay strong!"

After our mini-war together that day, I trusted Lindsay. For that matter, I also believed that if journalists had the correct information, they would hold themselves to high journalistic standards.

Lindsay reported from Florida in the morning that her husband had given her a pep talk. "He said, 'go work your ass off and take care of her. That is what you are there for. Assume no one is helping, and fuck them for it.' It's my motto today!"

I thought, *You go, girl!*

Melania invited Mrs. Abe to ride with her on Saturday morning to visit the Morikami Museum and Japanese Gardens. Betsy Klein asked for a comment, and I gave her a statement. Next, I had to prepare the exclusive fashion coverage for *WWD*. I texted Lindsay, who was glued to Melania's side, "What is she wearing?"

"It is a long white dress and matching cardigan," she replied.

Hervé had sent me a dozen photos for her looks for the weekend. "Calvin Klein?" I asked.

"CALVIN KLEIN CONFIRMED."

I said, "Please tell me she has a slip on?" The white fabric would leave little to the imagination.

"No slip. ☺ "

To bounce back, I wanted to make sure Melania and Mrs. Abe had a meaningful day. A garden tour didn't seem impactful enough, given Mrs. Abe's political activism and general gravitas. I texted Lindsay to ask Melania if it was possible for them to go to a church. I'd read in the State Department briefing that Mrs. Abe had grown up Catholic and was very involved with the Church.

I knew the Secret Service wouldn't be too thrilled that I was suggesting an OTR (off-the-record stop), but they were *so much easier*. No one was alerted that she'd be there. It was less time consuming, with fewer budget burdens.

Lindsay texted back: "MT said she wants to drive Mrs. Abe down Ocean and Worth Avenue and then turn around at Bethesda-by-the-Sea Church where MT goes." The same church she'd gotten married in. "Then Mrs. Abe wants MT to take her to Mar-a-Lago gift shop before they eat lunch."

But . . . were they stopping at the church or not? Were they going to take pictures? I needed to know to prepare Melania's social media postings. I was in charge of posting these items myself on her Facebook, Instagram, and Twitter, in addition to all my other duties. Melania was picky about the captions, so the photos went through a rigorous vetting process.

They went to the church and took photos, but Melania didn't like any of the pictures of the two of them—"too common, not artistic enough"—so she sent me a shot of the church itself and told me to "post this one with the cross." The photos of the garden tour were much more flattering. She sent two pictures and instructed me to "get them online."

A bit curt, I thought, but it's hard to interpret the tone of texts. She followed that up with rapid-fire instructions that made my head spin: *Only #1 first tweet with picture. #2 and #3 tweet no pic. Facebook #1 with photo #2 and #3 no photo just post. Instagram no #2 or #3.*

The whole time she was sending me my posting orders, she was sitting next to Mrs. Abe in the car.

Personal pictures were not "official" FLOTUS pictures on Instagram. We posted them anyway, a small act of rebellion to try to get some power back. We had no control over what the press would publish.

I asked Lindsay how Melania was doing, which Lindsay promptly told Melania. She LOLed and 😝-ed at me, as if her well-being were a silly thing for me to worry about.

"Business as usual for me," Melania said. "As long as they all do the job they need to." Meaning, as long as someone told her where to go, all she had to do was stand there and pose for photos; she was good.

And she was. We all survived an exhausting run through the gauntlet of *hajimemashite.* That evening, I texted Lindsay to thank her for her support and work, which very few people could possibly begin to understand.

Her response rang true. "There will be good days and bad days. We earned the shit out of these good days!"

If you didn't count the Bennett article, Melania's first state visit had gone pretty well. The Abes and Trumps had a lovely time in Florida. After Donald took a call about missile testing in North Korea on an unsecure phone on the patio at Mar-a-Lago right in front of restaurant guests and Prime Minister Abe, no one in their right mind cared anymore about Melania's accidental diplomatic faux pas.

#Slutshame

On February 13, I had to make a quick stop at the hospital to get a cortisone shot in my neck. The pain was becoming unbearable. The shot did not help. If anything, it made my pain worse; I think the doctor hit a nerve.

Other pains in the neck were revealed by actor and model Emily Ratajkowski, who tweeted that day: "Sat next to a journalist from the NYT last night who told me 'Melania is a hooker.' Whatever your politics it's crucial to call this out for what it is: slut shaming. I don't care about her nudes or sexual history and no one should. Gender specific attacks are barbaric sexist bullshit."

This random encounter took place at a New York Fashion Week event. I made some calls and found out that the *New York Times* reporter who'd slut-shamed Melania to Ratajkowski was none other than Jacob Bernstein.

One month earlier, Bernstein had written a profile of me, and I had felt the sting of his gender-specific attacks. He took pains to describe my wardrobe and put a price tag on my handbag, questioned my résumé, all but said I took more credit than I deserved for my work on the Met Gala, and suggested that I buried my Catskills past so I could pretend I'd always been a Scarsdale "granddaughter" of Harry Winston. Bernstein could have researched his newspaper's own archives if he wanted to know the truth about my work and background, but he obviously had his hot take on me before we'd met, and he bent the facts to fit it. I had to wonder how much of it was Trump hate.

Melania was quoted in that article about why she'd tapped me, saying I had an "impressive work ethic" and "fantastic taste." "She has a way of connecting with people—motivating them to get the job done in the best way possible."

Melania was nonplussed—the media had struck again—but we both agreed that she could not ignore it and that she had to affirm Ratajkowski's message.

By seven forty-five p.m., I posted on the First Lady's official Twitter, "Applause to all women around the world who speak up, stand up and support other women! @emrata #PowerOfEveryWoman #PowerOfTheFirstLady."

The *Times* slapped Bernstein on the wrist, issuing a statement rebuking his loose lips. He wasn't even a political reporter, but he'd had a part in writing two flattering profiles on Princess, one that asked, "Will Ivanka Trump Be the Most Powerful First Daughter in History?"

Under fire, Bernstein tweeted, "I want to take ownership of a mistake I made. Speaking at a party in what I thought was a personal conversation, I nevertheless made a stupid remark about the first lady. My editors have made it clear my behavior was not in keeping with the standards of the *Times*, and I agree. My mistake, referring to unfounded rumors, shouldn't reflect on anyone else and I apologize profusely."

Glad he was sorry. Maybe he'd think twice next time before he degraded a woman.

Hearts, Flowers, Whatever

I told Melania I'd been looking into possible locations for her and Donald to have a Valentine's Day date. She found that hysterical. In the past, February 14 had never caused a ripple of romance at Trump Tower. One thing Donald and Melania have in common: they are not sentimental types. I can't recall her ever telling me about Donald sending her flowers or taking her out on Valentine's Day, or her girlishly planning a special surprise or treat for him.

Since they were the First Couple, however, I thought it'd be sweet and affirming for them to be seen in public, sitting across a table from each other with a candle between them. She wouldn't hear of it. "OMG. 😜 Don't like Valentine's Day. So commercial," she said.

I begged her to reconsider, if only to promote them as a normal couple who loved and cherished each other.

David Monn recommended the Inn at Little Washington—James Beard Award–winning chef Patrick O'Connell's Michelin three-star restaurant—in nearby Virginia, which was bucolic and adorable. I sent her a link.

She said, "I don't care to do it just for people, so they say 'how nice.' Donald thinks the same way. We don't care about Valentine's Day."

I texted, "♥ ♥ ♥ ♥ ♥ ♥ ♥ ♥ ♥ ♥ ♥ ♥ ♥ ♥ ♥ ♥ ♥"

She said she'd think about it, but "for now is no."

I kept at it, though. She finally shut me up when she sent me a text about her having made plans. She said, "I talked to Donald. He is having dinner with Murdoch on Tuesday night. All set." She would not be joining.

Donald and Rupert sitting in a tree?

In hindsight, it was ridiculous of me to push a romantic dinner at the inn. As if Donald would be seen anywhere but a Trump property!

Hervé Pierre texted that day. Bad news: his best hope for a paying job hadn't worked out, and he was starting to worry seriously about money. His total compensation so far for two months of nonstop work for Melania had been a small fee for designing the inauguration gown, and nothing for his work as a stylist. He said, "I may need to move back to France. I'm a little bit lost."

I lobbied for him, and Melania told me, "He needs to find a job."

Princess Makes Her Move

On February 14, I was cc'ed on an email from Katie Walsh to Lindsay and Dina Powell, Ivanka's advisor, that said, "Wednesday March 8 is International Women's Day. It could be a great opportunity for FLOTUS/Ivanka. Would love to discuss any ideas you may have or help craft some events."

Powell was way into it and replied, "Happy to work with you [Katie] and Lindsay. And agree it's a big opportunity."

What was going on here: the First Lady's office (me) and David Monn had been planning a lunch for International Women's Day already. It was going to be Melania's first White House event that we organized, and her big opportunity (indeed) to host, introduce the broad strokes of her platform, and talk about the UN Women for Peace Association and the importance of empowerment and education for girls. Now Ivanka, Katie, and Dina were swooping in?

Melania was not having it. She told me, "Are you kidding me? Seriously? I'm not cohosting."

Soon after, Melania texted to ask why Ivanka wanted to invite Republican and Democrat senators' spouses to the White House for a lunch that was traditionally the First Lady's event.

She was referring to the traditional lunch the day after the Governors' Dinner hosted by the First Lady for the spouses. The event location alternated yearly between the East Wing and George Washington's historic home, Mount Vernon. Cabinet members and APs were not included, but apparently Ivanka was trying to get in on this event, too. Did she know no shame?

I said to Melania, "Dina said it like it was a new idea."

"She can't do it," said Melania. "We need to let her know that I know that this is a First Lady event done every year." Of course Ivanka could be there as a guest, but the hosting duties belonged to Melania. Melania said, "OMG. They just want to take credit for it."

Ivanka was relentless and driven. Topic A in the East Wing: Ivanka would never stop trying to muscle in on Melania's events. We had to be vigilant.

Shalom

The second state visit, on February 15, was with Prime Minister Benjamin Netanyahu of Israel and his wife, Sara Netanyahu. Melania would be in DC this time and would play tour guide to Mrs. Netanyahu, with a media posse to report on their every movement.

We decided that Melania should take Mrs. Netanyahu to tour the Smithsonian's National Museum of African American History and Culture. Tim Tripepi kept sending me emails about Stephanie Grisham, of all people, saying that she was very eager to help FLOTUS in any way possible and wanted to know what she could do for us. My answer? Grisham could keep doing what she'd already been doing for us: nothing.

With the clearance and itinerary in place, Melania put her mind to the most important matter of all. What to wear?

Easy answer: "Lagerfeld!"

Melania could wear the suit Karl Lagerfeld had designed for her that she'd wanted to wear to the swearing-in. It was glorious, a white cashmere jacket and pencil skirt. She loved this suit the way a little girl loves a basket of kittens.

There she stood in resplendent white at the South Entrance to the White House to welcome the Netanyahus. She smiled and posed for photos, a gracious host and diplomat. Melania radiated First Lady–ness, albeit with a European flair.

She sat in the front row at the president and prime minister's news conference in the East Room and seemed to be concentrating on the content of the discussion. Her views on Israel were aligned with Donald's. When I asked her, for example, whether the capital of Israel should be in Jerusalem or Tel Aviv, she said, "Donald wants to recognize Jerusalem." She made her own sense of his views.

While I sat in the press conference, I received an email from Tim about a huge point of contention between the East Wing and the West Wing: Melania's plane. She wanted a bigger, nicer one. They wanted her to have a smaller one with no Wi-Fi for her flights between New York, DC, and Palm Beach. Tim wrote, "I would seriously tell MT to tell DJT to tell Joe Hagin that she needs the C-40B to be her dedicated plane."

Tim told me to tell Melania to tell Donald . . . What good did his nagging me to nag her do? Mansplaining alert. He began to step on Lindsay's toes, too, scheduling and showing up for meetings that he didn't need to attend and wanting to speak directly with Melania and not stick to protocol. As chief of staff, Lindsay had the authority to put Tim in his place, but he wasn't having any of it.

The press conference wrapped. With entourages and the press

in tow, they went to the Smithsonian's National Museum of African American History and Culture and took in the newly opened exhibit. We were entering touchy territory. To open Black History Month, which had started two weeks earlier, Donald had had a press conference and mentioned the exhibit. "I am very proud now that we have a museum on the National Mall where people can learn about Reverend King, so many other things," he said. "Frederick Douglass is an example of somebody who's done an amazing job and is being recognized more and more, I notice."

Activist Frederick Douglass was indeed a great man. Except he died in 1895 and Donald didn't seem to know that.

The risk of going to the exhibit two weeks after that gaffe was that it might feel like a stunt, and she'd be attacked and mocked alongside her husband. Her speech would matter.

She read the following, which I helped her to compose:

As we toured this awe-inspiring building, one could not help but be overcome by the bittersweet history of African Americans. Theirs is truly the story of the triumph of the human spirit over unthinkable inhumanity. . . . we rededicate ourselves to those powerful words that both our nations hold dear: NEVER AGAIN!

I was hopeful that, after such a successful visit, Melania would embrace her role and blossom into the kind of First Lady our country would be proud of.

My gratification was complete when Kate Bennett's report ran on CNN. It was a rave: "Her presence Wednesday is evidence she might indeed take a more active role in official duties."

Sam Feist, CNN's Washington Bureau chief, sent me a note that said, "You guys had a very good day."

What a breakthrough! A perfectly executed tour and speech. Favorable press. It went off without a hitch.

"Great event. You were fantastic!" I told her during our recap of the day. Unspoken were my thoughts about her bright future in international diplomacy.

Plus, she finally got to wear the suit!

The joy didn't last. On February 16, the New York *Daily News* ran a gossip item that quoted a White House insider as saying, "Not only is Ivanka moving into the First Lady's office, she's redecorating it. It's what they're going to call 'The First Family Office.'"

Melania said, "Ridiculous! This has got to stop."

Presidents' Day Weekend

For the long Presidents' Day weekend, my daughter, Alexi, and I flew to Florida with Melania, her parents, and Barron on her plane on Friday. David, Tyler, and Zach were going to meet us at Mar-a-Lago for dinner on Saturday night.

Melania asked if I wanted to go along to a big rally on Saturday to "experience the craziness." Or, she suggested, I could stay at the resort and go to the spa. "Let me know. 😉 Guess u prefer spa 😃 as I would. 😊"

The president's rallies were known to be unhinged, and I was curious. A facial and massage sounded incredible, but I couldn't pass up a chance to experience the rally energy firsthand.

Alexi and I wandered down to the restaurant for dinner Friday night. Donald and Melania were already seated, just the two of them. They waved us over and asked us to join them. Alexi had known the Trumps her whole life, but this was her first meal with the president and First Lady. She was polite and charming and sat through Donald's monologue about his Electoral College victory with the patience of a saint.

Saturday was busy. Donald had asked Melania to say a few words at the rally, so she asked me to come to her bedroom to work on her speech. I sat on the floor while she sat on her bed. When Donald came in to say hello, he couldn't have been friendlier. I walked out onto her portico to give them some privacy.

When he left, I returned and we resumed. Melania had it all planned out. "I was thinking we should come out together," she said (which they did). She continued, "I should start, and Donald stays next to me" (which he did), and [I'll say] 'Let us pray,' and they do." A minute later, she wanted to know if I had a contact for Tommy Hilfiger.

Afterward, I made time for a facial at the spa with Tammy Fender, Melania's longtime secret weapon, that was like a two-week vacation in Hawaii. During lunch, Alexi and I ran into Ivanka by the pool. She caught me off guard, saying, "Let's have lunch together when we're both back in DC." I bumped into Jared, too.

I texted Melania, "I saw IT & JK. They are not coming to the rally."

She said of course they weren't. It was the Sabbath. "They are being good."

I replied, " 😊 "

Around three forty-five p.m., we all gathered out front by the main entrance of the resort and piled into our assigned vans for a motorcade. There had to be twenty cars, two fire engines, and a horde of police vehicles to drive the twenty minutes to the Palm Beach airport. I loved the motorcade! It was impossible not to feel the excitement with so many flashing lights.

Waiting on the tarmac was Air Force One, a huge plane, with a drop-stairs entry right in the belly. Many familiar faces waited to board: advisors Gary Cohn, Steve Bannon, Stephen Miller, Hope Hicks, and a dozen more. Tim Tripepi came too, and I gave him Melania's Louis Vuitton bag to carry.

Upon boarding, Alexi and I were handed towels and mints. We found cards with our names at a table (and my last name was spelled wrong again! Instead of "Wilcox," it was "Wolcoff"—at least they were making progress) and sat down for takeoff. Once we were in the air, Melania came to get us to give us a tour. She showed us her room, the conference room, the lounge area, and the cockpit. The three of us goofed around, took selfies (including the photo on the front cover of this book), and used the face-swap filter to put Melania's face on Alexi's head.

We landed at the Orlando Melbourne International Airport about an hour after takeoff, at 5:42 p.m. The hangar was already packed with excited fans waiting for Donald. He and Melania deplaned to the tune of "Proud to Be an American" and continued walking, not breaking stride, right onto the hangar's stage. It reminded me of a model catwalk, actually.

While Alexi and I watched, Melania took the microphone and delivered the speech we'd written. People cheered. I couldn't stop smiling at how far she'd come since we first met, how far we'd come as friends. And now we got to share this almost unimaginable experience with our kids.

Donald took the microphone and riled up the crowd. Melania sat nearby in a chair. He finished his speech at 6:36, loosened his tie, and walked off to the song "You Can't Always Get What You Want" by the Rolling Stones, straight back toward the plane and up the stairs, with Melania by his side. We were wheels-up within minutes.

When we returned via motorcade to Mar-a-Lago, we quickly changed and met David and my sons at the restaurant for their celebratory birthday dinner. Tyler's actual birthday had been the day before, on February 17, and David and Zach were both born on February 21. When the cakes came out with sparklers, we gathered on one side of the table to take a picture. A waiter rushed over and said, "You're not allowed to take photos!" Apparently, when the president is at the Winter White House, cameras are banned. But then Donald and Melania came to our table and posed with us. Donald told the waiter we could snap away.

Our last night in Florida, David and I had dinner with Donald, Melania, Ivanka, Jared, Hope Hicks, and Amalija and Viktor Knavs. The kids sat at the next table. Throughout the meal, Melania kept looking over at me and smirking at the antics between Ivanka, Jared, and Donald as they hashed over the topic of the hour: Was Kellyanne Conway losing it on TV?

Onlookers watched our table, but the Secret Service worked double duty that night as bouncers, keeping well-wishers away. Even my kids needed permission to approach our table.

Zachary came up, wrapped his arm around my neck, leaned in between Melania and me, and asked if it was "safe" to eat what the chef had prepared for him. Melania gently reassured him that she had spoken with the staff and chef and that it was safe for him to eat whatever he wanted. Melania had a soft spot for Zach.

As relieved as I was, my son smiled and said, "Thank you. I guess there really couldn't be a safer place for my food to be prepared than with the president. Pretty cool." It was cute and the three of us laughed.

David and I, the Kushners, and the president rose from our seats to head over to the dessert buffet. (Melania loves a good crème brûlée.) Donald had his eye on a big piece of chocolate cake, so I handed him an empty plate, my fingers on the bottom and my thumb on the top edge, a perfectly natural and normal way to hand someone a plate. He stared at my thumb as if it were on fire. I thought, *Oh, shit, move your thumb!* He beamed at me as he took the plate, and then, when he thought I wasn't looking, he put it down and got another.

I'd seen his germaphobia in action over the years, how he always kept his hands in his pockets or close to his sides, a bottle of sanitizer at the ready. When he posed in photos, he gave the thumbs-up so he didn't have to touch the icky hands of admirers. He was even afraid of *my* germs. This man wouldn't eat off a plate that had been touched by a friend.

On Monday, Presidents' Day, my family of five, Melania, and Barron all flew back to New York on Melania's plane and took a motorcade into Manhattan. As soon as we landed, the Secret Service took my Presidential Guest badge. I could have it at Mar-a-Lago and on the planes, but forget about having a badge to get into the White House. Where I really needed it.

On that weekend, I felt like I was onstage with Mick Jagger and

Madonna both at once. I was thrilled to ride in three presidential planes, be in four motorcades, see a rally up close, and spend quality time with my friend and my family in a gorgeous setting. I felt included and appreciated, and I couldn't wait to help create an initiative that would change lives for generations to come. I was bursting with good vibes for Melania, my work, my family.

Lunch with Princess

Ivanka's assistant Mallory Harney sent me an email following up on Ivanka's invitation to schedule a lunch. I guess she had no clue that I worked with Melania, since she also requested my social security number and date of birth so that I could "be granted access to the White House."

I wrote back, "I am already inside the WH, I work here, but thank you." I noticed that Mallory was using the Ivanka and Jared family email domain, not the government domain. Still? It'd been a month already.

Ivanka usually emailed or texted me to ask about the dress code for events, or to get passes and tickets for her VIPs, or to recommend her friends for jobs. She once suggested I reach out to hire her ex-boyfriend's cousin, Marjorie Gubelmann, to DJ an inaugural event, and recommended photographers and decorators. Now Ivanka requested a face-to-face meeting. I wondered what she wanted this time. My marching orders from Melania were to hear Ivanka out and report back. We assumed she was going to appeal to me personally to let her cohost the spouses lunch after the Governors' Dinner and the International Women's Day lunch.

Lunch with Ivanka was at the White House mess hall. Only APs (and their guests) were allowed to eat in there. I'd never been there before because I had given up my AP title for Lindsay; otherwise, Ivanka and I would have had the same access. Instead I had no access at all.

Our meal couldn't have been more different from my lunches with

Melania, which were full of giggles, affection, and stories about our kids. Ivanka asked about my family only as a launch point for getting down to business.

Ivanka was so complimentary. "It's so great that you and David [Monn] are working here together," she said. I smiled.

She said, "I know how busy you both are preparing for all of the events and all of your efforts in the East Wing."

I nodded and said, "There's so much to do!" Meanwhile, I really wanted to say, "Let it go! Just let us work on Melania's initiative and leave us alone."

Instead, Ivanka continued with her inquiry. "What do you have going on?" she asked. "How's the Governors' Dinner?"

I told her about the invite, which had the silhouettes of all fifty state flowers and was absolutely glorious.

"Do you have a guest list?" she asked.

"We do," I said, "but it's a work in progress." I wasn't about to share the names with her.

Ivanka asked if I could let her know which governors were coming so she could request who she wanted to sit next to.

Ivanka switched topics, and thought it would be a great idea to discuss our various projects to see if there was any overlap. She'd already put her stamp on STEM (science, technology, engineering, and math), which Melania had been focused on, so I knew whatever I said would be food for thought.

"Tell me more about the International Women's Day luncheon," she said.

I told her, "We are working with the UN Women for Peace Association."

She said, "I'd really appreciate it if you could send me more info about it. I can make suggestions for guests and maybe say a few words."

I said, "I'll let Melania know."

From lunch with Ivanka, I headed for the high-security Situation Room to attend a meeting about the president's first address to the joint session of Congress, which the staff was calling the State of the

Union address (although, technically, it wasn't). I'd only heard about this meeting a couple of days ago when Lindsay mentioned it. Lindsay and Tim attended senior staff meetings but never had much to report back. Katie and company from the West Wing rolled all over them. They had told Melania, "You will need to attend this nationally televised event. Takes place at the Capitol. You are seated in a box."

Melania had asked me, "What time is the event? Dress code?"

I asked, "What's a box? All they know is departure and arrival time? Makes no sense."

"You go to the next meeting," she told me. "Find out what's going on." Although I didn't have the clearance to attend, I showed up at the Situation Room anyway. I had to go to protect Melania's interests.

Thankfully, Katie had added my name to the appointment list. I felt excited and hesitant handing over my phone to enter. President Obama and his staff had sat in the Sit Room and watched as Navy SEALs killed Osama bin Laden. Critical decisions about covert operations and classified information were made at this very table.

The high of that feeling lasted for a few seconds.

At the meeting, I finally understood that we knew nothing. The West Wing press people in charge of organizing the event and the seating at the address informed me that there were no available seats left in the First Lady's box.

I said, "How can that be? We haven't invited anyone yet."

"They're already taken," said one of the bureaucrats.

"By who?"

"Cabinet members and other guests of Ivanka Trump."

There it was. Ivanka had set up her seats in Melania's section. It occurred to me: Had she scheduled our lunch for the same day as this meeting because she hoped I'd miss it and be none the wiser about her appropriating Melania's seats?

"The First Lady needs eight seats," I declared.

After much hemming and hawing, they agreed to free up four seats for the First Lady.

I marched right over to the East Wing and asked for an explanation. Lindsay pointed at Tim, and he pointed back at her. "We need a solution," I said. Not just to this but moving forward, too.

Rickie suggested a very organic fit. "Children's National is opening the Bunny Mellon Healing Garden, dedicated to the First Ladies of the United States, in a couple of months," she told us. Rickie organized a meeting with Kurt Newman, MD, the president and chief executive officer of Children's National Hospital. With their help, Melania invited Sheila Gregory and her daughter Jessica, who would come to the Capitol Building and sit with Melania in her box. We rushed their vetting, which thankfully cleared in time.

The next day, I texted Ivanka, "It was so great seeing you yesterday. I'm finishing up seating for the governors' dinner. Which governors do you want [to sit with]?"

Her answer came quickly. Ivanka's choices were California's Jerry Brown, Massachusetts's Charlie Baker, and New York's Andrew Cuomo. (She ended up sitting with the only Republican of the three, Charlie Baker.) If she knew that I'd reclaimed four seats for Melania for the congressional address, she did not mention it. It was always sunshine and light with Ivanka on the surface, in person and by email and text. She never let down her mask, not an inch, not for a second.

Mike Has Needs

The Governors' Dinner was the first large-scale undertaking of the Trump administration, with dinner in the State Dining Room and a sit-down performance in the East Room.

During the planning, Angella Reid, frustratingly, insisted she couldn't show David Monn and me the budget of the previous year's event.

Hedieh Ghaffarian, the White House florist, who wanted to use orange flowers only, wasn't too thrilled when David removed every orange petal in the East and the West Wing and replaced them with white viburnums, lilacs, roses, anemones, and sweet pea vines.

David and Rickie had a tense moment over turf; she was social secretary, but he was doing all the planning. I smoothed that over by inviting Rickie to meet with Melania and me.

There was the never-ending problem of getting talent to entertain the guests. Melania fixed that by suggesting, "We should use the Army Chorus you used for the concert at the mall." She was referring to the US Army Chorus, a group that sang at the Lincoln Memorial as part of the MAGA concert during the inauguration; we'd have them sing classics from the American songbook in their first performance at the White House.

On top of everything else, we had to organize a seven thirty p.m. small dessert reception in the Diplomatic Reception Room for Trump's advisors and cabinet members, followed by the performance. Senior advisors weren't traditionally included, but two broke with tradition.

Ivanka and Jared didn't seem to think protocol applied to them.

Planning the seating was intense, with lots of mixed emotions. Rickie and I went back and forth with Hope, Melania, and Donald over which governors would sit where. Even Ivanka made sure to speak up!

Regarding Virginia's Terry McAuliffe, a Clinton loyalist, Rickie thought it was "appropriate that he be seated next to POTUS. He is also a Dem so we truly cover two birds with one stone."

Hope wrote, "Terry McAuliffe has been very hard on the President. But DJT can charm him."

Donald said, "We used to be great friends . . . before."

Of course, we had to beg for a budget to pay for the event, and learned about the byzantine channels and three-letter agencies that controlled the purse strings.

FLOTUS, the host of the event, was still in New York while David Monn and I oversaw the final setup. When her plane landed an hour before the party and I got notification, I texted Rickie and Lindsay, "The eagle has landed," while they were doing their hair and getting dressed.

The White House photographer, Melania, and I went into the State Dining Room before the guests arrived and took some pictures of her in the beautiful, elegant room. David had outdone himself with a green and white "eternal spring" theme, with light green damask table coverings, the George W. Bush state china with its green lattice pattern, and an eclectic combination of round and rectangular tables.

Lindsay's frustration with her job was starting to show. I got it. This was a highly unusual situation, in a highly unusual White House. She was the chief of staff, but every decision went through me. That morning, she'd said, "I had only half an hour with FLOTUS, and she talked about flowers the whole time." But meanwhile, I'd had private time with Melania to review her schedule and spent the night in the Residence. I would relay to Lindsay everything she needed to know.

FLOTUS wore a black Dolce & Gabbana gown with a slit to her midthigh, sexy, dramatic, and regal. I was still very much on the American-only bandwagon and had tried to pair her with designers Ken Kaufman and Isaac Franco for this event. But after hearing that Ivanka had worn a KaufmanFranco dress for a different event, she said, "Forget it." If Ivanka was dressed by a designer, Melania would cross them off her list. *Too bad for her*, I thought, *they make the sexiest red carpet looks!*

We disagreed over the press release, with a surprise combatant. David and I worked on one that described the menu and the flowers, and included a nice quote from Melania about bringing together all fifty governors in the spirit of bipartisan unity. On top of the usual hurdles we had to go through to get West Wing approval, Melania decided she didn't want us releasing too much information.

"I don't want to put out the details," she said. "No one needs to know what we're eating."

It was an early sign of how Melania's intense privacy would affect her role as First Lady. Refusing to share the menu with the media seemed like passive-aggressive withholding to me. The press kept emailing questions about the food, the décor, the band, the china, the seating, but Melania said, "Nope." It was almost as if divulging the details spoiled the experience for her.

After a (delicious) dinner, the president and First Lady left the

State Dining Room first, followed by the vice president and Mrs. Pence. The four of them—and me—waited in the Red Room for the guests to assemble in the East Room for the entertainment. The four of them took a seat and got to talking. I decided to stand right next to Melania. Mike Pence brought up Trump's Justice Department and Department of Education's rescinding of Obama's federal protections for transgender students that allowed kids to use whichever bathroom they wanted to.

Jackie Evancho, the *America's Got Talent* singer who performed at the inauguration when no one else would, has a transgender sister. On February 22, four days earlier, she'd tweeted, "@realDonaldTrump u gave me the honor 2 sing at your inauguration. Pls give me & my sis the honor 2 meet with u 2 talk #transgender rights ♥" Trump didn't acknowledge the tweet or reply to Evancho. I don't think Vice President Pence did either.

The Supreme Court would soon be hearing a case about the same issue. Melania was confused about why Donald felt compelled to put himself front and center on the bathroom issue. He could have done nothing and avoided upsetting the LGBTQ+ community.

Once the Pences were gone and it was just the three of us, Melania asked Donald, "Why did you get involved?"

I asked, "In what, that bathroom thing?"

He said, "You're right." Then he clasped his hands and looked into her eyes and said, "I didn't need to get involved. I could have let the Supreme Court deal with it. But it was very important to Mike."

Mike Pence really, really cares about where people go to the bathroom.

The next day, February 27, Melania, Karen Pence, their various team members, and I attended the National Governors Association luncheon for the governors' spouses. I asked Melania to enter the room arm in arm with Karen, in a show of solidarity. She did. Terry McAuliffe's wife, Virginia First Lady Dorothy McAuliffe, chose the theme for the event: childhood hunger prevention and nutrition.

I'd written Melania's speech with her. She told the room that she cared about children's issues and invited the guests to get involved with her initiatives. I sat at her table next to Mrs. McAuliffe, who was so polite and engaging, and, as Melania's senior advisor, spoke to her and others about what Melania and her team planned to do to benefit children. It was so gratifying, I forgot about the pain in my neck for an hour there.

Afterward, Melania and I went up to the Residence, talking about the warm welcome she'd received and some details about the upcoming Easter Egg Roll on the White House lawn, and that night I went to sleep in my usual room, number 326. It had been a good day.

State of the Union

On Tuesday, February 28, 2017, President Trump was giving his first speech before a joint session of the United States Congress.

I woke up at three a.m. with a debilitating cramp in my leg. It felt like I'd been shot. I texted Lindsay to ask for the address of the nearest hospital. She gave me the information, but I didn't go. I knew that if I went to the hospital, I wouldn't come out for days.

I'd planned on flying home, but Melania decided that she wanted me to stay in DC and invited me to her husband's address to Congress. I'd already peeled off my fake eyelashes from the spouses lunch and was looking forward to returning to my family. But Melania said, "Please stay." I couldn't say no.

I was upstairs in the Residence with Melania when Jared came up to bring Donald his speech to review. Jared said a quick hello to us and asked if it was okay for him to enter Donald's bedroom. Melania thought the president might be taking a nap. She said, "Go ahead." Jared went inside.

An hour before the address, Melania and I were taken to a holding room in the Capitol Building, right across from the congressional chamber. Jared and Ivanka were also there, just the four of us, waiting to be announced. We took a bunch of pictures (as we do), and Ivanka was as sweet as always. Melania wore Michael Kors, a black skirt that showed a lot of leg. I told her to place the event pamphlet in her lap to cover up some skin. I felt like hell because of my neck and tingling leg.

Lindsay and Tim had told me what a big deal it was that I got to hang out in that holding area with the family before the address, and they couldn't believe I was going to be in the chamber when the president spoke. "No one gets to go to the Congressional address," Lindsay had said. "The staff stays downstairs." I still couldn't understand why Lindsay and Tim didn't demand that the First Lady's box be occupied by her guests, rather than Ivanka's and the cabinet secretaries.

Melania was announced and called to enter the chamber. She said, "Walk with me."

I walked behind her and tried to duck out of camera range. We were led to her box. Sheila and Jessica Gregory from Children's National Hospital were there, as well as Susan Oliver and Jessica Davis, wives of Deputy Sheriff Danny Oliver and Detective Michael Davis Jr., pillars of their community who were slain in the line of duty in California. It was an honor to be in the room with the families of these heroes. Only after Melania sat did I realize that the seats were all full. I was standing on the steps next to Melania's aisle seat with nowhere to go.

She looked at me and glanced down, signaling me to plop down on the stairs next to her. My wobbly leg and aching back groaned in protest as I sat on the hard step. When the camera came our way, I ducked and slid over, or bent down, so that I wasn't in the shot with Melania or blocking the people being honored behind me.

Every time we had to rise to our feet and applaud something Donald said, I hauled my large frame off that step and came all the way back down. Dozens and dozens of times. I squatted more in two hours in front of the entire world than I had in a gym for over two years. The stress on my back was beyond. During those ovations, Melania picked and chose when to stand. I told her through my teeth, "Stand up!" It was as if she didn't think she had to. The queen does not stand with the masses to praise the king.

Ivanka sat with Carryn Owens, the widow of Navy SEAL William Ryan Owens, who'd recently been killed in Yemen. The crowd gave the widow an ovation for more than a minute. Mrs. Owens was sobbing openly throughout. Ivanka stood next to her. At one point, she comforted the widow with a pat on her back.

I whispered to Melania, "You should turn around."

She shook her head. When we had the chance to talk, she explained she didn't want "just to do that," and I knew she was referring to how Ivanka used that moment. Melania did not do what people expected her to do, period; she'd only do what felt right for her.

That night, Melania and Donald were sitting out in the sofa area of the Residence. I didn't want to intrude. I told Angella Reid, "I'm just going to peek in and wave good night before heading upstairs to my bedroom."

Not wanting to intrude, I kept my distance from the sofa area, but when Melania saw me lurking, she patted the seat next to her on the couch. Some advisors stopped by to talk politics and I mainly listened as they spoke. At the end of the night, Ivanka and Jared had to go, but I got to stay.

I had a big realization that night about the difference between Melania and Ivanka. Melania would not play the sympathy or the drama card. Ivanka stacked the deck with them and made sure the cameras captured every moment. Although Ivanka gave the appearance of warmth, people questioned her sincerity, even if it was genuine. Melania gave the appearance of coldness, but she was authentic and genuinely felt sorry for Mrs. Owens.

Her authenticity and common sense were what drew me to her, again and again. She was who she was, and that had been fine in New York. But in Washington, compared to ingratiating Ivanka, Melania's refusal to go through the motions was not sitting well with the press.

My job, among all my other responsibilities, was to convince Melania to dance. Just a little! Baby steps.

— 8 —

The Shutdown

I chalked up the congressional address as a win for Team Melania. We had fought for and gotten those box seats, and Melania had appeared dignified and real. But it was exhausting to fight these battles. Attempting to match Ivanka's insincerity was wearing me out and I started to feel guilty about my own. I wish I could have been authentic and told her how I felt about her and her attempts to sabotage her stepmother, the First Lady, and maybe we could even have hashed out our differences, but that wasn't in the cards. Every day, every hour, felt to me like drawing fresh lines in the shifting sand between the two women. I knew where I stood: on Melania's side, no matter what.

On March 1, 2017, I awoke in the White House, and it all seemed like a dream. I couldn't believe it: there I was, sleeping right above the president and First Lady of the United States. At the time, I truly did care for them both, despite the fact that his policies were making me and many others very uncomfortable. I met Melania in her living room and we took some great pictures of her leaning casually against the piano in the center hall. She was wearing a bright red dress—one she'd worn before—for the planned visit to Children's National Hospital that day. She was careful to drape the dress with a cream coat, just in case someone noticed her repeat wearing of it.

Lindsay and Vanessa had scoured DC the night before to find and buy Tibetan singing bowls, recommended to me by sage-of-all-things David Monn. The bowls make a lovely sound that enhances meditation. We would donate them to the hospital in the morning. Lindsay didn't outright object to running errands as long as she could make Diet Coke runs to McDonald's in her truck.

At the hospital, Melania said a few words that were in essence the hallmarks of the First Lady's initiative, which was starting to take shape after months of hard work together. "I am a passionate believer in integrating and interpreting nature's elements into our daily lives to create a warm, nurturing and positive environment. I believe that these same natural benefits can be instrumental to enhancing the health and well-being of all children. It is important to me that children can recognize, identify and express their feelings in order to promote their mental wellness and healing process."

We went into the hospital's Bunny Mellon Healing Garden, where Melania dug in some dirt with a little shovel and dropped a few flower seeds—morning glories, symbols of love and renewal—into the holes.

See, Melania can garden, too!

The hospital tour and seed planting lasted about two hours, and Melania shook hands with every single kid, parent, doctor, and nurse. One girl, a cancer patient, and Melania made an emotional connection and the girl said meeting the First Lady made her feel better. When they hugged, it truly was a touching moment.

I thought to myself that moments like this were exactly why I'd signed on, for this adventure. As long as we focused on the well-being of children, we were on the right track. That day, Melania fulfilled her promise.

The two of us took her plane to fly back to New York that day for another hospital visit the following morning. We sat in her cabin alone, facing each other. I won't travel backward in a moving vehicle—I'm not sure if I really get nauseated from it or if it's just a superstition. But in her private cabin, I had no choice. There were only two seats and they were facing.

"Switch?" she asked.

"You're so sweet," I said. "I'm sure I won't feel a thing, but if I do, I'll let you know." I took tons of pictures of her in her seat, profile, full face. It was fun and casual, although my continuing neck pain did distract me.

When I got back to my apartment, Alexi said, "The First Lady is home," as I came through the door. She meant it as a joke, but I burst into tears. I'd neglected my kids. The stress and pain were grinding me down.

I still had to send out Melania's social media. I wrote, "The pictures are on their way. Please approve: 'Thank you for welcoming me @ChildrensHealth. My prayers and thoughts are with all of the children and families. #GROWUPSTRONGER.'"

"You are the best!" she emailed me.

On March 2, we went on another "OTR" visit, to the pediatric playroom at NewYork-Presbyterian/Weill Cornell Medical Center in Manhattan. She and I were both affiliated with the hospital and their word was golden to me. All three of my children were born at NYP. For many years, I'd donated a percentage of proceeds from charitable fashion events I'd hosted to the hospital.

Lindsay's search-and-buy errand for that event was to go to Target and purchase a bunch of Dr. Seuss books to put into a gift basket. Melania intended to read to the kids from *Oh, the Places You'll Go!*. We'd tried to get books from Random House, the publisher, but they couldn't deliver in time. The event coincided with the late author's birthday, too. Like I said, this was all carefully planned.

The press release for the event mentioned National Read Across America Day, which, as it turned out, isn't really a thing in the US. Melania approved the statement in full, but she asked for one line to be edited out: "Barron and I have read *Oh, the Places You'll Go!* repeatedly, and it inspires and captivates us each time."

Why cut that sentence? Because her private life was not for public consumption. "It's no one's business what I read to my son," she said. She just didn't want anyone to know the details of their intimate interactions.

A small press pool was permitted to come to the event, with strict stipulations. Melania said, "No audio of me reading on camera." She would shoot B-roll only, meaning press photographers could get shots of her walking and greeting the kids. No audio. No interviews. No questions.

Tim Tripepi played the big man and said, "They may try [to get audio]. I'll push them out if they do!"

You go, Tim. Flex those muscles.

The NewYork-Presbyterian event went well. The kids, wearing pajamas, gathered around Melania. "So you know what is today?" she asked. "It's a reading day. So I came to encourage you to read, and to think about what you want to achieve in life." I watched from just outside the circle of kids. She seemed to be in her element, and the children were captivated by her beauty and warmth.

My phone ringer was off, but I noticed a call come in from Ivanka, quickly followed by a text asking me to get back to her. What did she want now?

About halfway through Melania's reading, I could no longer move my neck and my left side went completely numb. Something was definitely wrong with my body. This was obviously more than a sore neck or cramping leg. Fortunately, I was already in a hospital—my hospital, in my town. I turned to my friend Peggy Oswald-Manning, now deceased and dearly missed, the director of VIP services at the hospital, and said, "I need to see a doctor." She looked into getting me some appointments.

After the event, we motorcaded back to Trump Tower. I walked home in agony.

Tim called me angling for Easter Egg Roll tickets for himself and all his friends. Tickets were hard to come by because Melania had ruled that the event would be scaled way, way back from the Obama administration, when it used to draw thirty-five thousand visitors.

Melania said, "Why do we have to do this so big? It's not necessary. Cut it back." Her decision was to gear it toward military families only.

The next day, I returned to the hospital and began what seemed like an endless series of medical tests, X-rays, scans, blood samples.

I wasn't able to reply to Ivanka until the next day. "Hi, Ivanka," I wrote. "Catching up after a very busy week. I have a few personal appointments in the a.m. that I have been neglecting, but, in between, I will call your cell."

She replied immediately, "Call my cell. If you could send me the one pager [about the International Women's Day luncheon] beforehand that would be great. I may have some ideas of interesting people you could invite as well."

This again? Ivanka was still trying to insert herself into a First Lady–hosted event? On a group text, I alerted Lindsay and Rickie that I was making some changes to the list, adding Ivanka, Dina Powell, and Rachel Roy. Rickie, who continued working closely with David Monn on this event, wrote, "Got email addresses for those beauties?"

Lindsay replied, "Sending get well thoughts your way. I'm glad you're at the hospital. Get some rest and meds! Xoxo."

Rickie wrote, "Please get rest. Please take care. You are loved and we are right here to help."

Throughout the day, I kept them updated about my MRIs and CAT scans. Rickie wrote, "We love you. Just get better. We have your back!"

Lindsay quickly added, "Even if it's a bad back with pinched nerves!"

Rickie said, "Shut up! I was emotional. How is our fearless leader?"

Meanwhile, Ivanka received her International Women's Day invite but nothing else. She texted me on March 4, "I received the invitation from someone on your team but I have no context on what the event is about. Karen Pence asked me as well. It would be great to have some details (who will be attending, topic of discussion, etc.). I appreciate your guidance. Thanks."

I didn't reply for a whole day, then wrote apologetically on March 5,

"I didn't call during the Shabbas. We are still revising all elements. Can send you and Mrs. Pence an overview once Melania signs off. Please send me any names you have, and MT is happy to review and invite. Please don't say anything but I am in the hospital. There is a disc or spur against my spine and pinching a nerve. A few more tests . . ."

She replied, "I am so sorry. Hopefully you will recover quickly! Once the overview/guest list is approved, send it my way. Based on the event theme/topic, I will suggest women you may want to consider including. Sounds great!"

Two whole sentences of sympathy before she went right back into what I could do for her.

Melania and I were in contact by phone, LOLing about Ivanka's trying to get into the loop. I told Melania about her sympathy for my health. If I'd said that I had a week to live, she would have written, "So sorry! Hope it'll be okay! About that guest list . . ."

The following evening, my husband, David, was out to dinner with his friend Ian. I texted him that I'd checked into New York-Presbyterian because the pain in my neck was excruciating and I was in a dire state. They immediately came over to be with me. Once I'd finally acknowledged that something serious was happening to my body, my physical symptoms went into overdrive. For months, I'd been writing checks that my body couldn't cash. Months of no sleep, bad nutrition, constant stress, traveling, hauling my heavy bags. Months of tension and burnout. Months of my body's screaming at me and my turning a deaf ear. I was now paying the price for all of it.

And yet . . . the show had to go on.

From my hospital bed, IVs in my arms, I continued to work on the IWD lunch scheduled for the following day. Emails between Lindsay, Rickie, and me flew. David Monn texted updates about table placement and seating charts. Tim kept me abreast of his management of the press pool's no-audio rule during Melania's speech, which I was still in the process of helping compose.

I wouldn't delegate, not for something this important. The IWD lunch, Melania's first solo event in the White House, was her moment, her first chance to step up and put herself forward as the First Lady. It had to be perfect, and it had to be hers alone.

Ivanka hadn't let up asking for info about the event, in particular to get a copy of Melania's speech. The team would never send her *anything*.

Rickie got it. Regarding one of Ivanka's repeated requests, she wrote, "[Ivanka] does not know her place. Inappropriate of her to demand."

Lindsay, on the other hand, kept pestering me about releasing the speech to the West Wing. I wrote, "You can tell them that Mrs. Trump is still working on it and when she is ready she will send it to them. Lindsay, you have sent us the same request 4 days in a row! We are not READY!! Have you told them that?!" I knew she was under pressure by Hope Hicks about our press release and the speech, but what about "Not yet!" didn't she understand? Whose side was she on? She was Melania's COS, not Ivanka and Hope's lackey.

Meanwhile, Melania was sending me a million ♥s per day. On March 7, I woke up to her text, "Good morning! ♥ How are you feeling? ♥ I love you! ♥ Donald is saying get well soon. That he loves having you around in the White House. ♥" She sent a link, too, to a glowing article in the *Washington Post* with the headline "Melania Trump to Host White House Luncheon Marking International Women's Day." She was happy and proud of the portrayal.

I busted my ass to make her look good. I worked hard to create a positive persona for her by collaborating with the media. She was the First Lady. That was my job. I was doing all this work in secret, with no official title, and no salary. I believed she wanted this, because she told me so. I didn't need to be recognized publicly, but I did feel a need to be respected for the work I was doing and acknowledged as a member of Melania's team by the people who *needed* to know.

As the sacrifices I endured grew daily, I questioned myself more and more over why I was destroying myself for her legacy—or lack thereof. I'd put myself in the hospital, ignored mounting pain to keep working for her.

I kept going back to the fact that this was my patriotic duty, to help our country in any way I could. But, as time went on, it seemed more and more like Melania's interest(s) were being stonewalled and thwarted, with constant interference and road blocks. At one point, I thought perhaps Melania's interests in fulfilling her role as First Lady were waning, and the drive to see them through to fruition was mostly coming from me. I felt like I was a passenger in a speeding car, heading into gridlock, and realizing no one was behind the wheel.

David didn't leave my side at the hospital while we waited for news about what was wrong with me physically. Nor did my parents and in-laws. The diagnosis was yet to be determined. I heard one of the doctors say the word "mental." As in, the pain was all in my head. I wanted to install him in my body so he could feel the pain himself and then comment.

The International Women's Day (IWD) lunch at the White House, meanwhile, went off without a hitch on March 8. Melania had the support of the UN Women for Peace Association, whose mission is to build awareness for, and help prevent violence against, women and girls all around the world. I'd reached out to the president of the organization, my mother, Barbara Winston, as well as to Muna Rihani al-Nasser, the chairwoman, so we could work together to recognize and honor IWD. Their dedication and tireless work to end violence against women and girls is critical. They sat on either side of Melania. Although I was too sick to attend, FLOTUS was protected.

Rickie and David Monn sent me peppy updates throughout the event. Melania's speech had gone over well, apparently. It hit on the themes we hoped to promote in Melania's as-yet-unnamed initiative, like gender equality; the rights of women and girls; the betterment of society through the collaboration of women; ensuring a just, safe, and kind planet for children; and the power of education to promote children's rights. She also announced the Girl Scouts' Global Action Award, to encourage girls from ninety countries to learn about global issues affecting girls, young women, and their communities and to sow the seeds of global social change. She gave a special mention to author, engineer, and businesswoman Sylvia Acevedo, the CEO of Girl Scouts of the USA, as she discussed the initiative to mentor girls in STEM education.

David Monn texted, "It was a huge success based on the accolades of the guests! I hope you are feeling better!"

A few days went by, and the doctors still didn't know what was causing me such pain; some started to suggest that I might have lost it. Melania's support and concern flowed my way with constant texts and calls. She asked to visit, but my husband told her it wasn't a good day.

I was in New York, strapped to a hospital bed in pain and agony, and didn't have the ability to go anywhere. I missed Melania's first solo event as First Lady in the White House, the IWD Luncheon, but I knew she was in the best of hands.

However, on Friday, March 10, 2017, my doctors hesitantly discharged me from the hospital so I could go to the United Nations. I am grateful to Dr. Neel Mehta for accompanying me to make sure I didn't fall down, get sick, or pass out.

I'd made a commitment to deliver the opening remarks as a representative of the First Lady at the UN Women for Peace Association's annual awards luncheon at the UN Headquarters, which reiterated the same messages as her remarks at the IWD lunch. I wasn't going to miss this one, too. As board secretary for Hopeland (a children's advocacy organization), and as a board member of the UN Women for Peace Association, it didn't matter if I was on my deathbed, I was going to be there. And I was. I returned to the hospital immediately after.

That night, we celebrated my daughter's tenth birthday. We had a party for Alexi in my room on the twelfth floor of the hospital with balloons, sushi, cake, and the whole family. I smiled and laughed with IVs in both arms and a brace around my neck, but I was gritting my teeth the entire time.

Then CNN's Kate Bennett reached out and I took the call. We

spoke about Melania's initiative and next steps. My mind was racing, so at 1:24 a.m. on March 11, I sent Bennett an email saying, "I will no longer sit back and allow the media to scrutinize our First Lady, whose actions and abilities speak far greater than anyone is even aware of. My hope, one day, is that thru her humanitarian work and achievements, her true empowerment will prevail and she'll be recognized and appreciated for her true qualities."

Kate's response: "As with any First Lady, the platforms and initiatives are vitally important, and an integral component of this presidential administration." She went on to say, "I sincerely hope you're feeling better. I understand the monster responsibility it must be to operate all of Mrs. Trump's events and initiatives with a scant staff, while navigating a new world in the White House."

"Hope you are feeling better today," Melania texted the next morning. "Peggy [Oswald-Manning] request I postpone my visit to you today. You are going for testing. 🙏 🙏 🙏 🙏 Stay strong. Call me later I love you. 🖤"

Also that day, I received a communication that sent a chill along my damaged nerves. It was from Stephanie Grisham, underminer and all-around bad apple, asking to FaceTime, perhaps to see with her own eyes that I was in no shape to argue with her about Melania's messaging. "Hi Stephanie," she wrote. "I don't know if Tim told you where I am. Really look forward to 'meeting' you and hope you're feeling better! All my best, Stephanie. P.S. About to watch the CNN segment about the First Lady. From the tease it looks like it will be a positive piece. If it is, you guys may want to tweet it out or post it on Facebook."

Oh, shit. Why was she reaching out to "meet"? Why was she telling me how to do my job? I wondered if Melania was aware of Grisham's run-ins with the law?

Of course she was dropping Tim Tripepi's name. I'd tried to maintain a firewall between the East Wing and the West Wing, but he and Lindsay had been in contact with Katie and Hope—and Grisham, evidently. In my absence, the wall had come down.

I was flat on my back, barely able to walk or talk, on so much pain medication I could hardly see straight. While I was incapacitated, Ivanka had pounced and moved her girl Grisham into the East Wing.

My worst fears were confirmed when I got a text from Melania that said, "I met with Stephanie Grisham about communications. When you feel better, you should FaceTime her. How are you?"

How was I? I was freaking out!

Grisham was known for being combative with the press. I'd been trying to get journalists on our side from the beginning. All of the inroads I'd made would be destroyed if Grisham took over.

Hands shaking, I called Pamela Gross, who had been asking to join Melania's staff since the transition. I'd kept her at arm's length at the First Lady's request. From her years as a correspondent on CNN and as the wife of the *Hill* owner Jimmy Finkelstein, Pamela knew everyone in politics. Before Melania officially offered Stephanie Grisham the as-yet-unfilled job as communications director, I needed to find someone else ASAP.

Pamela recommended Mercedes Schlapp, a lobbyist, National Rifle Association board member, Fox News correspondent, and long-time Republican Party veteran. She was an easy sell. So much for a politically balanced team. I texted Melania that afternoon, "Do you know Mercedes Schlapp? Pamela loves her. Could we meet her?"

"Don't know her. Yes, you can meet her."

"Might be better than Grisham," I said.

"We need communication and press," wrote Melania. "Grisham can be communication."

"Mercedes can be director? Pamela advisor."

"Meet her and let me know what you think."

I wasn't exactly in a position to do job interviews, but I might have bought some time.

The most excruciating aspect of my hospitalization was feeling stuck in the bed, unable to escape my pain, with no treatment plan. But at least I wasn't afraid for my life, nor my child's life. I'd been there. My darkest day had been when two-year-old Zach's lips blew up bigger than his head when he got his hands on a French fry cross-contaminated with peanut oil and David and I rushed him to the emergency room in terror.

If the best doctors in the world couldn't figure out what to do for me, I might be in physical agony forever, and I didn't think I would be able to stand it. What made it even worse was that my doctors kept telling me they didn't see anything on my scans. One of them mentioned relocating me to the psych ward.

"The *what* ward?" my mom asked. My mother-in-law, Michele, put her hand over her mouth. They thought I'd lost my marbles.

Dexter Sun, MD, board-certified neurologist and a clinical professor of neurology, and Roger Hartl, MD, professor of neurological surgery and director of spinal surgery and neurotrauma, came to see me. Regular CAT scans and MRIs couldn't identify the problem, so they brought a colleague who specializes in radiology. He looked at my MRI and dissected the images, splicing and dicing the film into sections, first by halves and then by quarters, and with God's intervention, because I was about to be sent to the loony bin, the radiologist was able to see a sliver of fragmented bone or cartilage lodged against a nerve.

By March 16—eleven days after I'd checked myself in—I finally had a diagnosis: a bulging disc and a large bone fragment were compressing the nerve root where it exited the cranial spine. I needed to have the disc and fragment removed, followed by multilevel cervical fusion.

When they wheeled me into the operating room, I wept in anticipation of the relief I'd one day feel. The surgeon, Dr. Hartl, made a three-inch vertical slash at the nape of my neck and inserted metal rods in my spine. Melania was in contact with David all day. She sent flowers and texts.

My room on the twelfth floor of the hospital had two huge windows. When I opened my eyes the next morning, I saw my mom on the black sofa, the sun shining into the room through the window over her head, giving her a halo effect. I knew it was a new day.

My doctors saved my life in more ways than one. Dr. Sun and Dr. Hartl made sure I didn't end up in a straitjacket for the rest of my life.

Zach later told me that that afternoon, which I don't remember because I was on enough oxycodone and morphine to tranquilize a horse, we were having a conversation and I took a bite of food, and boom, my head fell forward, right into my food, and I was completely out. The kids laughed at how sudden it was, and seeing them smile was the best medicine in the world. Granted, the punch line was how drugged up I was post-op, but I'd take it. My family had been through hell and any joy in that hospital room was welcome. Tyler cuddled up next to me and told me, "Everything is going to be okay."

Melania visited the day after my surgery, although I don't remember that either. David told me she showed up unannounced (another OTR), Secret Service swarming, no doubt, and stayed for over an hour, graciously offering her assistance in any way possible. I remember her calling me a couple of times a day and not being able to talk to her very well. David took her calls; he took all my calls and was the hero of my heart and my life for the duration of my hospital stay. I hadn't been around him or the kids enough since I'd joined Trump World the previous November, but David was always there for me, never more so than when I was at my absolute worst.

The relief I'd prayed for? It was short-lived. After a few days, my pain came roaring back, and no amount of morphine dulled it. Everyone thought I'd actually lost my mind. I was screaming, slouched over, unable to keep myself calm. Once again, the doctors were left scratching their heads.

Days in a miasma of pain passed. I was swimming in drugs.

On March 25, I had my second operation. The postoperative diagnosis: disc herniation, more pressure on a different vertebrae. This time, the incision was a two-inch horizontal slash across my throat, a truncated coup de grâce. A titanium plate was inserted, and bone screws were placed on my cervical spine.

A side effect of my two spinal fusions was a pair of pulmonary embolisms that, had I traveled on a plane in pressurized air, would have killed me. Another fun one: edema had made my ankles look like they belonged to the Elephant Man. They were so swollen, I couldn't find socks big enough. I wish this were an exaggeration. My eyes were black-and-blue. I wore a thick neck brace. "Today is the first day I've been able to walk," I texted Melania on March 27. As always, she sent ♥s, 🙏s, X's, and O's.

That same day, Stephanie Grisham was announced as the First Lady's new director of communications. Melania didn't send me any accompanying links, texts, or emails. It was almost as if she was hiding the news from me. Through Melania, I learned that the West Wing was in the process of vetting Mercedes Schlapp for a position in *their* communications shop. Melania told Donald that Jared and Ivanka "knew [she] was vetting her and took her!"

Two weeks later, to my complete shock, I discovered that I'd been locked out of my government email and contacts. Using my personal address, I wrote to Reince Priebus and Katie Walsh, cc'ing Melania, and asked what the fuck was going on. "No clearance? I have not been able to be at the office due to medically unstable flying conditions but have been working as a volunteer for the First Lady on ALL of her events, platforms and major initiatives. I would like an explanation immediately please," I wrote. As if they didn't already know.

Twelve hours later, Lindsay confirmed that things were even worse than I thought. Not only was I locked out of my email, the volunteer advisor contract that my lawyer Bob Rizzi and White House counsels Don McGahn and Stefan Passantino had been finalizing for months, which had been on the verge of readiness for signing, had abruptly been killed. Plus, my secure phone had been deactivated.

"Hello. Give me a ring if you have a moment and want to discuss," wrote Lindsay. "BB [Bella Blue, a.k.a. Melania] tried to call you and asked me to relay that White House counsel has spoken to your lawyer

Bob Rizzi a couple of times this week and can relay the status of your agreement. If you could call them and then let me know if you need anything. I am not privy to those conversations and the current status. The temporary suspension of the email and phone is standard for all 'extended leave' cases. I had made our East Wing team aware of your position but did not share the information with the West Wing. All best, call when you can, Lindsay."

No contract, no phone, no communications. I'd already had my neck sliced open, and this felt like multiple stabs in the back. I didn't blame Lindsay or Melania. The West Wingers had wanted me gone from my first day. I was nothing but a thorn in their side, the one person who fought for Melania and her office and made demands on her behalf. Now, with my being out of commission, they could finally get rid of me.

I checked out of the hospital on March 29 at eight p.m., still in bad shape, walking unsteadily like a newborn giraffe, my throat so sore I could only eat baby food. For the first two weeks post-op, I struggled to find flavors of Earth's Best that didn't make me gag. I was so frustrated (and hungry), I just wanted to scream, but I couldn't do that either! My voice was gone.

I was disheartened and furious about all the time I'd invested and money I'd wasted on that now-dead contract. Couldn't Melania reinstate my email and phone? Then again, I wasn't recovered enough to go back to working in any capacity. I was physically and emotionally devastated and needed time to heal. My mind, however, would not stop churning.

Where were those Tibetan singing bowls when I needed them?

On top of all that, the members of the press—the colleagues I'd known for decades—noticed that I wasn't around anymore, and they had questions. Texts and emails came in daily from the *Wall Street Journal*, the *New York Post*, CNN, the *Washington Post*, ProPublica, *WWD*, and others asking, "Where *are* you?" The same queries reached the press offices at the White House, but Grisham and Hicks were not releasing any information about where I'd been. With the truth withheld, it looked like I was another casualty of the Trumps' "Off with their heads!" employee retention style.

I sent Melania an email on April 2 that was probably way too raw for someone with her emotional detachment to deal with, but I had to get the feelings out. It's a bit rambling, but I was on pain meds . . .

> Hi BB,
>
> It has taken me quite some time to get this to you properly. The daily grief I have felt has been overwhelming and the anger is self-explanatory, not only for what I have endured in the past month, but for what this inauguration has done to us. I committed myself to you and DJT in hopes that your strength and ability to make a difference in this world would have me by your side making this a better world, too. I would do anything for you and I love you and trust you and will always be your trusted Senior Advisor, Chief Strategist, Best Friend and sister . . . and I hope you know that.
>
> Look at what WE did and prepared!! With NO help. NO guidance. And no support. We will prevail my dear First Lady. I must recover. I love you!! ♥ ♥ ♥ ♥ ♥

I also sent her grisly info about my surgeries and half a dozen graphic photos of my scars. I closed with a request for her to call me.

I wasn't the only one having problems with Melania. Hervé Pierre had been in loose touch. He was at his wit's end. He still didn't have a contract and was in urgent financial straits.

At the end of March, he texted, "I really enjoy working for her, but I need to get compensated!" He wrote that he'd heard Ivanka's stylist was paid $5,000 a day. I don't know if that's true, but it wasn't so far-fetched. "You know you are the reason I designed the gown," he wrote to me, "but I have to move to Europe in the next three months if I don't have a revenue!" He hadn't been reimbursed for months' worth of cabs and expenses. He asked me to ask Melania for an Uber account, which I did, of course. She said she would speak directly with him about that. I hoped she would.

On April 4, I sent her a picture of my medication bag with the caption "more issues than *Vogue*" and its contents styled like the "What's in your bag?" feature in the magazine. It was basically bottles of pills and medical supplies. She replied by sending me back my photo filtered to black and white to make it look "more editorial," just like in *Vogue*.

Because of my close relationship with Melania and the mutual trust I had with my colleagues in the media, we had kept Melania's messaging on point, consistent, and separate from Donald's. Kate Bennett explained Melania's favorable ratings: "For a long time she hid in obscurity, so people made their own narratives." In truth, now Bennett and Grisham were creating the narrative about Melania together. I told Melania, "You've lost your voice!" Melania noticed all her quotes came out of Grisham's mouth.

During the inauguration, CNN had reached out to request Melania's involvement in a one-hour special. Melania's participation was contingent on my involvement. At the time, I was swamped; it was not happening. But Melania gave me the authority to help produce a segment about her. CNN's Jake Tapper was hosting an hour-long special each night during the week of April 24 on President Trump's first hundred days in office and offered to pretape a segment with Melania "to include her very important voice regarding her many initiatives as First Lady," wrote his team.

Stephanie Grisham emailed me a week later with nauseating perkiness. "Hi Stephanie! Hope you are on the mend and feeling much better." She wanted to let me know that Melania had passed on—or Grisham had talked her out of—the request from CNN. "FLOTUS forwarded this to me, and I will let them know that she will pass. Going forward, feel free to send me any media inquiries that you receive, and I will handle. Really look forward to meeting you, I've heard great things. All my best, Stephanie."

Grisham's attitude with the press was apathetic and purely adversarial (during her nine-month stint as White House press secretary she held precisely zero press conferences). There is a difference between protecting Melania and hiding her. Grisham wrote that I should forward any requests to her and that she'd manage them. More like she'd delete the requests, insult the journalists, and isolate Melania. This really burned me up. Not to mention, if Melania didn't do TV specials or talk to the media, they'd create their own narrative and turn to Ivanka, who would trample her own stepmother for more attention.

A couple of days later Tyler and I went to see Melania and Barron at Trump Tower. The boys went upstairs and I visited with Melania for as long as I could stay upright. Between the pain in my neck, the medication, and my exhaustion, I still wanted to spend some quiet time with her.

Afterward she wrote, "Loved seeing you!"

It had been nice to be together again. But I was still very weak, and needed to heal.

In mid-April, I began the process of getting my phone and email back. Melania told me to connect first with Don McGahn, White House counsel (later to become a key source of information, and whose name appears more than one hundred fifty times in the redacted version of the Mueller report). I was quickly passed on to Stefan Passantino and Katie Walsh, like a hot potato. It was as if I needed every person in the entire building to approve the items I'd had just two weeks ago.

By April 22, nearly a month after I'd left the hospital, after several requests from the media about my whereabouts, I wrote a draft of a press release and sent it to Melania directly, bypassing Grisham and Lindsay. It covered all the necessary information about who I was, what had happened to me, and where I'd been, and I even supplied a quote from Melania that read, "Stephanie was in the best hands at NYP Hospital. My speaking with Stephanie daily reassured her that she would be fine and I was only a phone call away if she needed me."

Melania replied with her approval: "Is good."

Ten minutes later, she texted me that the White House lawyers said not to do it.

By late April, I'd all but given up completely on working with the West Wing lawyers on anything. I needed a new strategy and a new legal team for a new contract, since the old one had been killed while I was lying in my hospital bed.

I shared the news with Melania, who wrote, "Good luck. ♥ 🙏 XXOO."

"Thank you, MT!! I am very hopeful. XXOO."

Despite all I'd been through and the way they'd treated me, I was still dedicated to helping Melania in the East Wing. The path wasn't clear, and I'd have to limp. But I didn't come this far to give up now.

The East Wing staffers, most of whom I'd hired, must have thought I was gone for good and happy about it. I had been tough on them, and now they could assume more powerful roles without my being on-site telling them what to do. With Grisham in place in the East Wing, the West Wing must have believed I'd *never* return. But they had no idea just how committed I was. They would have to do more than rip up my contract and cut off my phone to get rid of me.

But they kept trying. They dangled a huge carrot right in front of my face, and, at first, I hopped right after it. On May 9, I received an offer from the US State Department to be an ambassador to the United Nations General Assembly. Melania herself sent the details of the job.

For fourteen months, I would represent the US State Department as an ambassador of the USA for the seventy-second session of the United Nations General Assembly (UNGA), to serve as a public-sector advisor to the US permanent representative to the UN on issues that came before the UNGA, attend formal sessions, and work with ambassadors, counselors, delegates, and officers to develop strategies for furthering US policy goals, support sponsored resolutions, provide advice and assistance in individual areas of expertise, and represent the US at functions and social events.

To qualify, I'd have to be confirmed by the Senate and turn over a financial disclosure statement. The vetting process would *not* require me or my husband to divest. I needed to give my answer soon so they could get started on the vetting process in time for me to step into the role by September 2017.

"Please let me know if you have any questions, and I can try to get additional answers. Pls let me know if you are interested. XXOO ♥," wrote Melania.

It was perfect for me; the people who wanted me gone knew it. No way would I pass up an ambassadorship. It was a natural fit. I'd worked with the UN for years. As magnificent as this offer was, in my heart, I couldn't help thinking, *What about Melania?*

I accepted the role with the State Department.

The East Wingers said they were overjoyed for me. Lindsay pushed me to accept the appointment. "Hi SWW!!!! I have attached the Appointee form for you to complete for the UN position. . . . We are all thrilled that you are willing to accept this role and look forward to working together again!" she emailed.

The vetting process began. The first link I received was the SF-86 security form, the one I'd been waiting for Katie Walsh to send me while I was in the hospital. She'd told me she'd sent it, but if she did, I never got it. I'd begged, borrowed, and pleaded for that link. It held up my security clearance and without it, the White House was able to cancel my contract.

I supplied every document they asked for. As the month wore on, I was more and more conflicted about taking the position. In mid-June, I concluded that as much as I wanted to represent the United States in the seventy-second session of the United Nations, if I wasn't in the East Wing, Melania's initiative would probably go nowhere. She would be isolated by Grisham and her role would be usurped by Ivanka.

I talked about it with Melania, and she said the decision was mine alone to make, but she was grateful when I told her I'd return to serve as her advisor. We knew it was us against them and there wasn't any-one we could trust. She assured me that she was still passionate about working on the initiative for children, and I believed that we would succeed in our plans.

On June 14, I wrote a letter to Jennifer Wicks in the State Department and declined the position, citing my recent medical crisis. I rejoined Melania's team in an unofficial capacity to work on her initiatives.

I could only imagine how Lindsay, Tim, Grisham, and the whole West Wing crew felt when they learned they hadn't seen the last of me yet. Picturing the looks on their faces when I walked into the East Wing and said, "I'm back, bitches!" probably speeded up my recovery time by weeks.

— 9 —

Be Best

I laid low through the spring of 2017, healing from my surgeries, detoxing from the pain medication, but Melania and I stayed in touch, texting and sending links to articles and information daily. She made it clear to me that she wanted me back in the East Wing as soon as possible. I missed the adrenaline and the feeling that what I did really mattered. From New York, barely able to speak, I renewed my commitment to Melania and the Office of the First Lady and promised that I'd do my best on her initiative, and as her friend.

Grisham contacted me in the middle of June: "We still haven't officially met but I wanted to reach out and say I really hope you are feeling better and hopefully we get to meet sometime soon!"

Al Dente

In June 2017, David and I attended the wedding of Steve Mnuchin and his third wife, Louise Linton, at the Andrew W. Mellon Auditorium in Washington, DC. The wedding was my first trip back to DC post-op, so it was sort of like a reunion. So many familiar faces, not all of whom I was thrilled to see.

Full disclosure: Mnuchin's second wife, Heather, the mother of his children, is a very good friend of mine, and I asked her if it would upset her if I attended his wedding. Her response? She was fine with it. She's as good as it gets.

I didn't make time to go to the dentist before the nuptials and was wearing two temporary front teeth, one implant and one cap, what David called my "chompers." (My real teeth were knocked out in a childhood accident.) My dentist had wanted me back in his chair months earlier, the day of my Jean-Georges lunch with Melania and Rachel, which wasn't possible. When I asked him if I could wear the falsies just a little bit longer, he said, "Bring Polident!"

Following the ceremony, I went to the bar and got a drink. I took one sip, and when I looked up, Brad Parscale, Trump's "digital mastermind," whom I'd worked with during the inauguration, was standing right in front of me. He said, "How are you? I heard you had an operation."

I had started to say, "Actually, I had two," when my temporary tooth went flying out of my mouth. I'm not so sure who turned a brighter shade of red, Brad or me. I picked up my tooth off the dirty floor, placed it in my mouth, and said, "I'll be right back." I was mortified!

I kept my head down, hoping not to be stopped by anyone else. I spotted Steven and Heather's oldest child, Emma, whom I've known since her birth, and she helped me avoid a stop-and-chat with Ivanka (of all people). When I found David, I grabbed him by the arm and said, "Follow me."

He knew there were at least a hundred reasons why I'd want to ditch this shindig and asked, "What happened?"

Once we were out of sight of the reception crowd, I took the tooth from my mouth and smiled at him, big gap showing. He said, "Let's go! I'll get your coat."

"No, we have to stay. We're at Donald and Melania's table. They can't have empty chairs." This was an inner-circle event, and it would be glaringly obvious if we were missing.

In the bathroom, I washed my temporary tooth in hot water, put it under the blower for a hot second, dried it off, and placed it carefully back in my mouth, and then we went back upstairs to our table for dinner.

Along with Donald and Melania, we sat with Thomas Barrack and his girlfriend, Cio Soler; Dr. Patrick Soon-Shiong, a South African biotech multibillionaire, owner of the *Los Angeles Times*, and minority owner of the LA Lakers, who, people said, had met with Trump advisors about replacing the Affordable Care Act and a possible role as "health care czar"; his wife, Michele Chan, president of NantStudio; and Karen and Richard LeFrak, who was heading up Trump's new "infrastructure council" with real estate investor Steve Roth. *Cozy!*

Dinner was served. I spent the entire meal with my index finger on my lip holding my tooth in place. I tried not to smile and didn't do too much talking.

After Melania and Donald had gone for the evening, everyone loosened up. I was happy to see Tom. I leaned over David's lap to hear their conversation. Tom looked at me, his smile contagious. I told myself not to smile back. David, sitting in between us, started telling Tom what had happened earlier with Brad, and I laughed so hard, my tooth went flying out again and hit Tom right on his bald head. We were all cracking up. Tom was a sport about it.

The next morning, David got me Krazy Glue from a drugstore, and I glued my tooth back in place before heading over to the White House.

David and I spent the afternoon with Melania at the White House Residence. Sitting in the West Sitting Hall, we rehashed the whole tooth saga. I was laughing so hard when I described the expression on Tom's face when the incisor bounced off his head that my tooth fell out yet *again*. Best comic timing of any artificial body part ever.

I started to shove it back in, but Melania said, "What does it matter? Just leave it out!"

She could be cool, so unfazed by things that would make others, including myself, cringe. So I did as she asked and the three of us sat in the Residence gossiping about the wedding while I whistled through my gap. Melania and I talked about next steps on the initiative, too, until Donald returned from playing a round of golf. I quickly reinserted my tooth. I didn't care if Melania saw me like that. But Donald would have been taken aback. Fortunately, he was so busy talking about himself, I didn't have to say a word.

Laughing together like that and being comfortable enough with her that I could be toothless, and that she even welcomed it, reminded me what I loved about Melania, and why I needed to keep working with her.

"Welcome Back!"

If you judged solely by texts, Lindsay Reynolds was excited to have me back in the East Wing. "Welcome back!!!!!!" she texted that summer, with "Love you!!!"s galore. But deep down in her heart, I'd bet bigly that she would have been happy never to see me again. When I returned to the East Wing, the team was back together. It was great to see Lindsay, Rickie, Vanessa, Emily, Tim, Stephanie [Grisham], and Mary-Kate congregating in one room—we were all there for the same reason: to take care of FLOTUS.

Lindsay told me, "I negotiated a great deal!" She'd traded Melania's gift-wrapping room in the East Wing to the Military Office in exchange for upgrading Melania's plane. Granted, the plane had been a real bone of contention. But we'd been guarding every inch of office space for Melania. When the initiative got rolling, we'd need all of it. And Lindsay had just given away a prime piece of White House real estate behind the First Lady's back. Melania loved the military, but she was none too happy to lose her gift-wrapping room. I was furious. No one should go behind the First Lady's back. Melania was puzzled when she heard, and Lindsay was mad that I'd told Melania. It was like junior high, but with much higher stakes.

With Pamela's help, Melania and I created a wish list of candidates for key positions like director of communications, and perhaps a new chief of staff. The list included Millie Hallow, an executive at the National Rifle Association, and, for the position of director of policy, Kayleigh McEnany, a graduate of Georgetown and Harvard Law, a veteran of the George W. Bush administration, and a CNN contributor. McEnany was more interested in being the First Lady's chief of staff, and she certainly was qualified. But Melania had gotten used to Lindsay. She really liked McEnany, though, especially her law degree, so without deciding on a specific role, we notified the West Wing that they should begin the vetting process. Of course, we got into the weeds with them yet again about salary and title.

The vetting took forever, and it became apparent that the West Wing wasn't doing anything to speed it along. During the intervening months, McEnany was writing a book (what became 2018's *The New American Revolution: The Making of a Populist Movement*) and was leaving CNN—not to be a senior advisor in the First Lady's office, though. She'd been offered the job of national spokesperson for the Republican National Committee.

Melania texted, "She prefer to do this than being [my] senior advisor? Seriously?"

I called McEnany to ask, "What happened?"

She said, "I met with the family and they wanted me to be their spokesperson."

"The family." Ivanka's phrase. They were meeting with her behind our backs after we sent her name to the West Wing to be vetted. Melania and I were livid.

"Did you ask Ivanka if it was the same position or a different position than the East Wing was looking into for you?"

"No," she said, "I just assumed 'the family' meant all of them."

"The family" was Ivanka, the only Trump given the power of the purse, and she had offered Kayleigh a job.

I explained to Melania what happened and how the West Wing had thwarted us again. She texted, "You know how they are snakes."

They were that and so much more. Melania still couldn't believe

Kayleigh had chosen "the family" over her and texted, "Newscaster 😊."
(She is currently the White House press secretary.)

Ivanka was a serial poacher. She'd diverted McEnany and hired
Mercedes Schlapp out from under us. And she'd installed Stepha-
nie Grisham in the East Wing to keep an eye on things and isolate
Melania. The pattern had clearly emerged: Princess wanted to render
Melania irrelevant.

In July, Melania finally agreed to pay Hervé Pierre a monthly salary, albeit one that was far less than he'd received at previous jobs. The
package was not retroactive to include the seven months he'd been
working for her, nor would he be given a credit card or access badge.
(She did reimburse him for months of taxis, though.) He said he would
not be paid for original creations, just the labor of creating them and
for the fabrics. I suggested he add a commission for the garments he
scouted and purchased on her behalf, which is standard for stylists. He
refused to do it. I remember saying to Melania that his agreement was
low, considering she spends $20,000 on a single dress off the rack. She
said, "No, it's good. It's a lot."

He must have accepted the situation or figured out a way to work
around it, because he stuck with Melania and is still working with her
today. I never asked Hervé why he stayed, despite his agony over the
money. I didn't need to. I clung to the East Wing, too, just like he did.
We did it for her.

Get Your Narrative Straight

On August 7, Tom Barrack, Jon Reynaga, and I had a conference
call about the financing and accounting of the Presidential Inaugural
Committee (PIC). Tom said he was preparing to release the Form 990.
"The what?" I asked. Form 990 is the mandatory tax return filed with
the Internal Revenue Service revealing the expenses associated with
the planning of the inauguration.

"What was the total raised?" Jon asked.

"Somewhere between one hundred seven and one hundred twelve million dollars," Tom said.

"Cool, cool," Jon replied.

So what did he need to talk to us about?

Tom said, "I just wanted to touch base and let you know what's been going on."

Jon interrupted, "Tom, I want to make sure that you know on March 26, 2017 [while Stephanie was in the hospital], Mel and I sent the PIC [Douglas Ammerman and Heather Martin] WIS's fully audited accounting report with every expenditure down to the penny."

"Yes! Got that," Tom said. "This is what I need from you."

"Sure," Jon said.

"Okay," I replied.

"What I need from you is a one-pager," said Tom. "No reason to hide the ball. We just want to be up front about the spending. It won't be an issue if we have the one-pager we all agree on."

Agree on? The math was the math. There was nothing to agree about.

He said, "We need to take care of this so there's no issue with Stephanie in the press."

Me? WTF was he talking about? Why would the press even mention my name?

Jon said, "I thought the 990 only listed the vendors."

"Right," Tom said. "Just the top five vendors."

"Just the names of the companies, right? Not individuals?" I asked. I wanted to know why I would be part of the conversation. "Why would the press ask about me?"

Jon said, "Do you mean her friendship with the First Lady might be seen as cronyism?"

Tom said, "There's that potential and we need to take care of it and make sure nepotism or cronyism doesn't come up. That's why we need to do this correctly now, so if that comes up, I will say 'hell no.'"

But Ivanka was the one who had brought me in, and we were not friends.

Jon and I hung up with Tom, and for the first time, I felt a little scared. I didn't know everything that was going on, nor did I understand it at the time. But I mentally pushed aside a nagging worry about the one-pager. I was back at work and fully engaged with Melania.

The Storm Stilettos

In August 2017, Melania and Donald traveled to Corpus Christi, Texas, to view the damage done by Hurricane Harvey. Melania wore Manolo Blahnik stiletto heels from the White House to Air Force One, setting off a storm of her own. Headlines, like this one from *Vanity Fair*, asked, "Who Wears Stilettos to a Hurricane?" Inappropriate footwear would be the death of her.

The story behind Melania's "storm stilettos" or "flood heels" has more to do with office politics than shoes. By the summer of Donald's first year as president, Melania had had enough of the West Wing's expectation that she drop everything to be available at a moment's notice for her husband. Part of her resentment about it had to do with the West Wing's glacial pace whenever she asked for anything from them. Everything she did was met with the same resistance: sending a press release, hiring staff, a contract (hello), granting interviews—everything had to be approved by the West Wing, and they moved at the speed of continental drift on all of her requests.

The only way Melania could exert any power was by saying no. She wasn't going to cancel a facial because Hope Hicks or General John Kelly (Donald's new chief of staff) asked her to, say, accompany her husband on a tour of a storm-ravaged region, shake hands, and throw paper towels so that he'd appear to be caring and human. Her reply, which she relayed through Lindsay and which eventually got to me, was to say that she couldn't possibly be ready to get on a plane without several days' advance warning. Does it take three days to pack for a four-hour trip? No. But that was not the point.

My perspective on these power games was that every time Melania said no, it gave Ivanka a chance to step into her place. I begged Melania to be more flexible about certain requests, like going to Texas. She hesitated, but she knew it was the right thing to do.

That day, her en-route-to-the-airport, Manolos-and-bomber-jacket look was Outfit #1. She changed on the plane into Outfit #2, different pants and blinding-white tennis shoes that had obviously never been worn before. Even if she'd thought for a second that her stiletto heels would cause controversy, she wouldn't have cared. She liked how she looked, and That. Was. That.

"Ronald Reagan always wore a suit to the Oval Office out of respect for his position," she would say. "It's the same thing."

Soon after, Melania and Donald made another catastrophe-related trip to San Juan, Puerto Rico. The island had been devastated by Hurricane Maria. The Trumps took their time before making that flight, which was controversial in and of itself. They flew to red-state Texas a day or two after Hurricane Harvey but waited nearly two weeks before going to Puerto Rico? It looked bad.

Between the two hurricanes, I thought a lot about rain boots and how the hell I was going to get her to wear them. I couldn't even begin to count the number of shoes she owned, but I wasn't so sure about a pair of rubber boots. I happened to be buying some cute Sorel ones for Alexi and me and thought that Melania might like a pair, too.

"Have you seen the Sorel Joan Rain Wedge Chelsea?" I texted. "Love them!"

She said, "Send me pic."

So I did, in eight different colors. "I can't wait to hear what you say 😄. I can get you a pair."

She said, "No thank you. Love you. 😘"

Well, I tried.

For the Puerto Rico trip, Melania's Outfit #1, worn between the White House and Air Force One, was stilettos and cropped navy trousers. By the time they touched down in San Juan, she'd changed into Outfit #2, just-out-of-the-box Timberland boots and white pants. Naturally, Twitter asked, "Who wears white pants to a city in rubble?"

As far as Melania was concerned, it did not matter whether her clothing met whatever standard the public and media required, or whether it was appropriate for the weather, location, or occasion. Nothing mattered to her but her opinion of how she looked. And to be fair, she usually looked pretty great.

Gratuity Included

The impossible task of hiring qualified people only intensified my desire to get my role defined and made official. I still needed the help of a qualified person with political experience and was thrilled to enlist Pamela Gross again. She was fine with being an unsung, unpaid volunteer, too. Melania wasn't so keen about it at first, but Pamela said that she'd report directly to me so, as she put it, "we are sure it's one voice and message and Melania is not bothered."

Melania pushed for the contract on her end. She sent an email to Stefan that said, "Please contact Stephanie and Pamela. You need to work out the contract for both ASAP. I need them to work with me and connect with the right people on my behalf for my initiative. I am losing a lot of time to start with initiative. Thank you."

My legal bills were mounting. I'd been working with two sets of lawyers: one from the firm Steptoe & Johnson, and the other from Jones Day, who'd been negotiating a new contract with the White House legal team, Stefan Passantino and Don McGahn. Naturally, the process took *forever*.

On August 22, 2017, after many long months of waiting, my contract was executed. It was a first-of-its-kind "White House gratuitous service agreement." (I found out later that my lawyers had also represented various Trump-related entities. I wish I'd known sooner.)

The finer points: (1) I would *volunteer* as a trusted advisor, (2) my duties were limited to providing advice and guidance on policy initiatives, speeches, and social media, as expressly requested by FLOTUS,

(3) I was forbidden from interacting with third parties (journalists, etc.) unless explicitly authorized by the Office of the First Lady and only as a "trusted advisor" or "longtime friend," not as a member of Melania's office, the White House, or the US government, (4) I'd submit to being investigated by the FBI, and (5) the agreement could be discontinued at any time or for any reason by myself or at the sole discretion of FLOTUS.

I paid my (and Trump's) lawyers tens of thousands of dollars for the privilege of working my ass off for free without acknowledgment, under intense scrutiny, with no job security. It was a legal muzzle that only made the job of launching the initiative harder. Unless Melania gave me written permission, I couldn't speak for the Office of the First Lady. Melania wrote an email that permitted me to speak with and meet experts about her initiative, which she did the very next day after I signed my gratuitous service agreement.

It was absurd. And yet I'd *fought* to make this happen. I was thrilled it was finally done. I definitely have a few screws loose.

In a move of pure genius, Pamela used the exact same gratuitous service agreement my lawyers created for me, so the legal eagles in the White House couldn't object.

The girls in the East Wing were not Pamela fans. They asked me not to bring her around. Grisham complained that Pamela was too "high-maintenance" and made too much noise in meetings. I didn't care what Lindsay and Grisham said about her. Pamela's heart was in the right place. She was there for the right reasons. She is brilliant and I knew I could trust her.

On September 2, before visiting a distribution center at First Church of Pearland in Texas, in an area hit hard by Hurricane Harvey, Melania was getting her Twitter locked and loaded. She asked me whether she should tweet "The First Lady brought books, crayons, and games for children" or "for children who have nothing left."

For children. Period.

"Those kids will be so happy to have you, your smile and hugs today," I said.

"Love you!"

I gave her two recommendations for what she should tweet: "Option one: 'So happy to have spent the day with the wonderful families helping each other after Hurricane Harvey' with a picture of you and a child. Option two: 'I was so honored to meet so many heroes who have saved thousands of lives in Texas' with photo of rescue workers or coast guard."

Melania's response, "Got it. Thank you! Love you."

Kate Bennett was on the beat, writing a CNN story about Melania and on a hard deadline. I made a call to get her deadline extended. I asked Melania, "Do you want to tell Grisham the deadline was extended or should Kate?"

Playing the diplomat, Melania said, "Kate should reach out to SG." She told me Grisham would not have been able to extend a deadline in that way. If Grisham knew I'd been working with Bennett behind her back, she would have had a conniption.

Children First

We must have come up with a hundred names for Melania's initiative. I bought dozens of domain names on GoDaddy on my own dime. All rejected: Children First ("too much like America First"), Shield Your Children ("don't like 'shield'"), Be a Cyber Buddy ("don't like buddy, too casual"), Protect Our Children ("too long"), Speak Up ("nope"). I pushed Let's Talk, a natural continuation of Michelle Obama's Let's Move, but Melania rejected anything that would remind people of someone else. It had to be original, hers alone.

The biggest issue with creating a program about the emotional wellness and mindfulness of children was the president. He bullied everyone. Ironically, the guiding quote we used for the initiative from the very beginning came from Frederick Douglass: "It's easier to build strong children than to repair broken men." Donald was the walking antithesis of what we were trying to create.

There was no way for Melania to present her initiative to the world without first accepting the obvious about her husband's profile. She knew she'd get roasted about her anti-cyberbullying agenda. It was evident that cyberbullying caused life-threatening depression and suicidal ideation in teens and kids. And yet, her husband was an adult offender. I'd warned her about what the reaction would be if she focused solely on cyber. She texted, "I already know the reaction. Start at home."

My intentions with the initiatives were always pure. I have dedicated my life to supporting children's causes. This is personal for me. Always has been, always will be.

I wanted it to be personal for Melania, too.

While we were talking about mental health issues and kids, I asked her, "Do you think Donald has attention deficit hyperactivity disorder?"

Children with ADHD have symptoms that include difficulty forming and maintaining friendships, a limited ability to develop social skills by observing others, failure to notice social cues, impulsive behavior, and a tendency to engage in disruptive behavior.

What I should have really asked her was, "Do you think Donald has borderline personality disorder?" Symptoms include having no empathy or flexibility and rigidly clinging to problematic beliefs and behaviors that are way outside societal norms.

She laughed at my question and said, "ADHD, what? Are you kidding me?"

I was dead serious! I know what ADHD looks and feels like. I'd been diagnosed with attention deficit hyperactivity disorder (ADHD) and expressive language disorder. At times, I find myself at a loss for words, which, if you heard me ramble, might seem impossible.

I said, "If Donald actually went on television and said to the world, 'I've got it!' it would be huge! Imagine the impact it would have in our society." I wasn't only referring to raising awareness for ADHD. His owning up to a disorder would explain his impulsiveness and inability to stop tweeting and saying stupid things.

Then she *really* laughed. "Boys will be boys," she said. "They're all like that."

I laughed along, but I knew not all "boys" behaved like Donald.

The irony of ironies: I was working with Melania on an initiative to promote social and emotional well-being and awareness through educating kids about how to express their feelings when she so rarely expressed her own. Her emotional reticence and blanket acceptance of Donald's behavior in public will never change. I had to tread lightly and keep looking for cracks in her armor and opportunities to overcome the obstacles we faced. We needed experts to help try to shape her into a champion of emotional health and wellness.

Pamela and I enlisted some heavy hitters, a group of dynamic forward-thinkers, the most highly regarded professors and leaders in the field of social and emotional learning (SEL), with twenty-five years' worth of scientific evidence-based research backing them up. These superstars included Marc Brackett, PhD, director of the Yale Center for Emotional Intelligence, and Robin Stern, PhD, the Yale Center's associate director. Our ultimate goal was to use Melania's platform to incorporate SEL into the curriculum of every public elementary school in America. We wanted children to learn how to express themselves, and her primary focus was in their well-being.

These were serious people, and they weren't going to be involved in anything they couldn't be proud of. The First Lady's initiative had to live up to its promise. Melania believed children were America's most valuable asset, and that it was their right to feel safe and supported.

We declared, "Let's make America care again, especially for America's most valuable asset and our collective brighter future: our children." This comprehensive and multifaceted vision to teach children how to care for themselves and society was based on several systems that had been researched and developed by experts in the fields of psychology and education, and implemented with the support of think tanks and community leaders around the world, including the Aspen Institute, the Centre for Advanced Strategic Leadership, and Yale University's Center for Emotional Intelligence. These scientific, evidence-based approaches concluded that developing the tools and skills of SEL and emotional intelligence, starting when children are toddlers, leads to greater well-being and the freedom to make your own choices at an early age.

Marc and Robin sat down with Melania, Pamela, and me at the penthouse in Trump Tower and explained how decades of research has proven, with these tools, that children and adults alike learn how to feel, which in turn enables them to know what to say and how to say it. It was simple and yet profound.

To prove its effectiveness and relatability, I was the first guinea pig. I opened up and shared my life's journey with Marc and Robin, expressing how I'd learned many coping mechanisms. What they taught me was that, without first being able to identify my emotions and accept and express my feelings, I wasn't self-aware. Further, because I didn't have the skills, at times I didn't know how to nurture and support myself, which I now see leads down a path of depression, isolation, and addictive behaviors. It was fascinating.

After Marc and Robin brought us up to speed and Melania understood the power of this information, she was engaged and excited about the idea of adapting this multipronged approach as a part of her platform. She elaborated: "We must join together to protect ALL children from the terrible suffering caused by our opioid epidemic and the unthinkable pain caused by bullying in all its many forms."

Pamela, Melania, and I—and zero support staff—along with our experts, refined the mission of the First Lady's as-yet-unnamed initiative. It had to be a platform, not a single issue, that was bipartisan, could rally and inspire the whole country, and encompassed a range of child and adolescent wellness issues, especially teaching kids how to express themselves. I remember saying to Melania, "We can use the line 'Children should be seen *and* heard.'"

"What do you mean?" she asked. She'd never heard the common phrase before, that children should be seen and not heard. She grew up in a culture that taught kids to hide their feelings and show nothing. We presented her with Marc and Robin's compelling research that proved children who could learn to talk about their feelings and received validation from parents and teachers were more confident and compassionate, and grew into empathetic, considerate adults. Melania was warming to the idea.

Her strength, that she cared deeply about her own child and was a loving mother, could be extrapolated to her caring about all children. Melania *was* motivated to create a successful platform that would resonate with American families and also tamp down some of her husband's most inflammatory chatter.

Before an upcoming interview, I asked her how she would respond to the Donald question, and she said, "Don't care what they ask. Will always answer what I want. They don't deserve more." Way to kick off our initiative about teaching noncombative communication skills with a great, open attitude!

The UN Lunch

The September 20, 2017, US Mission to the United Nations luncheon with the First Lady was traditionally intended for ambassadors' and world leaders' spouses only. But if Melania was interested, we could invite individuals and experts from the private sector who we believed would be supportive of her initiative, in the interest of children. She approved. Pamela and I reached out to our contacts. Those in attendance included Harold S. Koplewicz, founding president of the Child Mind Institute; philanthropist Ronald Lauder; Deborra-lee Furness of Hopeland; Dr. Shefali Tsabary; Dr. Marc Brackett; Dr. Robin Stern; philanthropists Allison Lutnick and Julia Koch; and, of course, Rachel Roy.

The girls in the East Wing, especially Lindsay, Rickie, and Grisham, had been icing me out about the details, menu, press invites, State Department details . . . the things I used to handle. Their exclusion felt personal, and it was. I couldn't get access to the information or do anything on my own because I was locked out of my computer again. I apologized to Melania numerous times for bothering her about the details, but her guests were going to miss the State Department's submission deadline. I explained I was being thwarted by people who didn't like me or didn't want me around, but I still needed to get things done. Melania asked, "Why do you allow your-self to care what they think about you?" I cared, A. L.O.T. I felt they were out to get me.

Rachel, who'd had to send in her info at least twice, said, "Those people don't care about her. They just want their positions and titles. Melania needs you now more than ever. Friends that are family. That's what we are, through ups and downs."

Grisham demanded that all requests go through her. This is typi-cally how the press should be handled, but she and her obstructionist ways made me anxious. When I realized she hadn't invited *Women's Wear Daily*, I connected her directly to Rosemary Feitelberg. Grisham's response was, "I checked all of my mailboxes and had White House IT do a search, but oddly, neither of your initial emails came through to me. That being said, we didn't connect until after the US Secret Service deadline had passed."

Was she kidding me? She didn't want *WWD* to cover the First Lady's appearance at the United Nations? Sure enough, almost eigh-teen hours later, Grisham made it sound like she'd accomplished the impossible and wrote to Rosemary, "Great news, I was able to get you added to our press pool."

Like all speechwriters, I helped Melania write her address, as directed by her, and even made a recording for her to use when she rehearsed. Melania did a good job on her delivery: "We must teach each child the values of empathy and communication that are at the core of the kindness, mindfulness, integrity and leadership which can only be taught by example. By our own example we must teach children to be good stewards of the world they will inherit. We must remember that they are watching and listening so we must never miss an opportunity to teach life's many ethical lessons along the way. No child should ever feel hungry, stalked, frightened, terrorized, bullied, isolated or afraid, with nowhere to turn. . . . "

I noticed more than a few smirks in the room when she said chil-dren needed to be taught by example about kindness, integrity, and leadership. Three days earlier, Donald had retweeted a manufactured

GIF of him hitting a golf ball into Hillary Clinton's back, knocking her down. The line "no child should ever feel hungry" was also hard to swallow from a woman in a $3,000 hot-pink dress by Delpozo.

During the hour she spent there, it would have been appropriate for Melania to work the room a bit. Instead, once all the guests were seated, she entered from the back of the room, walked straight up onto the stage, delivered the speech, and then made a beeline to her table. She left without shaking anyone's hand. She could have shown her respect to the guests by stopping at each table to say hello. I was bothered by that. We'd invited many of these people to meet her and sign on to be a part of this mission.

When Katie Rogers of the *New York Times* asked her to comment on the rumor that I'd written Melania's speech, Grisham replied to her directly, "Mrs. Trump was the main driver on the content and subject matter of the speech. Stephanie Wolkoff contributed to the speech in her role as a consultant to the Office of the First Lady, along with others."

Finally, Grisham is doing her job, I thought. I was stuck because she called me a "consultant," but per my contract, I was told I had to use the terms "friend" and "trusted advisor." No idea why I'd spent tens of thousands of dollars on lawyers and more than a hundred hours of time so I could call myself a "friend." Made no sense. But I went with it to get my work done.

Rogers sent me a separate email saying, "She [Melania] seems to be growing into the job. I would love to hear whether that's true from someone who knows her as well as you do." She asked if I had "at least partially been behind some of the more sophisticated messaging choices FLOTUS ha[d] been making lately," adding, "Her Twitter videos, for example, are heartfelt and seem effective. I also heard that you helped write her UN speech! Is that true?"

I forwarded it to Melania and wrote, "Please read this!"

Melania responded, "Pls send me what you will send her. Will look over. Thank you 😊"

I forwarded Melania the following statement, which she had approved before: "Mrs. Trump has welcomed the return of Stephanie Winston Wolkoff, the former *Vogue* Director of Special Events and Founding Fashion Director of Lincoln Center. Wolkoff was sidelined with a spinal fusion and away for several months after the inauguration and establishing the East Wing. Ms. Wolkoff, a friend of Mrs. Trump's, and one of her trusted advisors on her staff, has returned as a consultant in recent weeks to help advise the first lady on her initiatives, events, messaging, and speech writing. She works closely with Mrs. Trump on drafting her speeches and most recently for her speech at the United Nations. Ms. Wolkoff remains based in New York City."

Melania said, "This is too much information. You should write her back that you were director with Vogue. And that you are back as a consultant to the office of the First Lady. Will send you what SG sent already on the record and you need to stick with that off the record."

Her next email said, "You want to say to her to keep you out of the story."

Almost every politician works with a speechwriter, and certainly no one suspected that Melania was writing all of her own speeches without assistance, especially after her plagiarism debacle. And helping her craft speeches had always been part of my job description. I started to sense that someone was trying to make it seem to Melania like I was attempting to undermine her (with my need for credit). I had my suspicions who it was.

I was chastised by Stephanie Grisham a few days later for corresponding directly with Katie Rogers. She texted that I could only describe myself as a "consultant."

I replied that I'd only corrected some facts for her story, to which Grisham replied, "Tell her that is all wrong. She can't write it if you tell her she has facts wrong."

This was how Grisham treated journalists? Keeping them out of events and telling them they're wrong? Even when they're not? I mentioned to Melania that Grisham was increasingly hostile and that Lindsay was chronically unprepared. Melania 💀 ed and said, "They're here. If you want to come live here, great. What am I going to do?"

Stephanie Grisham started throwing her weight around and portrayed me as a cat among the pigeons, causing commotion, speaking to the press, and stepping out of line, but all I was was a cat chasing her tail. I returned to the White House to assist the First Lady. I wanted to show up to work without being harassed or having to keep explaining who I was. If I didn't say I was there working for Melania, I wouldn't get past the front gate. What was I supposed to say? I was delivering a pizza?

I couldn't help noticing a chill in the air between Melania and me. It had been on and off since the UN lunch. As quickly as Trump's wall on the Mexican border went up, so did Melania's. But hers was more impenetrable. Things were just *different*. Little did I know that the powers that be had concocted a brilliant plan that involved Melania and me, and the wheels were now in motion. The plan, in fact, had been in place, for almost a year.

The complex and destructive motivations and behaviors from all of the personalities that joined the bandwagon made the dynamic of Melania and my relationship, once fenced off with boundaries and barriers, explode at the seams with intrigue, secrecy, and, ultimately, betrayal.

The next day, Melania reached out and told me, "Don't talk or meet with Nina [Burleigh] of *Newsweek*," whom I'd been planning on seeing for an off-the-record discussion. Attached was a screenshot of Burleigh's article about the recently released archives of Donald on Howard Stern's radio show, including the nugget, "Trump says he got Melania for the 'right price' and he likes to grope her in public."

On September 27, Pamela and I were taken aback when Melania texted, "Doing a round table and listening session on opioids in the WH tomorrow." Addiction was a pillar of our initiative. Children turned to opioids and designer drugs as a coping mechanism. As she learned about the opioid epidemic, she said, "Reading all the stories and stats. Scary."

"I wish we were going to be there," I said. "Are you hosting it?"

"Yes," she replied.

"You didn't want Pamela and me to come?"

"Doing with the Presidential Opioid Commission. In the White House. Not East Wing."

Melania's first informational session was on Ivanka's turf.

I texted Melania on the day of the roundtable, "Big day for this initiative. Wishing you all the best." What I really wanted to say was, "Why didn't you include Pamela and me?"

A couple of days later, I sent Melania an article from the *New York Post* headlined, "White House Launches Probe into Private Email Accounts." We all knew that Ivanka used her personal email account for official business.

Melania had explained to Rachel Roy and me at Trump Tower months ago when Ivanka's email issue first came up that it wouldn't be good "for any of us."

Pamela and I went to DC on October 3 and 4, and both mornings, I had to text to Melania, "We can't get in." We were stuck outside the White House gate, in so many ways.

Failure to Launch

Bad week for Melania. On October 10, Donald's first wife, Ivana Trump, released her memoir about motherhood, *Raising Trump*, and told ABC News, "I have the direct number to the White House but I don't really want to call him there because Melania is there, and I don't really want to cause any kind of jealousy or something like that because I'm basically first Trump wife, okay? I'm first lady, okay?"

When I saw the video, I texted Melania the unflattering photo of Ivana that was all over the news, which was mean-girl of me, but I was only supporting my girl. I said, "By commenting, you're promoting her book. You know that!"

Melania declared, "No more Mar-a-Lago for her!"

Grisham issued the statement, "Mrs. Trump has made the White

House a home for Barron and the President. She loves living in Washington, DC, and is honored by her role as First Lady of the United States. She plans to use her title and role to help children, not sell books. There is clearly no substance to this statement from an ex, this is unfortunately only attention-seeking and self-serving noise."

On October 18, Second Lady Karen Pence, a former art teacher, held a press conference at Florida State University in Tallahassee and presented her art therapy initiative with the cute motto "Healing with HeART." In her interview with Fox News, she explained that arts and crafts were proven to be beneficial for mental health and could be used to treat cancer, anxiety, eating disorders, and autism.

In its coverage, *Vogue* reported, "As the country patiently waits for First Lady Melania Trump to actually begin implementing her murky anti-cyberbullying agenda (starting, presumably, with her own husband?), Second Lady Karen Pence has beaten her to the punch, formally announcing today that *her* chosen cause will be art therapy."

Keep in mind that Karen Pence was not a threat to Ivanka. She also had a qualified staff and prior personal experience doing art therapy. We had no staff, there was nothing in Melania's history or experience to form the basis of our program, and we were fighting resistance from forces in the East Wing and West Wing.

Melania wanted to launch! She was frustrated that she hadn't.

Pamela and I would meet with Dr. Marc Brackett and Dr. Robin Stern with and without Melania, and we'd go back and forth with presentations about using the RULER Method (recognizing, understanding, labeling, expressing, and regulating) to teach SEL in an educational environment starting in kindergarten. Since all of us were helping the First Lady without a budget, we figured out a way to launch her initiative without one. We were undecided if we should launch in partnership with the Department of Health and Human Services or the Centers for Disease Control and Prevention. We had no budget and no support, but we plowed forward.

The initiative was now known as Be Best. Melania had come up with that. I warned her that the phrase sounded illiterate. What about changing it to Be *the* Best or Be *Your* Best? No. Melania, lover of Sharpies, drew the two-word logo with block letters and said, "I drew it myself, so no one can say I plagiarized it."

As the days went on, I felt less and less in touch with the East Wing. I knew I was being squeezed out. They no longer included me in meetings or agenda items and would occasionally send me dribs and drabs of information. Melania kept up our friendship but was mostly focused on making sure I delivered all aspects of everything Be Best related.

Despite feeling marginalized, I did deliver everything to her. I presented the ideas and still hoped, at the very least, they'd be executed, and all of our efforts would bear fruit, whether I was involved or not. Although I had my doubts that anyone running the East Wing would know how to implement any of it, I gave it all to them.

Hopefully, Melania would do some good with her position as First Lady, which was why I got involved in the first place. At least there'd be something to show for it.

Every time Melania's name appeared in the press, Stephanie Grisham's name was right there with it. Pamela sent me the link to Kate Bennett's article "Melania Trump Does Things Her Way," with Grisham's name all over it. Pamela said, "[Grisham] is building her brand on Bella's back. The chutzpah!"

Melania was distant, not always replying to my messages. She asked me to delete our texts, reminding me that it was "no one's business what we talk[ed] about."

Hervé Gets His Moment

On October 20, Melania and Hervé Pierre went to the ceremony at the National Museum of American History where the First Lady formally presented the gown they'd collaborated on for the inaugural balls to the Smithsonian's *First Ladies Collection*.

I would have loved to attend, but I wasn't really invited. Melania told me, "Come if you want," a few days before. Instead, I offered to help her write her speech.

She said, "I have my remarks."

Grisham must have written them. With some hesitation, I emailed Grisham, suggesting that she invite *WWD* to cover the Smithsonian presentation exclusively. Instead of just sending me a press invitation to forward to *WWD*, Grisham sent me a link with info about the event, but I couldn't open it on my government phone. I went back to her, and she blew me off. "I'm too busy preparing for the Asia trip," she wrote. Soon, Melania was going to be in Tokyo and Seoul, traveling the world without a care.

I asked Melania directly about a *WWD* exclusive.

She said, "Yes, I talked to [Grisham]. Won't give an exclusive to WWD. My statement will go out to everyone."

Grisham's reasoning was that no one would get an exclusive interview with the First Lady. Was she a press secretary or a prison warden? I knew the answer to that. The East Wing felt more like a jail every day.

I told Melania, "Just so you know, I suggested WWD because they have been a part of your fashion legacy since the inauguration. Never mind if Grisham said no. I think they should be invited, like all the other press."

"They can be invited, but no Q&A."

Well, at least I tried.

I had been part of the collaboration between Hervé and Melania, but I wasn't included in their celebration.

Melania's speech was brief. "To be honest, what I would wear to the inaugural ball was the last thing on my mind," she said, though of course it had been item number one on her to-do list. "Poor Hervé was given only two weeks to design and produce this couture piece. We had never worked together before, but I knew of his stellar reputation and wanted to work with someone who would do more than just design a dress. I wanted to work with someone who would be willing to collaborate with me. And Hervé exceeded my expectations. I was so pleased with our end results and it is my hope that this piece is one of the many great beginnings of our family's history here in Washington, DC. Thank you all for being with me here today. God bless you and God bless the United States of America."

The Melania I knew would never say "our family." That's Ivanka-speak. Hervé, beaming, stood next to her in front of the gown, which was displayed in a glass box, and I was thrilled for him.

Hervé sweetly reached out to thank me. On October 26, Melania told me that the ceremony was no big deal. Instead, we talked about Anna Wintour's appearance on *The Late Late Show* with James Corden. He asked her, "Who would you never invite back to the Met?"

Her answer: "Donald Trump."

Melania said, "Oh we are crying 😂😂😂."

The Justice Department special counsel Robert Mueller's investigation was heating up. It was rumored two indictments were going to be served. Melania and I had our hunches about one of them. On October 30, news broke that Rick Gates (yes, *that* Rick Gates, the one who Donald said he didn't know in his living room at Trump Tower over a year before), Trump's former deputy campaign chairman and deputy chairman for the 58th Presidential Inauguration, and Paul Manafort, Trump's former campaign chairman, were charged with twelve counts that included conspiracy against the United States, conspiracy to launder money, and acting as an unregistered agent of a foreign principal.

Trunk Show

On November 16, 2017, Melania and I were flying to New York on her plane, along with her parents, when I showed her a *New York Post* article titled "Trump to Lift Ban on Importing Elephant Trophies from Africa." The Fish and Wildlife Service had something to do with it, but for the most part, Trump was to blame.

"The family" strikes again.

"Such cruelty! The brutality of killing elephants, it's horrifying," I said. "The boys should be ashamed of themselves." The story gave credit where it was due: "President Trump has decided to let big game hunters like his sons Eric and Donald Jr. import the heads of elephants into the United States, reversing an Obama-era ban from 2014." The National Rifle Association trumpeted the decision.

Melania was not sympathetic to "the boys'" lobbying efforts for guns and hunting or the bizarre need to hang a dead animal head on the wall. That night, she did some lobbying of her own, and her plea directly to Donald actually worked. It didn't always, but this time, thankfully, it did.

The next day, Trump tweeted, "Put big game trophy decision on hold until such time as I review all conservation facts."

The sudden change of heart was because of Melania, not because of pressure from foreign governments or Ellen DeGeneres, or his seeing gruesome animal-slaughter images on the Internet. I felt proud to have had something to do with it.

She was able to make a difference that day and would have done so much more had she not been derailed so often, so aggressively.

Another One Bites the Dust

Tim Tripepi had been warned over the last nine months about bandying about Melania's name. He'd hired his friend to do advance work with him and gotten in screaming matches with Lindsay and Rickie about his not doing his job and spending way too much time kissing ass in the West Wing and feeding them lots of intel.

So Melania fired him.

He wrote me an apologetic email on November 16, 2017: "I am sure you heard about today. I am sorry it didn't work out with me and Lindsay. I hope I didn't let down FLOTUS but I always had her best interest first. I just want to thank you for the greatest experience of my life working for her. I would have never had that opportunity without you and I will always be indebted to you. If I can ever be of assistance to you, please don't hesitate to reach out to me."

I wasn't surprised he'd been let go. And I thought to myself, *Better him than me.*

What's the Story?

On December 8, Tom Barrack followed up with Jon Reynaga and me about the Form 990. Tom told us it hadn't yet been filed. After some small talk, Tom said, "Jon, what I need from you is the story. The narrative. [The press] is going to say, 'Obama's cost X, so why did ours cost Y?'"

The "narrative" we'd heard was, "The broadcast was so expensive because we didn't have any underwriters or sponsors. The PIC paid for it itself." So I didn't understand the question.

Jon said, "Do you mean about the events that fell under WIS and Inaugural Productions? Or the other events?"

I chimed in, "All eighteen events?"

I didn't really understand what he wanted from us. The WIS accounting was done.

"I'm not asking you to invent it," said Tom. "But I need you to write a one-pager about WIS's spending on events and on the broadcast." Again, with the one-pager. Back in August, Jon and I'd had the same conversation with Tom.

"Does this have anything to do with Rick Gates?" asked Jon.

"Gates?" asked Tom. I was in a time warp; he sounded just like Donald had that night in Trump Tower. "No! That's about [Paul] Manafort and Ukraine. No questions have been raised about the PIC." Not yet, anyway. "I want you to give me the narrative you want to see on the cover of the *Washington Post*," he said. "We need a narrative, not numbers."

Instantly, my stomach clenched.

He was the chairman and had approved and signed off on *everything.* Why did he need us to write a one-pager on our scope of work?

I hung up the phone more confused than ever. I looked Jon dead in the eyes and said, "I've never even seen the numbers." I'd never seen the audited budgets sent to the PIC. I'd been in the hospital when WIS prepared them and sent them in. I couldn't even tell you what bank WIS used. I had no signatory powers.

"I'll talk to Mel and get back to you," Jon said before heading out.

At 3:07 p.m. I received an email from Jon saying, "Knock yourself out!" The subject line: "FW: Presidential Inaugural Broadcast Events: Calendar/Budget/Budget Assumptions (V3)," forwarded from Chris Wagner of Inaugural Productions, with the "approved bottom line of $24,805,499."

I told my WIS partners Jon and Mel, "Meet me at my lawyer's office to explain the finances." I hadn't been privy to them all.

The whole thing was so upsetting. I was worried about seeing Tom Barrack at the White House Christmas party. I told Melania I was considering not going. She asked, "Hope you are not stressing it out about TB. I hope your headaches go away soon."

"I was awake until 5:00 a.m. preparing all the paperwork Tom requested," I said. "I think it best for me not to be there to see him. I love you."

Melania said, "Go to rest. Don't give up your life because of him. Love you. ♥"

Instead, I went with David and the kids to an intimate friends and family party at the White House on the weekend of December 2. Zachary and Tyler were running free around the White House with Barron, making a stop in the Oval Office. After a ballet performance, David, Alexi, and I joined Melania, Donald, Phil Ruffin and his wife, Oleksandra, and Rachel Roy upstairs in the Residence living room for lunch, where we ate shrimp cocktail and pigs in a blanket. When Zachary and Tyler joined us, Tyler whispered in my ear, "Did you know the president has a red button on his desk to order Diet Cokes?" We laughed. "No!" I said.

The president, David, and Mr. Ruffin were talking politics. Donald asked David, "What do you think of Rex Tillerson?" David said, "I thought he was okay." Donald was silent. He then asked, "What do you think of Nikki Haley?" David told him, "I think she's a rock star!" Donald nodded and smiled. He was also very interested in knowing what David thought about moving our embassy from Tel Aviv to Jerusalem. I heard David say, "That's a very bold move." Mr. Ruffin interjected. "We should negotiate more before we move the embassy." David said, "I didn't know we were negotiating."

Fire and Fury

On January 2, 2018, I was back in New York. I was relieved we'd finally hired a policy director, our "go-to" inside the White House, Reagan Thompson. She'd been an executive assistant on the National Security Council and served as a communications and policy advisor for then-congressman Mike Pompeo. After I FaceTimed her several times, I told Melania that Reagan would be a great middleman for Pamela and me in dealing with the East Wing and White House, especially with her experience on the hill.

I needed to spend time catching up on my life. I had 4,541 unopened emails, 213 unopened text messages, and 140 voicemails to listen to. I was on a mission to get my own paperwork done. That lasted about thirty minutes before I got sidetracked.

I texted Melania, "What are you doing?"

"Working on pictures for albums of all of my trips and if I don't do now, will never do." I stared at the word "albums" for a good five seconds. So that was what she'd been up to? Albuming?

I thought to myself, *Want to switch jobs?*

"I still don't have a wedding album," she wrote.

I didn't either. Albuming seemed fun, actually. No wonder she was so excited about it. "I wish you were next door so I could come in 😊," I wrote.

She said, "👍 😊 Move to DC. It is beautiful here. Don't miss NYC at all."

The next day, Melania reached out: "Did you send papers to TB [Tom Barrack]? He is still calling."

I told her, "Jon and Mel are still working on them."

About five minutes later, Katie Rogers of the *New York Times* got in touch with me about the recent book release that had captivated the nation, *Fire and Fury*, the White House exposé by Michael Wolff. In the book, he wrote that Melania hadn't wanted Donald to run and that she'd been crying bitter tears on election night. Rogers said, "I was just wondering if you had any idea if that was actually true."

I asked Melania how to respond. "Say it is not true," she told me. "Whatever is about MT in the book is total fiction. Never happened. Wonder where they get all this info? They don't know real MT." Like DJT, MT sometimes spoke about herself in the third person.

Melania and I revised her statement, and after her approval, I answered Rogers's question: "She was neither crying nor surprised on election night. She and Donald worked very hard to achieve victory on election night."

In her article, Rogers wrote, "Nearly a year into her tenure as first lady—and after a week of intense scrutiny prompted by a new book that claims she had dreaded life in the White House—Melania Trump has hired a director of policy to advance her nascent platform. On Thursday, the White House announced the first lady's choice: Reagan Thompson, 27." It seemed to imply Thompson had been hired to oversee the initiatives in response to *Fire and Fury*. Not true.

I texted FLOTUS, "The fact that no one knows we've been working with you for almost a year on your initiative is absurd. That's why these articles come out. It sounds like you hired an inexperienced 27-year-old."

Melania replied, "Are you surprised they wrote that? What did you expect from NYT and Katie? Do you want to be announced in the press? Or that is a stupid question? ☻ I googled your name and is saying senior advisor. Now they say trusted advisor and why is she hired again?"

The truth would have been nice for once! Press outlets had mentioned me as Melania's advisor since the inauguration, but in all this time, the White House had never announced me.

My reply: "Whatever you think." I knew no one in either wing of the White House was going to allow her to put my name on a press release. They hadn't yet, so why would they now? No one wanted the truth about all the work we'd done to come out.

She wrote, "I feel it means a lot to you that you are announced. I will talk to legal AGAIN. As per now, they said because of different contract and contractors form, and as volunteer, legally cannot be formally announced. Will try again. XO ❤"

If I hadn't been prohibited by my nondisclosure agreement from speaking with the media as Melania's "trusted advisor," the American people would have known about the initiative, our working with experts, and what Reagan Thompson's role was.

It was almost midnight. I texted, "🙂," and went to sleep.

In the morning, I found her reply text. "I want you are happy. I feel you are not. ☹ I fight my best but can't go against the law. Love you. 💋"

WTF were they telling her? *Against the law?* What law would it break to share the work we'd been doing?

On January 12, 2018, a week before Donald and Melania's thirteenth wedding anniversary, a *Wall Street Journal* article, "Trump Lawyer Arranged $130,000 Payment for Adult-Film Star's Silence," reported that a woman named Stephanie Clifford, a.k.a. porn star Stormy Daniels, had received a secret payoff from Michael Cohen in October 2016, around the time of the "pussy" tape reveal, to keep quiet about having sex with Donald in 2006 when Barron was just a baby.

I sent Melania an "URGENT" text. She didn't reply all day.

I was horrified by the Stormy Daniels story. And Michael Cohen was in deep, deep shit.

When Melania finally replied, she wrote off the story and said, "It's just politics."

That year on my birthday, Melania sent me the usual white orchid, as well as a luxurious Louis Vuitton travel case just like the one she had. It was very thoughtful of her.

Not Listening

Melania gave Pamela and me permission to host an official lunch meeting in the East Wing on behalf of the First Lady's initiatives. I set it up to coincide with a conference when all the experts were going to be in DC already, so we wouldn't need to pay for their travel. Rickie told me that there was no budget to pay for the expert lunch. It was just a dozen people. I offered to pay for sandwiches and soda myself.

Instead of greeting these experts with open arms as they came into the East Wing, Stefan Passantino, who was suddenly involved, kicked things off by dismissing the First Lady's guests. He handed out a memo that said: "The First Lady is seeking information and perspectives from a diverse range of thought leaders to provide her with insights and perspective regarding issues that are of great importance to her. These individuals will not, however, be making policy recommendations to the First Lady or the president in the form of a 'council,' an 'advisory committee,' a 'commission,' or through 'subcommittees.'"

I was mortified. He basically said, "You can talk all you want, but none of what you say will ever be used or credited."

Par for the course.

Never Forget

In late January, Melania was supposed to join Donald in Davos, Switzerland, for the World Economic Forum, the annual gathering where billionaires talk about how to rule the world. Grisham's statement about why FLOTUS decided at the last minute to blow off Davos was, "It was determined there were too many scheduling and logistical issues, so Mrs. Trump will not travel to Davos."

Many speculated that Melania wasn't going because she was furious about Stormy Daniels. She told me she didn't feel like going and just waiting around.

So what would the First Lady do instead?

On January 25, she went to the US Holocaust Memorial Museum. International Holocaust Remembrance Day was a few days away. The visit was politically acceptable and close to home, and she could control it completely.

Melania asked me to come with her and her mother. I was supposed to be on a flight back to New York, but I stayed for that. No press was invited, which was how things were done now, with Grisham calling the shots. But the visit would be chronicled by the White House photographer.

The museum director, Sara Bloomfield, gave Melania a private tour, and the photographer captured every solemn moment. At one point, I nudged Mrs. Knavs to stand with her daughter in a photo. Except for that one moment, Melania walked with Bloomfield, learning about the museum, while the rest of us trailed behind.

Melania knew that my grandparents were Holocaust survivors. I would have loved to have walked with her to hear what the museum director had to say about the exhibition. I'd stayed in DC just to follow her around? Especially here, in a place that had meaning to me and my family? This push-pull feeling, the back-and-forth of her being cold on Monday and warm on Tuesday, asking me to come on an outing and then not including me in the museum director's tour? Sending "love you" texts and then not replying to calls was wearing on me.

At that time, the news cycle was about Melania's renegotiating her prenup with Donald, and the Stormy Daniels story only helped her cause. While Donald was in Davos, hobnobbing with elites, his wife would be remembering the six million dead, wearing black, and being strategically photographed alone against tragic backdrops, as if she were a serious, solemn human being.

At the Hall of Remembrance's eternal flame memorial, Melania paused to light a candle at the starkly beautiful prayer wall. I thought of Bobie and Papa and missed them so viscerally, my throat and stomach tightened.

Did Melania notice my emotion and call me over to light a candle with her for my grandparents? Nope.

She was my friend, someone I loved, remembering people I'd loved before, acknowledging their survival and their suffering. Any normal person with a human heart would have understood why that was important to me. But I was coming to realize what was really important to her. She just wanted a picture to post on social media.

As we rode back to the White House, I said, "That was hard for me. I miss my grandparents." Melania looked at me sympathetically. I said, "Thank you for bringing me with you today."

And then she went back to looking at the images.

Later that day, she posted a few of them and released a statement, written by Grisham, no doubt: "My thoughts and prayers are with the people whose lives and families were broken by the horrors of the Holocaust . . ."

But not with the person standing right behind her whose family had experienced those horrors.

The White Suit

The Holocaust Memorial Museum was a rare outing for Melania in January 2018. The press assumed her not appearing in public had to do with shame about her husband's infidelity. The truth is, no one in the West Wing would dare apply pressure to her now to appear, and Melania wasn't offering.

She had to go to the State of the Union address, though. We talked about what she'd wear for her reentry into the public eye, and she had her heart set on a Christian Dior white suit with cropped pants, a fitted jacket, and a ruffled blouse.

"You cannot wear a white suit," I said. "You know that, right? I'm begging you not to wear a white suit!" I enlisted Hervé to send texts to Melania that said the same thing. She was onto us, though, LOLing about how we were tag-team texting her to convince her to leave the Dior in the closet.

Why was it so important that Melania Trump *not* wear a white suit to the State of the Union in 2018? For starters, the white suit was practically Hillary Clinton's trademark, the uniform of anti-Trumpers, a symbol of female empowerment and the #MeToo movement, which had exploded a few months earlier in October 2017 when reporters from the *New York Times* and the *New Yorker* exposed the serial assaults of movie producer Harvey Weinstein. If Melania wore a white suit, it would look like she was sending a coded message to the world. The press would go nuts for days with assorted #FreeMelania hot takes. We were trying to keep the focus on Be Best, which was within weeks of being presented to the world. Her ambiguously political fashion choices would be a distraction.

The more I begged, the more she laughed it off, saying, "Oh, Stephanie! Come on. I mean, really. Get over it!" She wore the Dior, and the media predictably twisted itself in knots trying to interpret the message of her ivory suit.

I'll give her one thing: No one remembers a word of Donald's speech. All they remember is Melania's white suit.

— 10 —

The Takedown

*N*o matter what else was happening with Donald's presidency, Melania's initiative, or my feelings of frustration, Melania and I never stopped 😗 😗 😗 😗 😗 ing. On January 6, in a series of tweets, Donald said, "I went from VERY successful businessman to top TV star to President of the United States (on my first try). I think that would qualify as not smart, but genius . . . and a very stable genius at that!" I sent Melania a link to an article about his remark, and she texted 🤓, the nerd-face emoji, which we used to denote goofy affection for each other. It was a favorite of ours, along with 😆. The Mueller investigation was in full swing. The country was deeply divided. But we were 😆ing. It was all silliness . . . until things turned 😩.

First Warning

On January 11, 2018, over in the East Wing, Lindsay swung by my office and asked, "Are you free now by any chance to meet with Heather?" She was referring to Heather Martin, formerly the PIC's director of budget and treasury (currently the chief financial officer in the Office of the Administration).

I stood up and together we walked down the hallway. Along the way, we knocked on Rickie's door, and the three of us met Heather in Lindsay's East Wing corner office.

"Heather!" I shouted. "It's so good to see you!" We all hugged her hello. We shared a common bond. We were all willing participants with leading roles in the planning of the 58th Presidential Inauguration.

"Did they make your position full-time yet?" Lindsay asked Heather.

"Not yet," she said, "it's worrying me." Back then, she worked part-time for Joe Hagin, in the West Wing, overseeing Melania's budget. I asked Melania if we should hire her "to keep her close" since she knew everything about the PIC's and the White House's finances, but Melania said, "No way!"

The purpose of the meeting was to talk about the imminent filing of the Form 990.

I thought to myself, *Here we go again. The one-pager!*

Heather reported the PIC had filed several filing extensions, which had delayed releasing the 990 for nearly a year. The PIC and the White House were under pressure from the press about the timing of the release. She said that Barrack's office and the White House were keeping track of all the press requests. "The *Washington Post* and other media outlets were working on stories."

Heather's mission in bringing us all together: "We want to be prepared to mitigate any negative press the 990 release may generate for the First Lady," she said.

I was on the edge of my chair with anticipation. "What's been the focus?" I asked.

"Are you concerned?" Rickie asked Heather.

We stared at one another.

WIS was preparing the "one-pager." I had known this day would come. But why was this about Melania?

Heather walked us through the PIC's yearlong process of preparing the Form 990. She told us she'd been working with Tom Barrack, treasurer Douglas Ammerman, and Rick Gates on its preparation. Despite Rick Gates's indictment, he was still involved in the 990 filing. My spidey senses were going full tilt. I was practically a tarantula by now.

She explained, "It's taking longer than they expected."

"Why?" I asked.

Apparently, Barrack and Ammerman were having a rough time preparing the form because the actual numbers didn't add up.

That set off a sudden headache. The numbers were the numbers. Why didn't they add up?

Heather told us the two main areas of concern, which hadn't escaped the notice of the press, were Tom's Chairman's Global Dinner and Mark Burnett's close involvement at every stage of the presidential inaugural planning.

Sitting there with Rickie and Lindsay and listening to Heather talk about the PIC's financials was surreal. "What's been your response so far?" I asked.

Heather said, "No comment," and we all nervously laughed.

"What do they want to know about Mark?" I asked.

"If he was paid," Heather said.

That was the million-dollar question.

I flashed back to that weeks-ago phone call I'd had with Tom about writing a "one-pager" about the PIC, when he asked how Jon and I would like to see the story covered on the front page of the *Washington Post.* I thought he had meant it ironically!

Heather informed us that Tom Barrack's advisor Tommy Davis (former chief spokesperson for the Church of Scientology, son of actor Anne Archer, and friend of Tom Cruise) had been fending off media requests that asked, "Where is the 990?" for months.

"And the budget breakout?" I asked.

"No, not necessary!" Heather said. "We only list the top five vendors, no individual names."

As far as the 990 was concerned, WIS Media Partners was listed at number one, *the* top vendor.

Hearing all this, a kernel of worry lodged in my gut, but I told myself that, however obtuse the 990 would be, WIS Media was safe because Jon Reynaga and Mel Johnson had submitted WIS's fully audited and approved accounting ten months ago, while I was in the hospital. WIS and IP's budgets had been pre-submitted, approved, and signed off on by Barrack, Gates, Ammerman, and PIC CEO Sara Armstrong (currently the vice president of political affairs and federation relations at the US Chamber of Commerce).

We all left the meeting knowing a lot more than we had walking into it.

The next day, as promised, Heather sent an email to Rickie and asked her to share it with me. Why not send it directly to me? Because I was locked out of my government email again, for some strange reason. "As discussed yesterday, I told Stephanie I would write two blurbs," said Heather. "The first is the suggested response she gives when a reporter calls her and the second is the suggested for Tom B. Bear in mind, this is specific to SWW. As other, more general questions come in, the responses will be drafted and discussed. Generally, the concept is going to be that this Inauguration was consistent with every Inauguration in history, we raised more money and spent more money, but the scope was proportional. Let me know what you think."

Heather's two blurbs:

For me to use with press: "It was an honor and privilege to be a part of the most historic Inauguration our country has ever witnessed. I was so grateful for the opportunity to help usher in the peaceful transition of power, and I would be humbled to do it again." Beyond that, I would refer any questions to the inaugural committee.

For Tom to use when asked about me: "We were very fortunate to have someone of Stephanie's caliber on our team. Her exceptional vision transformed our Inaugural events into an elegant masterpiece never seen before in the history of Inaugurations. She was able to bring a unique style to the events throughout the week that captured the interest of people, not just in the US, but around the world. There is no doubt she has raised the bar for future Inaugurations to come."

It sounded great, but why were these blurbs necessary at all? I didn't need Tom to gush about my aesthetic or justify my work on the inauguration. I willfully decided that all of this was just their watching out for me. In a previous phone call, Tom had told me, "Your name is already linked to the First Lady's. Because you did such a great job on the inauguration, she brought you in to work in her administration. If we don't release your name, you know . . . it'll look like we're trying to hide something." The press was well aware of my work on behalf of the PIC, as well as my work for the First Lady, despite the White House's never announcing me. It still makes no sense that *I* was a part of the discussion. I was one of the founding partners in WIS Media Partners. The 990 lists the top five vendors' company names, not individuals who worked at any of those companies!

That kernel in my gut started growing. After the meeting, I called Melania, told her about the meeting with Heather, and said, "This feels off."

"What are you worried about?" she said. "You didn't do anything wrong."

Later, I texted to her, "Did you get the update from LR [Lindsay Reynolds] about the Heather [Martin] mtg? I prepared a document from that meeting—would you like it? I LOVE YOU ♥♥♥ XOXO."

Melania replied with a " ▯ ♥ XO ☺ ♥♥♥ " and asked, "What specifics?"

"Heather told us EVERYTHING. Lindsay and Rickie were there but they had no idea of the information that Heather was providing. I have it ALL now. [I'll send you] the pdf when I get home. On way to watch Alexi perform and sing. ♥♥♥ 😘😘 XO."

Melania replied with a " ▯ ♥ Have fun and good luck to Alexi ✏▯."

Rickie and I had some late-night calls and text exchanges that week and talked about how hard it was to balance work and family. The conversation turned to our meeting with Heather Martin. Rickie texted, "I miss the days of picking linens and pretty lighting. I spoke to legal seven times today," meaning she had spoken to Stefan Passantino.

Why would she need to be speaking with legal? And seven times?

Back in DC, I went to speak with Rickie alone. We may have had our differences here and there, but we both knew each other to be pure to the core. I closed the double doors to her office behind me and took a seat. I told her I'd begun to feel uneasy about it all.

"Take your things and leave," she said. "You don't need to be here."

Huh? Was she really telling me to pack up my shit and go home?

"You are killing yourself," she said. "Your heart and loyalty are so deep—you have taken on too much. You can still do your work, but you don't need the headache of the White House."

Upset and panicky, I went to see Melania in the Residence. "Rickie said I needed to pack up and leave," I said.

"What do you mean?" she asked. "When did she say that to you?"

"Rickie said that I don't need to be at the White House to do the work I'm doing with you." I interpreted the comment as disrespectful to Melania, and to me. Were the powers that be kicking me out? Melania assured me that wasn't going to happen.

In hindsight, Rickie was just trying to warn me. If I hadn't been so defensive, I might have seen that.

Second Warning

On January 20, Heather sent me a link to a *Washington Post* article about Russian nationals attending inaugural events and wrote, "Here is the article I was mentioning (it just came out). It's not bad at all for 1 month's work and pestering from the Post. Much ado about nothing." It was about Russians at inauguration events who'd gotten tickets from a straw donor.

The 990's top five vendors, the Chairman's Global Dinner, and Burnett weren't the only PIC controversies at the moment. Heather told us that Walter Kinzie, CEO of Encore Live, was threatening to sue the PIC for $1.7 million, claiming that the Opening Day

Foundation—a nonprofit created by Don Jr., Eric, and their cohorts Thomas O. Hicks Jr. and Gentry Beach—had hired his firm to produce the concert at the Verizon Center, a.k.a. Camouflage and Cufflinks, and then canceled it. Heather also told me Barrack's lawyer had sent Kinzie a cease-and-desist letter in response.

Heather wrote again, on January 22, and said, "I just had a call with Tom, Douglas Ammerman, and their press people. Tom separately emailed me afterwards and asked for your résumé. The direction, I believe, is that they're going to say we brought in the best of the best of the best!"

Once again, I had to wonder why Tom's press team needed to know anything more about me. What more did they need? Why was I "the direction"? My reaction was to stall. I didn't send my résumé as requested, and Heather nudged me about it.

Melania, Pamela Gross, and I met in the First Lady's East Wing office to talk about initiative matters. The First Lady was sitting at her desk; Pamela and I were in chairs facing her. I said, "I don't know what the fuck is going on." They sat there looking at me with puppy-dog eyes. "I'm worried about the inauguration filing and all these emails from Heather."

"I'm not worried about you," said Melania. "You will be fine."

"The truth is the truth," I replied, and slumped down in the chair. I heaved a sigh of relief.

Gesturing to the three of us, she added, "We all know the truth. We'll all protect you."

What did I need protection from, though? "Do I need to hire a lawyer?" I asked.

"*Yes!* You should have one," said Melania. "You did nothing wrong!"

The room fell into silence.

And then, out of nowhere, the chair Pamela was sitting on broke and she fell straight to the floor! She's a tiny woman; that chair was not even fit for a bird. We burst out laughing. It was a deep laughter filled with relief but also born out of dread. Her falling was a sign that the proverbial shit was about to hit the proverbial fan and we were all about to be thrown on our asses, myself included. Who in the PIC would fall on theirs over the 990?

The next day, I connected with a lawyer, a partner at Paul, Weiss, Rifkind, Wharton & Garrison, the same firm that had run an internal investigation about Roger Ailes at Fox News and Harvey Weinstein at the Weinstein Company. I felt I was in good hands with him, and from that point on, I didn't make a move without his counsel. I was a political neophyte who had stepped right into the center of one of the most divisive political and ideological battles this country has ever known, and I didn't like what was happening around me.

Final Warning

On January 30, I received a document from Heather that became known as "the sixty-seven questions." The document was being prepared and was approved for release by "the family" and other "operatives" affiliated with the White House. The timing of the release was being handled by Heather, Hope Hicks, and Grisham. It was a list of press questions about the inauguration the West Wing communications shop had received and compiled (and ignored) for the last year, and their cookie-cutter answers.

I don't think Heather was supposed to send me the entire document, but she did.

Rick Gates had his own section:

Question #32: "What did Rick Gates have to do with the PIC?"

The White House answer: "*Need answer.*"

Question #33: "Was Rick Gates in charge of the PIC money?"

The White House answer: "*No.*"

Question #34: "Are there any outstanding PIC issues related to Rick Gates or PIC money he handled?"

The White House answer: "*No.*"

And that was the moment I realized that there was a *major problem*. Gates had had *everything* to do with the money!

Reading ahead, I found a section about *me* personally—not WIS

Media Partners. My name was not supposed to appear on any PIC documents. But there it was. All by its lonesome self. The WIS partners' names were nowhere to be found and neither was Inaugural Productions.

To make matters worse, all of the information was wrong; dates, details, amounts, the scope of my work, and major clarifications needed to be noted. I got to work making the changes in consultation with my attorney and my partners Jon and Mel—and even Melania; she read everything. Melania herself addressed the potentially controversial question "Is Wolkoff a good friend of the First Lady?" and suggested I cross the word "good" out of the question. At the time, I assumed it was to protect myself from a cronyism charge.

I sent back a heavily redlined document that set the record straight, with Melania's edits too, to Heather, in good time and with a good-faith understanding that they'd use them.

"We are not going to file until next Thursday or Friday to coincide with the next round of the government shut-down possibility," Heather informed me. So their strategy was to bury the release during the shutdown? I wasn't so sure that would work. The information had to be corrected in any event.

Heather said, "I got [your corrections]. I am going to talk to Tommy [Davis] again this morning and tell him we need to release to a friendly." She meant a friendly journalist who would tell the story the way they wanted it to be told. "We have to get ahead of it. There were two more articles yesterday wondering where the money is."

By "the money," did she mean the $80 million–plus of the $107 million in inaugural donations that hadn't been adequately accounted for yet? The only money that we knew *had* been accounted for was WIS's budget, most of which had been transferred to Inaugural Productions for the concert and the balls.

On January 31, I had no time to think about the 990. We were on the last push for the initiative presentation. I felt like a child telling Melania, "I asked Lindsay for your official picture so I could incorporate into the presentation . . . didn't get it. I also asked for your past year of visits [to schools and hospitals] so I could use as the guideline."

Melania's response felt distant and cold. She said she would need to look for pictures herself. "Just do without them. Get it done." It was a command.

After our listening session in the East Wing, the West Wing's interest in our initiative was heating up. "All of a sudden everyone is so interested in your initiatives . . . because of the experts on your team! Yale! Marc Brackett! Robin Stern! Tim Shriver! A real Kennedy," I wrote. "All of this started right after our meeting."

Lindsay had reached out to Jared's Office of American Innovation to inform them of what we were doing, which made no sense, unless Ivanka intended to swoop in at the last minute and usurp the First Lady's initiative right out from under her, or at the very least, sabotage it. I alerted the designated White House ethics czar, Stefan Passantino, about all of it. He was a lawyer; I could trust him. Right?

Wrong.

I'd later learn that Stefan was a part of "the family." The only reason he showed up and gave us such a hard time is *because* of my email. I'd given him the inside scoop without even realizing what I'd done.

Jared, Ivanka, the whole West Wing, and the East Wing, for that matter, were sick of my trying to make the First Lady look good. I told Melania, "They all want me out of the way." She knew I was right.

But I didn't give up. On February 8, Pamela and I made a detailed, evidence-based presentation to the East Wing staff that succinctly laid out the initiative and our months' worth of research in partnership with experts. I highlighted the phrases "Children should be seen and not heard" with a ⊘ symbol over the word "not." We wrote easy-to-remember rules like "Think before you hit send" and "If you feel something, say something," and walked through the steps of ending the "cycle of silence" to teach kids the skills they needed to understand their emotions and instill positive feelings in them about themselves, the keys to stopping bullying and addiction.

The staff sat in chairs in a semicircle; Melania sat right in front of me in the middle of the room. But she was different. She looked like a queen on her throne waiting for us all to kiss the ring.

Halfway through my presentation, Stephanie Grisham got up, left, and never came back. Melania didn't bat an eyelash, which seemed so strange. Grisham's rudeness actually gave me a moment to pause and reflect on the image on my computer screen, the Frederick Douglass quote, "It is easier to build strong children than to repair broken men." Everyone stared at me blankly, so I kept going and finished the unveiling of the First Lady's initiative. I asked Pamela, seated in back, if she had anything to add. She gave me a supportive smile but didn't speak.

Everyone filed out of our office. Melania was last. Pamela and I congratulated her. She'd lived and breathed every step of the way with us. We were proud of our work and honored to have served our friend. Melania was all smiles, but something was off.

Pamela and I accompanied Melania on the three-minute walk from her office in the East Wing to the Residence elevator. At the same time, Donald walked over from the West Wing.

The four of stopped at the elevator, Melania standing between Pamela and me. Donald kept two feet back from us, legs clamped together—I could have sworn I heard his heels click—and arms at his sides. He said, "Hello, ladies." Usually when Donald saw Pamela and me, he greeted us with a big smile and hug and a few pleasantries. This greeting was cold and abrupt. Melania smiled, stepped into the elevator with him, and gave us the British royal wave she'd mastered.

I brushed it off. Surely he had more pressing things on his mind than being his jovial self, but his behavior was markedly different. For some reason, the 990 popped into my head.

Pamela and I did an about-face and walked back to our office in the East Wing; closed the door, hoping no one would hear us; and sat down in disbelief. We stared at each other for about a minute. She said, "What was *that*?!"

Later that night, Melania texted to thank me for the meeting and to ask if there was anything I needed from her or if I had any questions.

I replied, "I just received an email about the government shutdown. I am not allowed to come into the White House, only your staff can come. So I won't be able to work in office while I'm here. However, shall I arrange with Tim [Harleth, the White House usher] to come as a visitor to residence?"

She said she'd take care of it. "I will let Timothy know. See you at 10:30."

That day, February 9, 2018, the approved PIC press release arrived in my inbox. It was bland and generic—and intentionally vague on the burning question, "How was the $107 million spent?"

"This is the largest amount ever raised for a Presidential Inaugural Committee. All of the funds were raised from private sources and no taxpayer money was expended for any PIC activities," it said. The underlying message was classic Trump. Biggest amount ever! But that didn't provide substantive details about where the money had gone.

Thomas Barrack's quote: "This inauguration represented the hallmark of American democracy in the unique and cherished American tradition of a peaceful transfer of power from the President to the President-Elect. The day of the 58th Presidential Inauguration, as well as the more than 20 events surrounding it, was conceived, planned, financed, staffed, and executed in 69 days. And it was executed in elegance and seamless excellence without incident or interruption, befitting the legacy and tradition that has preceded us."

There were echoes of that first lunch I had had with him and Rick Gates at Le Bilboquet about excellence and legacy. I'd been suckered then, and now here he was smooth-talking the American people.

The release also stated that millions had been donated to charities, such as the American Red Cross, Samaritan's Purse, the Salvation Army, the Smithsonian Institution, and the White House Historical Association.

My name was not mentioned. I exhaled weeks of stress.

By evening, the statement had not been sent to the media. I asked Heather about the delay, and she said, "We are still tracking a release tomorrow but we are awaiting the final green light by Hope Hicks."

I told her, "TB [Tom Barrack] left me several messages."

Melania texted at 7:55 p.m., suddenly all eager to see my responses to the questions. She asked to see the ones that pertained to her ASAP. She also told me that Grisham and Barrack needed more time to ready the PR, so they weren't releasing anything that day. "Pls send me my Q&A for PIC. So I approve it." I had been double-checking her answers. "Show me mine," she demanded.

I wondered if I'd set off some alarms when I sent back the sixty-seven questions with all of that redlining. It'd been approved by my lawyer. I shouldn't have spoken with Stefan Passantino (who, unbeknownst to me at the time, was Ivanka's ethics lawyer) and shared my feelings about the PIC with him. Had I shown my hand too soon by demonstrating to Tom, Donald, Melania, and the powers that be that I was not, and would never be, prepared to just look the other way? Whatever *they* wanted "the narrative" to be, I was not on the same page.

On February 12, I sent Melania an email containing a draft of her "MESSAGE FROM FLOTUS" and asked her what she thought about the name "Speak UP +++." I still believed Be Best wasn't the best.

At 5:30 p.m. she texted tersely that she was just finishing her meetings. "Will go over tonight."

On February 13, Tuesday, Heather emailed, all jazzed up. "Spoke to Tommy [Davis], convinced him we need to go all in and be proactive! I am tweaking the press release they wrote and trying to get some surrogates ready to speak positive."

Later, she emailed about the journalist they'd given the exclusive to. Heather's text read, "We're all set, moving forward on Thursday [two days hence]. The plan is that Maggie Haberman [of the *New York Times*] will run the story on Thursday per Tom Barrack." Depending on whom you talked to, Haberman was either tough on Donald

Trump or a complete suck-up to him. That didn't matter. The issue was Haberman's relationship with Tom Barrack. According to Heather, Haberman was "a friendly." She would present the story the PIC wanted the world to read.

She continued, "And they will also give the package to [Sean] Hannity and [Laura] Ingraham [at Fox News]."

I didn't know anything about a "package." This was all making me very nervous.

Heather kept me up-to-date on everything. "The [990] report is officially filed," she texted at 11:00 p.m. "We're starting to get questions. The NY Times will likely be the first story." She said Tommy Davis was making sure that my credentials would be emphasized in the articles. Huh? But my name hadn't been on the press release . . .

I pulled up Google and began searching for the report. "I can't find it?" I texted Heather. "Are you sure it was filed?"

She said, "The IRS might not post it for months, but the federal law states that the moment it is placed in a mailbox we are legally required to provide the public copy."

I asked her, "Where does the public copy go?"

"Public copy is just held and provided as people ask for it."

Does she think the story about how Trump spent $107 million isn't going to hit every major network around the world?

On February 14, Melania and I texted repeatedly about Be Best and the launch that was coming up in just a couple of weeks. "They're sending me a new Be Best logo," I texted. "I will send the whole deck to *only* you when I am finished."

Melania was all "👍." I sent her the complete Be Best presentation that evening. Months of work, a true labor of love. The dream I'd had when I first joined forces with Melania.

She texted at 10:00 p.m. to thank me for sending my eight pages of summary and to say she would go over them. "Busy day. Will talk to you tomorrow." She directed me to combine social media and cyberbullying so that the initiative had only three points: well-being, social media, and opioids. She signed off with "Happy Valentine's Day."

To say I was crestfallen would be an understatement. Suddenly, the truth hit me like a ton of bricks: I'd been under such enormous pressure from all sides, I hadn't realized those feelings were because of her, too. I felt resentment. She decided it was easier to toe the line than step out of line. I wish she would have told me.

After all the battles I'd fought to do this, the attitudes and road-blocks, the lack of resources and no staff, not to mention the West Wing hurdles, just to get her initiative off the ground. There was a reason behind the tension and defensiveness I was feeling. I was offended and disheartened.

I thought about the question my mom had once asked me: "What would you tell your daughter to do if you saw her suffering the way I see you?"

She was right, and she wasn't alone. She, Bruce, David, my children, my brothers, my in-laws, and my friends all saw the emotional and physical toll working for Melania took on me and had begged me to walk away from that toxic environment. They worried about my overall health and well-being (how ironic). I made a promise to them all that as soon as I delivered Melania's initiative to her, I would walk away. Until then, I would bear the daily onslaught of hate, resentment, humiliation, and antagonistic behavior. Bullying, really.

I promised my mom I'd check in daily.

"Dear Mom," I wrote. "So proud. So sad," and attached the final deck for Melania's initiative.

"I adore you. Tomorrow would be Bobie and Papa's anniversary. All will be good," she replied.

I felt somewhat relieved. I had delivered on my promise both to the First Lady of the United States and to my family and friends.

I inhaled deeply, with dignity and grace, and then drafted my res-ignation letter at 11:44 p. m. that night.

Dear Melania,

As I sit here tonight, I am thinking about the past year and a half. I willingly opened my heart and sacrificed my health, my family, my relationships, my companies. I accepted the roles with honor to produce the Inauguration and work with you on everything (despite the intense hostility everywhere), followed by my role at the WH when no one else was there and I was taking care of it all alone. I would do it all over again for YOU.

I could go on and on, but you have heard it all already. Your staff—Lindsay and Stephanie are horribly disrespectful, and I can no longer be a part of such a toxic environment. Not only are they abrasive and hostile but they do it passive-aggressively. They only share what they want, and they don't collaborate. They just speak down to me and not speak with me.

I am heartbroken, truly heartbroken, that these people, who couldn't care less about anything but their resumes and next job, have made sure not to include me (when I ask every day to be called or conferenced in) but then USE all of my work.

I haven't taken care of my health, spent time with my children or enjoyed even a walk outside because I wanted to make sure you had it all complete for a perfect roll out in every area.

I can't believe these people have WON! They are in control of everything and want to glide on by.

They have completely stripped me of my dignity, and I can't be treated like a subordinate by someone with no experience.

I love you with all my heart and will be here always. I REALLY LOVED the initiatives because so much of it was personal about my difficult journey with Zach. This was a way to heal. All for what????????????????? So they can stand there and applaud themselves. We did all the work.

This has nothing to do with me wanting to leave. It has to do with them making me leave.

I am speechless. . . . . :

You are my best friend, and this isn't what I ever wanted. I am so dedicated to you, always and forever.

XOXO I LOVE YOU.

Stephanie

Cover Girl Strikes Again

I woke up the next morning, February 15, 2018, to see my name and picture splashed across the front page of the *New York Times* website under an article headlined "Trump's Inaugural Committee Paid $26 Million to First Lady's Friend" by Maggie Haberman and Kenneth P. Vogel.

With those ten words, life as I knew it ended.

Sitting at my desk alcove in my kitchen, I stared at the screen in disbelief. I kept hitting refresh, hoping it'd go away. The comments on the article started racking up, all of them hostile, hateful, and negative. By the headline alone, it seemed like the First Lady had handed her "party planner" friend a cushy job and that I had danced off with millions. It made our friendship the big scandal.

I was freaking out.

Heather said, "Seriously just annoyed at all the stupid spin. They write a perfectly boring article, but they paste your face on it to draw readers." The article was filled with lies! "Look, it's hard to be on the receiving end," Heather said. "Even Rick is behind the scenes telling reporters to get your record straight, all the while he has his own fake news out today!" Did she really think Rick was innocent of the Mueller charges? *Poor deluded Heather.*

The article said that WIS Media Partners had been "created in December 2016, about six weeks before the inauguration, and its founder, according to a person familiar with the firm, was Stephanie Winston Wolkoff, a longtime friend of Mrs. Trump's. Otherwise there is very little information available about the company." It implied that I had only gotten the job because of Melania and that I'd just opened some rinky-dink party-planning company for the very first time. No slam on party planners, but my life's work has been about producing large-scale epic events—the Met Gala, Fashion Week—and raising millions for scientific research and the emotional wellness of children. Also, it read as if I alone had created WIS Media Partners. Jon and Tiny Horse, or any of the other partners, were never mentioned.

Personally, I was characterized as a rich white lady society dilettante. "Ms. Winston Wolkoff made her name planning Manhattan society galas. An associate of the *Vogue* editor Anna Wintour, Ms. Winston Wolkoff traveled in the same circles as Mrs. Trump, who attended Ms. Winston Wolkoff's 40th birthday party in 2010. Ms. Winston Wolkoff has subsequently been brought on as a senior adviser to the first lady's official government office."

Oh, and I was a name-dropper, too. "Two people with direct knowledge of Ms. Winston Wolkoff's role, who asked to remain anonymous, said she often invoked Mrs. Trump's name with transition officials as she delivered instructions for the inauguration." No shit! I was working for Melania! I was delivering HER instructions for her husband's inauguration; I was interviewing her staff. Should I not have mentioned her name?

The two anonymous sources? Take your pick. Lindsay was no fan of mine. Grisham, obviously. Hope Hicks? Heather Martin? Tommy Davis? Ivanka? I'm sure they had all spoken to Haberman.

"Ms. Winston Wolkoff could not be reached for comment," the article claimed. Not true. Haberman and Vogel never called, texted, or emailed me.

This part killed me: "Stephanie Grisham, a spokeswoman for Mrs. Trump, said the first lady 'had no involvement' with the inaugural committee 'and had no knowledge of how funds were spent.'" Complete and utter horseshit! Melania knew it all, every detail, including who was screwing around, the type of salmon served at the Candlelight Dinner, the inconsistencies in Hargrove's budgets, and approving those Tiffany bowls, and she was the one who told me, regarding our quest for talent, "I don't think Donald likes Kenny Rogers."

"According to Ms. Grisham," said the article, "Ms. Winston Wolkoff is classified as 'a special government employee' and 'has specified duties as outlined in her contract.'" Per the contract I'd paid a heap of money to prepare, I was an UNPAID "trusted advisor."

"An operative," the piece continued, "who worked with the inaugural committee, who was not authorized to speak for attribution about its spending . . . said Ms. Winston Wolkoff personally received $1.62 million for her work through her consulting firm."

My head exploded right there, all over my white kitchen walls. People would read these falsehoods and believe them. I was completely unprepared for this. They wanted to pin the whole thing on me. No, correction—they *had* pinned it on me.

I sat in front of my computer screen most of the day, with fast-striking PTSD.

Per the *NYT* article, "An inaugural committee official, who spoke on the condition of anonymity because the official was not authorized to discuss the details publicly, said Ms. Winston Wolkoff's firm also paid the team used by Mark Burnett [referring to IP], the creator of 'The Apprentice,' whose involvement in the inaugural festivities was requested by Mr. Trump."

For the record, my personal compensation for my work on the inauguration that I retained was $480,000. That number seems like a lot. It is a lot. But to put it into perspective, imagine we had been making a $107 million movie. Producers' fees are typically 5 percent, and sometimes they are as high as 10 percent. My fee was less than half of 1 percent. Many people working on the inauguration made far more than I did.

Only after I went ballistic did Heather Martin and Tommy Davis tell me they'd "try to help [me] and clear up the confusion" that they'd caused with the *Times*. Later in the article, it was stated that ". . . although committee officials said she used that money to help pay other inaugural workers who reported to her," but it was already too late.

I don't need to defend my compensation. I'm a well-paid professional and I worked extremely hard, as I always do. I didn't take a penny to work with Melania during the transition or the inauguration, or for the year we spent together in the White House. I gave up my career. I gave up every partnership. *I gave up my salary* and title at the White House so that I could hire much-needed help and to support our initiatives. I landed in the hospital for a month and almost died.

I was not in this to get rich. And if you take into account the amount of money I have now spent on attorney fees to defend myself, I'm in the hole almost a million dollars. It was the worst mistake of my life to get involved with Melania and the Trumps: emotionally, mentally, physically, financially, socially, professionally. I thought I had an amazing friend. But when it really counted, Melania wasn't there for me. It suddenly became painfully clear to me that she wasn't really my friend, in the true sense of the word.

This reputation-decimating smear, in the *New York Times*, the so-called paper of record, was the price I paid for my devotion. And it was too high. It cost me the reputation I'd built for twenty-plus years in media and entertainment. I knew instantly the damage was extensive. Emails and texts were flooding in from journalists asking for comment (a courtesy the *Times* had not extended), but not from friends and colleagues. I think they were embarrassed for me and didn't know what to say.

I texted Melania with a link to the story. "URGENT! READ THIS!"

I sent an email to Grisham, cc'ing Lindsay, Melania, and Passantino: "Can you please explain to me why would you tell the press that I am 'a special government employee' and a 'contracted volunteer.' I have a 'Gratuitous Service Agreement'—attached. I am a Trusted Adviser and have worked on all of the Initiatives."

Grisham had gone ape-shit after the UN luncheon when Katie Rogers asked me to define my role. She said I was not allowed to answer *any* questions about my title or agreement. And now, she was spouting incorrect information to the *Times*.

The distinction in title language and the type of contract is important. A special government employee is hired by the federal government for a temporary, specific job. A contractor is also hired for a specific project. If I had been one of those, I would have gotten a contract and been paid, like David Monn had been. My agreement was not with the federal government. Nor could I be a contractor, because my role was too broad. It did not relate to a specific task and had no set time frame. Grisham and other forces in the White House didn't want people to know that I'd been working for the First Lady for more than a year on every aspect of her work.

Grisham replied, "I cleared all that I said through legal. I have been inundated with questions as to the unique nature of your employment situation here at the White House. This messaging is the best way to go in order to minimize the negative press stories of today and protect FLOTUS & this administration. Removing Mrs. Trump's personal email from this exchange." She didn't want Melania to see communications.

The next day, I fired off an email to "legal," a.k.a. Stefan Passantino. "Stephanie G. admitted that she lied and said she did so to do what is best to 'minimize the negative press stories of today and protect FLOTUS & this administration.' (Freedom of Information Act?????) The Inaugural stories are FAKE NEWS!!! Heather Martin knows all of this. And so does Lindsay, who spoke with Heather and me," I wrote. "I am a dedicated and loyal friend to FLOTUS. Everyone knows the truth about the Inauguration and all the fake news around me is to deflect attention. For the East Wing's staff to treat me this way is wrong. I'm surprised you didn't call me or speak with me when I told you two weeks ago that I had information to share with you about the Inauguration. I have removed everyone else from this email. You can decide who to share it with."

"Friendly" Haberman had taken the exclusive from the "operatives" who had "asked to remain anonymous" and had made me the scapegoat for suspicious inaugural accounting. I was the perfect distraction from the real story: the scores of millions that were insufficiently accounted for. Not one reporter was questioning the people who did the PIC financing? It was unbelievable.

Was I just collateral damage, or had someone set me up for this fall? Who would want to hurt me so badly? For that matter, was I the *real* target, or was I being used to discredit Melania by association?

I texted Melania, "Tom fucked me over! He made me the headline!"

She replied, "😡😡😡😡," and later, "Hope you are okay and talked to your lawyer."

You bet I did! He and I talked about next steps. I wanted to sue the *Times* for defamation and provide every scrap of paper that proved the story's inaccuracies. But if I did, the PIC could sue me. I'd signed a nondisclosure agreement that barred me from talking about my work on the inauguration. I was stuck, and the PIC and Trump knew it. It must have been part of the setup. (I'm able to write about some things now because these events have been investigated and reported on. I can comment on what's in the public record. What I've written about that happened between Melania and me during this time wasn't under an NDA.)

My mind was spinning. In the middle of my meltdown, I received calls from Heather and Tommy Davis, who were dealing with the press on this. Sometime during the course of that horrific day, the *Times* headline changed to "Trump Inaugural Committee Paid $26 Million to Firm of First Lady's Adviser," adding "Firm of" and changing "Friend" to "Adviser." The *Times* ditched the original defaming headline, but I have a screenshot, and it exists in the annals of Reddit.

Tommy told me, "We worked very hard to clear up the misconception about the one point six million dollars and to make clear your incredible reputation and outstanding qualifications to be picked for the job you did."

Heather said the headline change "was a slight improvement," but the lies in the body of the piece were unchanged. The paper never issued a retraction or an apology.

If I hadn't taken a screenshot of the original headline, I would have no record of it. But it got out there and thousands of people saw it nevertheless. Outlets around the world picked up the story. My face and name became synonymous with Trumpian self-dealing, graft, cronyism, and avarice. People believed I was the antithesis of the woman I actually was. Most still do.

The Trumps were experts at perception, so they had to know what this would do to me. I knew who I really was, but my identity had been stolen. The dichotomy was like being torn in half. The humiliation of the article triggered in me a terror of leaving my house.

My family was upset for me, of course, and tried to empathize with how cataclysmically devastated I was. Unless you've been wrongly, publicly shamed, it's hard to understand how seismic it feels when your core self is demolished. What a fool I was, thinking I could make a difference in the middle of this den of thieves.

That day, I remember staring at the screen for hours, hitting refresh on a Google search of my name, reading all the tweets, not able to stop myself. My body was racked with chills, covered in goose bumps. At one point, I crumpled into a ball on the floor and sobbed and cried out in anguish like a wounded animal. My only comfort was a cozy black sweatshirt that was big enough to bury my face in. In my head, I turned it into a life vest, the only thing that was keeping me afloat. I didn't take it off for days.

Melania ghosted me. She didn't comment on my resignation letter for two long days.

Finally, she texted, "How are you. Did you talk to your lawyer?"

She and I spoke for hours about how my lawyers were handling this, and the day after that and the day after that, "Did you talk to your lawyer?"

Melania's 😎 😝 🖤 💋 had been replaced with "lawyer lawyer lawyer."

Nothing Personal, Just Business

Meanwhile, Clown Prince Jared still didn't have security clearance to do classified work, and yet, there he was doing it, every day. On February 16, the *Times* reported that General John F. Kelly, Donald's chief of staff, had ordered an overhaul of all White House security clearances. It wasn't just Jared; presidential aide Rob Porter had somehow gotten FBI clearance to work in the White House despite the agency's knowledge that he'd been accused of domestic violence.

They'd let a twice-accused wife beater in the White House, no problem. But they'd escorted my potential hire out of the building for smoking pot once, decades ago.

Part of the fallout from General Kelly's sweeping overhaul was his decision to cancel all contracts for volunteers, which included my gratuitous service agreement. It'd been signed only six months before. If Melania had just accepted my resignation—which she never acknowledged, ever—I would have had the dignity to say, "I quit."

I genuinely believed, as did Marc and Robin, doctors, therapists, professors, researchers, and experts, that Melania wanted to effect change. Melania wanted to focus on cyberbullying and being a good digital citizen in today's world. Her mission was to stop individuals from hiding behind their screens to protect their identity.

I wanted this initiative to succeed against all odds and was willing to keep fighting for the greater good.

She'd always asked me, "Why do you care so much?" I had to care for the both of us until I realized how much she didn't really care at all.

While *loyalty* was everything to the Trumps, *honesty* was everything to me. Melania didn't respect me enough or have the decency to tell me the truth to my face or to pick up the phone and call me to tell me everything I'd predicted was coming true and that she was playing a role in it all. She hid behind a screen, dropping the news via email in a letter addressed to Pamela and me. No disrespect to Pamela, but Melania could have taken the time to send me my own letter.

I couldn't believe what I was reading.

Dear Stephanie and Pamela,

I know you both received a call from the White House, and that it was not news that you wanted. I will call each of you personally later this evening, but wanted to reach out immediately to express my gratitude for all that you have done.

The decision to terminate all gratuitous service contracts was made on a professional level by White House counsel and was not a personal attack or reflection on either of you. I consider you both my friends and appreciate all that you have done for me.

    I am sorry that the professional part of our relationship has come to an end. But I am comforted in the fact that our friendship far outweighs politics.

    Thank you again.

    Much love,

    Melania

    Much love?

From the tone of her letter, she expected me to buck up and be on my way, with my reputation stomped to bits and without a place on the initiative we'd worked so hard to accomplish. I was asking her to defend me, to clarify what I'd done for her and what she knew about the inauguration. Since "friendship far outweighs politics," as this almost certainly White House–written letter said, she should help me clear my name by just telling the truth.

As I was reading the letter, Stefan Passantino called.

He said, "The White House has made a decision globally that we are going to be terminating all gratuitous service agreements. This is not personal, and this is not related to you, and the decision was made by the president, the First Lady, and the White House that there's too much risk involved with folks [who are not] special government employees. I just wanted to call you and let you know, because I didn't want you to hear that from anyone else, and make sure that you knew that this is not personal."

"This is because of the bullshit *New York Times* story!" I exclaimed. "You know firsthand that's a cover-up!"

Stefan said, "I can't speak to any of that."

"This is going to make it look as though I was fired," I said.

"I don't want you to think that this has anything to do with PIC, so *this is not personal,*" he said. "We're not going to do any press or anything with it, but it's a decision we made at a White House–wide level to make sure we're not going to do this kind of contract. You didn't do anything wrong and there's nothing wrong with this kind of contract. It's just that the decision was made to operate this way going forward."

No one else had ever done an agreement like the one my former lawyers (who, unbeknownst to me at the time, were also representing Trump) had drawn up in consultation with the White House. It was the first of its kind—probably because no one else would be as eager and foolish as I was to beg to work for free with no protections. But it wasn't the last. Pamela Gross had the exact same agreement as I did.

"Pamela's contract was discontinued, too," he said. "They are both ended."

This was another key factor that, if it were disclosed to the public, would have exonerated me. It proved that "this type of contract [was] being discontinued" and "had nothing to do with the PIC." But since the White House insisted on not releasing the details, the public would believe I was fired because of the bogus claims made by the *New York Times*.

Melania called while I was on with Stefan. After I hung up with the lawyer, I called her back. "I can't believe this," I said.

"Stephanie, I know you're upset and so am I. I don't blame you."

"Stefan told me I am to stop working on everything. I have *no* role." I know I'd sent my resignation letter to Melania the night before the *NYT* story broke, but it's one thing to ask to leave and expect a transition period to wind down, and another to be "severed" and kicked out immediately.

"The lawyers say you can't work under this kind of contract," she said.

I finally lost it. "You know this isn't right! And you also know it makes no sense! The White House is going to make up the story they want to protect all their asses!" The narrative was so juicy, they knew the press and public would eat it up. Even though it was a blatant distortion of the facts, they let it fly. Melania's friend "got" $26 million and was "fired" because of it. "You have to make it right," I pleaded.

"My contract was discontinued due to security clearances. But you know people will assume I got fired because of the PIC financing."

I told Melania that Stefan had said it wasn't personal and that it had nothing to do with the PIC. He'd also claimed that the White House was not going to comment. "You know that's bullshit!" I told her.

On February 23, Rick Gates, someone my business partners and I had been forced to work with, pled guilty to lying and conspiracy against the United States. It didn't surprise me. Light was slowly being cast on the deceptions that were creeping into every corner of the inauguration, the transition, America First Policies, and the West Wing. These men left a trail of bread loaves behind them, leading investigators right to their doors.

I could only surmise that the price for informing Donald and Melania about the irregularities and problems, and executing my overload of work for the inauguration, was becoming the cover girl for the inauguration shenanigans, and having my name soiled by the *New York Times.*

Teflon Don was left completely unscathed as "the best people" were arrested, fired, and disgraced for their association with him. Logically, you would think the *New York Times* would have been investigating the overspending and asking about the other $80 million–plus spent by the PIC—the majority of the money—and the possible corruption of the PIC under the stewardship of Rick Gates, but as Melania would say, "*Nope!*"

Instead, on February 25, I received a text from Ken Vogel, the coauthor of the defamatory article. "Hey Stephanie," he wrote. "We are writing a story on the first lady's office firing you from your unpaid job as a result of the president's displeasure with the news that your firm was paid $26 million by the presidential inaugural committee. Wondering if you wanted to comment and/or provide context."

Immediately, I texted Melania and said, "My inbox is flooded with this. I would like to know how you plan on responding?"

Melania didn't reply. Her plan for responding was to do nothing.

Under the advisement of my lawyer, I emailed Vogel, "I encourage you to carefully evaluate your 'sources' and proceed with caution. Please do not exaggerate the facts or rely on false information and innuendo. I do not know why you and others seem to be trying to cause me reputational harm, but I do know that it is completely unfair. I am proud of the work that we did to support the inauguration."

Second Detonation

The second *New York Times* story was published on February 26, ten days after the first *Times* story and six days after my contract ended. Same picture, new headline: "Melania Trump Parts Ways with Adviser Amid Backlash over Inaugural Contract" by Kenneth P. Vogel and Maggie Haberman.

They'd taken another shot, this one straight to the kneecap.

"The first lady, Melania Trump, has parted ways with an adviser after news about the adviser's firm reaping $26 million in payments to help plan President Trump's inauguration," it said. "Stephanie Grisham, Mrs. Trump's spokeswoman, said the office had 'severed the gratuitous services contract with Ms. Wolkoff,' who Ms. Grisham said had been employed as a special government employee to work on specific projects. 'We thank her for her hard work and wish her all the best.'"

"Severed?!" I emailed Grisham, grabbing at my throat reflexively. It was a violent word.

"Keeping the response short and professional—confirming the contract has been severed, thanking you for your hard work and wishing you the best," she replied.

Their intention was to smear my name and long-standing credibility by implying that I had been chopped from the White House due to my role in the inauguration.

I was not a special government employee. I was not hired for one task for a specific period of time. I was contracted to be an advisor for as long as Melania and I cared to continue.

I know I sound like a broken record, but this detail was more critical than ever. The White House lawyers repeatedly claimed I couldn't be given a proper contract and salary because my work was open-ended, but now they were firing me because my work was open-ended? Damned if I do, damned if I don't. Any way you slice it, I lose.

The article claimed that two people "with direct knowledge of the situation" said that my contract termination was "prompted by displeasure from the Trumps over the news, first reported by the *New York Times*, that a firm created by Ms. Winston Wolkoff was paid nearly $26 million for event planning by a nonprofit group that oversaw Mr. Trump's inauguration and surrounding events in January 2017."

Donald and Melania had repeatedly told David Monn and me that we were doing a great job. I was now living in a completely alternative universe.

David was dragged into this, too. The *New York Times* reported that "Mr. Trump was reportedly enraged by the payment, and by the news that Ms. Winston Wolkoff had paid an associate, David Monn, $3.7m to help plan the festivities."

I didn't pay anyone a penny. I wasn't paid $26 million. I wasn't a part of the approval process, and I didn't have access to the financing, not even WIS's. Every budget was preapproved and authorized by Tom, Rick, Sara, and the PIC Finance Committee.

David and I worked on the Candlelight Dinner *with* Melania and had Donald's input, and we then helped renovate the East Wing and Executive Residence together. David had a contract with the White House, as a contractor, hired for a specific project, with a start and end date.

So, in this story, written by the *New York Times*, again, just like the first two stories by Maggie Haberman and Ken Vogel, there are no quotes from Donald or Melania, just a "source," "operatives," and "people who asked to remain anonymous." Wow!

Melania explained to me, "We didn't say it. The lawyers, they say we have to do it this way." Oh, I see, the lawyers made the president and First Lady not tell the truth? That explains it.

At least this time, the *New York Times* could say that they had called me, and they included a comment from me in the article: "I was informed by the White House counsel's office that all gratuitous volunteer contracts were ended." But I couldn't say more because of my NDA.

Vogel didn't mention that Pamela Gross's contract had also been "severed." If he had, then the story that mine had been "severed" because of the PIC financing would have been proven bogus. Tragically, it was my friends Melania and Pamela who insisted Pamela's involvement and contract remain a secret.

The follow-up article said I had been introduced to Tom Barrack by Melania. Also not true. I was introduced to him by Ivanka Trump. Her name was mysteriously absent from this story.

Dragging my name and photo in front of the public again, this time about my "firing," was an effective distraction from the real and totally embarrassing stories that were unfolding at the White House. The Mueller indictments. Other investigations under way. The security clearance debacle.

I would have given almost anything to have had Melania's coldness at that time to protect me from the wolves. But I couldn't stop myself from caring. I was way too sensitive for that.

"You Weren't Fired. Seriously."

I just couldn't let it go. I couldn't let the lies stand. I emailed Stefan, who promised there would be no comment from the White House, and demanded to know why he had allowed Grisham to say "severed" knowing its implication, knowing the truth about both Pamela and me. He said he'd get back to me.

I'm still waiting.

"How could you let Stephanie Grisham say I was severed?!" I asked Melania. "You know what it means?"

"The contract ended," she replied.

"No! 'Severed' means you cut my head off! Fired me!"

"Don't be so dramatic. You weren't fired," she said.

She'd never spoken to me with such contempt and impatience before, in over fifteen years of friendship. "I'd been in a meeting and I didn't know she was going to say that."

The next day, I begged Melania, "Please clear my name!"

The day after that: "You know I was thrown under the bus for nothing. At least be straight with me after all these years of friendship! All you have to do is tell the truth and stand up for your loyal friend. No one else was there for you like I was. How can you let this be?"

Finally, on March 2, five days after she'd allowed the world to believe I was fired for displeasing the First Couple, she texted, "I know you are still angry and upset." You bet your ass I was!

She had been informed by the White House counsel that because of the possible investigations into the PIC's finances, she was not allowed to say anything on my behalf. The American people had been told that she and the president had no involvement in the planning of events or how the PIC spent its money.

That triggered an epic letter-writing session that went on for hours. I couldn't put my feelings in a text. As Tom would say, I had to craft and sculpt a response, and let her know just how angry and upset I still was.

Melania,

ONLY YOU CAN REPAIR THIS TERRIBLE INJUSTICE TO ME, MY REPUTATION AND MY INTEGRITY BY ISSUING A STATEMENT.

I know the lawyers told you not to comment. But the facts speak for themselves. And you can say something for me.

You are the First Lady, and you have the authority to take care of this. You know I would do this for you a hundred times over. My family and friends, the ones who still talk to me, are horrified by your silence. There is no excuse for you not to defend me.

If [Grisham had] just repeated what Stefan told me—"You've done nothing wrong and this had nothing to do with the PIC"— none of this would be happening and I would not be begging for your help.

The moment you saw that headline, you should have issued a statement of your complete acknowledgement of my work, my integrity and my loyalty to you, POTUS and the country. You know that. The SILENCE from you is deafening and unfair. ONLY YOU can fix this. I love you.

Love,

Stephanie

I challenged her about saying she and Donald were displeased with me and David Monn. She said, "The lawyers made me and Donald say that. I would defend you, but I don't want to break the law."

What law says you are forbidden from defending a falsely accused and devoted friend? This was Melania Trump. A woman who does what she wants and what suits her own interests. In this case, that meant letting powerful forces (1) discredit me, (2) get rid of me, and (3) destroy me. By not protecting me, which she had promised to do, she was a tacit accomplice.

I'd been there for her. Whatever she asked for, whatever she needed, I supplied. The one time I asked for a precious thing—for her to speak the truth—she left my corner, leaving me bleeding in the ring.

When it really counted, Melania wasn't there for me. She wasn't really my friend. In fact, I wish I had never met her.

— 11 —

Just Friends

*I*n my thirties, I was on three magazine covers—*Avenue*, *Hamptons* and *Hampton Style*. Now I was the cover girl for the overspending and corruption of the Trump Presidential Inaugural Committee. It was not exactly the trajectory I had in mind when I signed up for this patriotic journey.

This was the price I paid for my own ignorance and not doing my homework, and jumping into the ring with people I really didn't know and trust, in an arena way dirtier and nastier than any I'd encountered before. I had been warned repeatedly to stay away from the Trumps but didn't listen. I'd naively believed that because of my proximity to them, I could help change them and make a positive difference in the world. The truth is, you can't change people. They are who they are. And when people show you, time and again, who they are, you need to listen even though you might wish with all of your heart that they were different.

From day one, I'd been in way over my head with the Trumps, and simply biding my time until they deemed I was no longer of value. At such time, I was supposed to disappear and join the long list of former friends who were now considered vanquished. If getting rid of you could help them in any way, they wouldn't blink an eye.

Even though the facts were wrong, the pain of public humiliation was very real. Once the headlines hit everyone's phone, television, and doorstep, I was afraid to leave my apartment. I embarrassed my children and my husband with my uncontrollable outbursts, and constantly looked over my shoulder in fear that I was being watched and followed. My solution was to stop going out, completely. I'd broken down entirely and my former self was a distant memory at best.

My friends worried about me. Many worried so much that they'd often show up at my front door, uninvited but always welcome. I'm grateful for every supportive email, text, voice message. I'm sorry I couldn't bring myself to reply to most of them.

Another drop-by guest was Michael Cohen. I'd known him for years; he had given me legal advice in passing. At the time, Michael was in the middle of his epic showdown with the president. He sat down with me, in my den, and said, "How are you, Steph?"

I was a freaking basket case. "I can't stop crying," I told him. "Those motherfuckers threw me under the bus! I got fucked, Michael!"

Only the few people who'd lived in the trenches with me could relate and empathize. David Monn wrote repeatedly. Pamela and I spoke and cried so often because no one truly saw her side of the story either.

My husband was furious about what had happened, because he knew the truth. He saw better than anyone how much I'd sacrificed to work on the inauguration and in the White House, chiefly my health and our family time together with our kids. He also knew exactly how much money I'd been paid by the PIC. If he had known how much I'd lost on attorney fees for my three contracts, expenses at the Trump International Hotel, travel, hundreds of domain names, and numerous other expenses, he would have been sick.

I reviewed old texts and emails, trying to figure out where things went sideways. I came across this text from Jon Reynaga, on February 15, 2017—exactly one year to the date before the scarlet letter *Times* article came out. At the time, I was in Washington working with Melania on the Israeli state visit, while Jon and Tom were having lunch in LA. Jon texted me after lunch. "I will be away for 2 weeks and then mad busy in a project in L.A. . . . I want to catch up. . . . Given how much scrutiny the media is giving the administration we cannot afford one single tiny mistake, so I need you to engage on this ASAP. Otherwise, in a few weeks/months time you'll be all over the press, negatively!"

I responded, "I am at the WH now and will call you at 11 a.m. tomorrow." Seriously? Negatively for what?! I had no idea what he was referring to, nor did I have the time to find out.

Jon replied, "Could do, hence wanting it never to be an issue. The press will be able to see the books and could say, 'SWW got paid $27m for her role in the inauguration' or something totally untrue."

And there it was in black and white. A narrative that could easily be sold to the press and the public. Jon and Tom had, apparently, talked about it over lunch. I believe Jon floated it out there to me as a subtle warning about what might happen if anyone poked around the PIC financing too closely. It hadn't even dawned on me at the time. Why would it?

It must have occurred to them that, if it became necessary to blame someone for the fuzzy finances, they could lay it at the feet of Melania's pal. It was a brilliantly conceived and even better executed plan. Jon had warned me but it went in one ear and out the other because I knew I was doing everything by the book. That didn't matter. Ivanka was right. Perception is more important than reality.

Right then and there, poring over year-old texts, I solved the riddle of "Who Is She?": She—me—is a *sucka*!

It wasn't until three years after the inauguration that I discovered the $1.62 million consulting and supervisory fee paid to WIS was earmarked as "SWW Executive Consultation/Management Fee." If anyone saw that, without knowing the facts, it would be construed that I, Stephanie Winston Wolkoff (SWW), personally received and retained the full amount. Could it be explained as an oversight? Or was it in fact well thought out with the goal of making me the scapegoat of overspending, if ever the time arrived? (And it certainly did!)

It was sleight of hand, creative accounting, bullshit at its finest, and the press ate it up, hook, line and sinker.

Catch and Kill

I was still in Mel-La-Lania Land. We continued to text and talk as if nothing had happened. I went along with it because I clung to the belief that she'd eventually defend me with the truth.

After one of her regular "How are you? Kids? XO ♥" texts, I couldn't bring myself to gloss over my feelings. I replied on March 13, "I am horrible. My kids are sad. None of this is easy." She sent ♥ and 🙏.

Jon Reynaga stayed around me a lot. He often slept over at our apartment and told me, "I am here for you!" And I loved him for that. "Promise me you won't do anything stupid." He was referring to the op-ed I was writing and rewriting over and over again, which never saw the light of day. Every day was Groundhog Day.

What crushed me the most was that not one person came forward to defend me.

Press requests came in from some journalists hoping to find the truth.

Melania told me, "Put out your papers!" She told me over and over to share all my receipts. I explained to her that, because of the PIC's nondisclosure agreement (NDA) I signed, I couldn't.

On March 22, CNN's Anderson Cooper interviewed Karen McDougal, the 1998 *Playboy* Playmate of the Year, about her alleged ten-month relationship with Donald, and the catch-and-kill deal she made with Trump friend and owner of American Media Inc. David Pecker to keep it quiet. Cooper asked McDougal what she'd say to Melania if the First Lady were watching. She said, "What can you say except 'I'm sorry'? I wouldn't want it done to me." A few days after that, Cooper interviewed Stormy Daniels on *60 Minutes* and pieced together a timeline of that one weekend in 2006 when Donald slept with the women on consecutive nights at Harrah's Lake Tahoe, while Melania was recovering from giving birth to Barron.

During the height of the Stormy Sturm und Drang, a reporter from the *Washington Post* sent me a list of questions about Melania's aims as First Lady. Believe it or not, I was *still* fielding her press requests—because Grisham was not responding. Melania most definitely did not have support, nor was her perspective covered by the press. The world only heard from Grisham—and not on behalf of the First Lady—in her inimitable combative tone. What this *WaPo* journalist didn't understand: Melania had no interest in revealing her thoughts, feelings, and perspectives about *anything*, let alone her friendships—including ours, which the reporter had asked about specifically—or Donald's affairs.

After I forwarded the request to Melania, she wrote, "Hi. How are you? I will pass on this XO ♥ ."

Right now, her nonresponse cast her as either a long-suffering victim of her unfaithful husband or a coldhearted gold digger. She refused to take action. I now realize Melania is not a normal woman. Two women had described having sex with her husband on national TV in graphic detail in the same week. Her private response: "It's politics." Her public response: dead silence. It just wasn't a human reaction.

Through the White House channels that remained open to me, I heard that Melania's staff was laughing at her behind her back. I texted Melania in April, "You should know that Lindsay Reynolds tells everyone that she gives you a list of only five items to choose from with your red sharpie, knowing you'll say 'no' to four of them, so that you'll say 'yes' to the one she wants you to choose."

Melania said, "That is laughable." She wrote that there was no red pen and no one gave her five things to do. "I am in charge of my own schedule." Then she said, "I know you are still upset."

Understatement of the century.

* * *

A few days after our exchange, Betsy Klein of CNN wrote an article about the First Lady's team. Grisham described them as "small but mighty." Klein had the audacity to claim that Melania's staff hadn't seen the rapid turnover and "palace intrigue of her husband's West Wing, although they have lost at least three members since inception." Considering the size of her office, that attrition rate might be on par with Donald's. Grisham said, "We are a close-knit team." And I almost spit out my coffee.

Poor Michael Cohen had admitted that he paid Stormy Daniels $130,000 in hush money but was still publicly denying that Donald knew about it. On April 9, Michael's home, office, and room at the Loews Regency Hotel were raided by the FBI. Agents claimed a reported 1.3 million files, acting on orders from the US Attorney's Office for the Southern District of New York (SDNY). They had been alerted to Michael's possible criminal activity by the special investigation led by Robert Mueller.

On April 10, Trump tweeted, "Attorney-client privilege is dead!" And on April 21: "I don't see Michael doing that [flipping] despite the horrible Witch Hunt and the dishonest media!"

The same day Donald was vouching for Michael Cohen's loyalty, Melania was at Barbara Bush's funeral. She famously smiled at Barack Obama, showing beautiful teeth, instead of giving him the pursed-lipped grin she used around her husband. Donald didn't go, since he knew his presence would not be welcomed by the Never-Trumper Bush family. Instead, Melania was accompanied by former White House head maître d' George Haney and Buddy Carter, the butler I'd met my first week in the White House, who gave me the biggest hug when he was retiring. He was one of the only gentlemen I'd met in Washington.

Nothing but the (Be) Best

On May 7, Melania presented her Be Best initiative in the Rose Garden at the White House. She said, "As a mother and as First Lady, it concerns me that in today's fast-paced and ever-connected world, children can be less prepared to express or manage their emotions and oftentimes turn to forms of destructive or addictive behavior such as bullying, drug addiction, or even suicide. I feel strongly that as adults we can and should *be best* at educating our children about the importance of a healthy and balanced life."

Pamela, Marc, Robin, our experts, and I were supposed to be standing with her. But we had been replaced by other people, other institutions.

Donald sat in the front row and made a big deal about signing her initiative with his illegible signature. He said, "Everywhere she has gone Americans have been touched by her sincerity, moved by her grace, and lifted by her love. Melania, your care and compassion for our nation's children, and I have to say this and I say it to you all the time, inspires us all."

Melania didn't take questions or give interviews.

Pamela texted me, "I'm numb."

I was, too. It was no longer the initiative we'd given life to, barely even a shadow of what it had been. Our ideas had been tossed around and chopped up. It was overwhelmingly obvious that Melania had been set up to fail.

When we spoke, I congratulated Melania on the launch. She sounded chipper! She was excited that Be Best was finally a reality.

The next day, her staff directed visitors to a downloadable "booklet by First Lady Melania Trump and the Federal Trade Commission" with tips on talking to kids about the Internet.

Except for tiny changes, the content was exactly the same as a booklet put out by the FTC in 2014. Melania's people had borrowed from the Obama administration *again*, presumably without Melania's knowledge.

They changed the booklet's authorship to "the Federal Trade Commission, promoted by First Lady Melania Trump."

FLOTUS MIA

On May 14, it was announced by the White House that Melania had checked into Walter Reed National Military Medical Center to be treated for a benign kidney condition. I knew all too well about her kidney stones. The procedure had been described on the news as minor, and yet she wasn't released from the hospital for a week? Or not? No one knew where she was. The media was not informed. Weeks went by without her attending an event or being seen in the White House. Naturally, her being missing in action again caused rampant speculation about her health, her recovery, and the state of her marriage.

Melania texted me back on May 17 that she was okay and recovering and not to worry. "Have a great specialist. Hope you and the kids are well! XO ♥. Good night. ᶻᶻ 🌙 ."

On May 22, one week into her three-week withdrawal from public view, we caught up by phone. She was in the White House, resting comfortably in the Residence, not giving a shit. We covered the usual subjects—the kids, their schools.

She was enjoying her game of hide-and-seek with the American people.

Melania was still laughing about the media reaction to her mysterious absence from public view. "Face lift? I'm too scared!" she said. "Nervous breakdown? I'm like, seriously? They don't even know me. My friend said, 'You *give* people nervous breakdown, you don't have it your own!'"

Tell me about it, sister.

"The funniest thing was when Donald told the press outside, 'She's right up there, looking at us!' And they look up!" she said, referring to an impromptu White House lawn interview with the press, during which Donald pointed up at her window. "I start laughing and said,

'Oh my God, do they really think I'd wait at the window and wave at them?'" As if she'd acknowledge their interest and concern for her well-being.

"Yup, they have no idea who you really are," I said.

"Seriously? For me, it's nothing. I start laughing. Come on, they don't have nothing better to do?" she asked.

The Jacket

On June 21, Melania wore a green Zara jacket with the words "I really don't care, do u?" on the back as she boarded her plane to visit immigrant children who'd been separated from their parents at the Texas border. The nation's eyes collectively bugged at the sentiment. What did it mean? Was the message for Ivanka? Donald? Democrats? The media? It couldn't possibly be about the caged children, could it?

On the day of, she texted me, "Liberals are getting crazy again! 😆"

For the record, Hervé had *nothing* to do with this. He didn't buy that jacket for Melania or design it. "I never saw that jacket!" he wrote. "It's a nightmare for me!"

But as her stylist, people thought he was responsible for her wearing it. Within minutes, "nasty horrible messages" started streaming to him, along with media requests and, in the days to come, "cold feedback from vendors" he was working with. I was also getting dozens of emails from reporters. I asked Hervé to get Grisham to do some damage control, but he was hesitant to insert himself. He was afraid to jeopardize his relationship with Melania. "I don't dare," he wrote, and added, "I am devastated."

The whole country could not stop talking about the jacket. I was appalled that no one in the East Wing even attempted to come up with a rationale for her insensitive fashion choice. In a *New York Times* photo, Melania strolled outside the White House in the jacket, Lindsay and Grisham walking directly behind her, the lettering plainly legible. No one in her "close-knit group" could or would dare tell her to take it off.

Melania and I had a seventy-minute phone call on June 26, several days post-jacket. For the first fifteen minutes, we did the usual catch-up. Kids, health, summer travel plans. She was still recovering from her hospital visit. I was dying to bring up the jacket, and when she mentioned an upcoming diplomatic trip, I segued in. I asked if Hervé was helping her for the trip and added, "You know, he almost had a heart attack with the jacket. People are writing terrible things to him about it on his Instagram and Facebook."

"Bad comments are expected," she said. "And that's too bad for him. He had nothing to do with it. My office had nothing to do with it. They are not my gatekeepers. I decide what I wear for myself."

"What prompted you to wear *that*?"

She laughed. "I'm driving liberals crazy! You know what? They deserve it!"

"I would have jumped on you to stop you," I said, which prompted a laugh as she imagined our rolling on the floor, my trying to get that jacket off.

"You warned me about the white suit," she said, laughing. "Some people get too much into it. They connect stuff to my clothes, but they don't really know me. They think so much, their heads will explode."

"So you make your decisions and you have your reasons, but if you don't tell people, they'll come up with reasons for you," I said.

"I don't care what they think. They're always negative," she said.

Melania wore the jacket to "get the media's attention," she said. "Otherwise no one would have covered the story.

"The media never covers the good things," she said. "They'd say, who cares she went to the border." This was a defining moment for Melania, and she wanted attention, just like Donald. Sure, the media would have covered it, but *not* the way they did.

"Melania," I said, "when Grisham finally did make a statement, she said, 'It's a jacket. There was no hidden message.' That was to your disadvantage and negated all of the good that could have come from your visit. Isn't your truth 'To my critics, I don't care what you think of me, and to my supporters, do you care what my critics think of me?' All you had to say was, 'I am doing what is the right thing to do and visiting the children at the border.' When you don't make a statement, people will go after you."

She said, "They're going to do it anyway, and they're always wrong. I wear what I wear because I like it." She mentioned that the day before, she had worn a pink Proenza Schouler dress to welcome Jordan's King Abdullah II and Queen Rania to the White House. It was the day after the Gay Pride parade, and Melania said she was shocked that the press surmised that she wore the brand as a secret nod to the LGBTQ+ community because Jack McCullough and Lazaro Hernandez, the designers, are gay. "I read it and it's like, 'Really? *Excuse me?*' Are you kidding me? It never even crossed my mind! These people are really crazy and obsessed and stuff!" she said.

She was in a groove now, hating on the media. "I've been getting visa questions again," she said, exasperated. "I did everything legal and perfect! They all went crazy about the zero-tolerance policy at the border. But they don't know what's going on. The kids I met were brought in by coyotes, the bad people who are trafficking, and that's why the kids were put in shelters. They're not with their parents, and it's sad. But the patrols told me the kids say, 'Wow, I get a bed? I will have a cabinet for my clothes?' It's more than they have in their own country where they sleep on the floor. They are taking care nicely there. And the mothers, they teach their kids to say, 'I'm going to be killed by gangs!' so they are allowed to stay. They are using that line and it's not true. They don't want to stay in Mexico because Mexico doesn't take care of them the same as America does."

Her comments made me queasy. But now I wanted to see how far she'd go. I'd been working with a few charities to get supplies like diapers and bottles to the shelters. I said, "If you're interested in getting the information I can send it to you, and we can try to do something."

She said, "I can give you the names of some shelters." In other words, she wasn't going to get personally involved to help these charitable efforts. It sounded like she was regurgitating rhetoric about asylum-seeking mothers, "criminals and murderers" that the government rightfully should separate from their children. "What about taking care of *our* people?" she said. "Many children in the United States are hungry. And now we're taking care of someone else's children? It's crazy! And then the media is negative about me going to the border to see those kids. Did Michelle Obama go to the border? She never did. Show me the pictures!"

Shifting gears abruptly (as she often does), Melania asked, "Did you go to the premiere of André's film?"

Is she really asking me if I've been to the movies? I looked around at the mayhem on my table and floor. It looked like I'd pillaged a Staples warehouse with all my binders of PIC records and printouts of emails and texts. Plus, I knew I looked haggard. I'd woken up with a migraine and black circles under my eyes. I'd been wearing the same flowered cotton pajamas for the last three days.

She was referring to *The Gospel According to André*, a documentary about *Vogue* editor-at-large André Leon Talley, which had come out in April.

I'd been cut off from the industry I once called home and my old friends, in part because I'd chosen to work for her. I simply said, "I haven't seen it."

"Me either, but I read it was sad."

It probably was. André had told the *Guardian* of his time since he'd left *Vogue* in 2013, "People have dropped me because I'm no longer viable on the front row.... I feel sort of lonely."

I could relate.

Did Melania have the first clue what "sad and lonely" felt like? I wasn't so sure.

I said, "I'm not going to watch it. It'll be too upsetting, and my emotions have been out of control enough already."

"Stephanie, what doesn't kill you only makes you stronger."

She'd said the cliché to me before, but this time, it didn't hold the same gravitas as it once had. I felt like replying, "Easy for you to say!"

André had emailed her, she revealed, to congratulate her on the white suit during the State of the Union. "He was very nice," she said.

As I listened to Melania ramble about her upcoming travel plans to Brussels and London, I realized she was oblivious to my reality. She was not weighed down by the burden of empathy, not one tiny bit, for me, André, or anyone.

But I still cared about her. Part of my mind yelled, *What is* wrong *with you?*

The Heat Is On

In July, the news broke that Michael Cohen had secretly recorded Donald talking about making the McDougal "catch-and-kill" secret hush money payment via David Pecker's company. On the tape, Donald asked whether the payment should be made "in cash," like a drug dealer or a john leaving money on the dresser on the way out. Donald tweeted his anger about being taped (but, astonishingly, continued to deny that it was his voice): "What kind of a lawyer would tape a client? So sad! Is this a first, never heard of it before?"

Melania and I had a two-hour conversation on July 31, but Michael came up only briefly. "I don't know what's going on," she said. "I'm not involved with it."

I expressed to her that I felt sorry for him because "what happened to him happened to me." Meaning, we'd been loyal to the Trumps and then dropped when convenient.

"You need to go day to day," she said. "Just know where the priorities are, and you cannot know what's happening tomorrow. You don't know what will happen in two days, or three days. Stuff like that, you know."

Platitudes! That was all she could give me. I played along, just to see what she'd say. "I love how you live your life," I replied.

"Nothing surprises me anymore," she said.

Melania was in a very chatty mood. "Anna [Wintour] gave the September issue of *Vogue* to Beyoncé. The cover, the articles, everything. . . . They say it might be [Anna's] last cover. I don't know. And Annie Leibovitz shot the porn hooker." She pronounced it HOO-car.

"The *what?*" I had no idea who or what she was referring to.

"Stormy," she said. "*She* will be in *Vogue*."

The buzzer in my apartment kept going off. I had to ask the First Lady to wait a sec while I opened the door. Another delivery. Thanks to my terrible insomnia, I'd been shopping online alone in bouts of midnight madness. The boxes would arrive, and then I'd return most of them; this was what my life had been reduced to.

Melania said that her White House closet was bursting and that "special stuff will go to a museum," adding, "Sometimes, I wear stuff a second time. It's only clothes. As long as I have a space to put it, I'm fine."

We talked about how she had worn a yellow dress that resembled Belle's gown from *Beauty and the Beast*. "So they called Donald and me Beauty and the Beast," Melania said. "They reported I wore a Raf Simons dress to Belgium because he's Belgian. I had no idea!"

Always the same, I thought. *She does what she wants and doesn't think anything through.*

She said, "I'm so glad I didn't do that profile in *Vogue*. You know, they came back two months ago and asked me to do it again. 'It might be a cover,' they said. Are you kidding me? I don't give a fuck about *Vogue* or any other magazine. They would never put me on the cover. All these people are so mad. Some people say, 'They're all jealous. They want to be you.' They cannot believe that [I still look good despite] all these designers who refused to dress me. Like I need their help. I don't need to prove anything to anyone. My life will not change if I'm on the cover or not."

She really did live in a fairy tale, where the queen rules from her throne and the little people were so far beneath her, she couldn't even see them. It was time for one of us to speak up. "I'm so depressed from what happened to me," I said. "I want to be positive, but I can't. I'm stuck."

"Maybe you think too much. You're analyzing too much. Maybe you should move forward and have different goals." This, from the person who never analyzed anything!

I replied, "I am still working with Marc Brackett and Robin Stern.

I still care about what we tried to do. I hate that the people who did this to me also took that away from you. You could have done something bipartisan and actually made a difference."

"They hate [Donald] so much, they hate on me, too. No matter what I say or do," Melania said. "They say I'm complicit, so I work on Christmas stuff. Who gives a fuck about decorations? But I need to do it, right? So I tell them I'm doing Christmas stuff, and they say, 'What about children at the border?' Give me a break. They will not do the story about the initiative. Yeah, if I went to Fox, they'd do it. But I don't want to go to Fox." She knew it would be a puff piece.

I had to agree with her, but she'd allowed the press-hate to happen. I told her, "The journalists call me say, 'The First Lady has no voice. Grisham took her voice away, and she's not nice.' You can make friends with the press, Melania. They're not the enemy. But not with Grisham. She's way too combative. You have to do it with kindness."

With a giant sigh, she said, "I don't give a fuck. It's true: as soon as I didn't give them enough access, they got upset with me. But no matter what I give the press, it'll never be enough."

"The First Lady can choose not to say anything, but her staff cannot," I told her. "You're private, but you're not mean. The way Grisham treats the press is mean. You've got three more years to try to build better relationships and do some good." That was what I'd done for her. Since I'd left, no one had bothered.

"I know, I know," she said. "But I don't think anything is going to change. There's no point in trying." She'd finally acknowledged that her staff wasn't doing anything for her since my departure.

Buzz. My door again, more packages.

We both laughed. My laugh was from the relief that she'd admitted to me that her staff wasn't helping her. She did know the truth about Lindsay and Grisham, but she had resigned herself to throwing her hands up and saying, "I give up." If I were still there, I would empower her to try harder. But I wasn't.

A Lucky Break

In mid-July, Kenneth Vogel and Katie Rogers of the *New York Times* came to my apartment to try to make amends. Ken brought me a gift of a bottle of wine. They apologized and they acknowledged Haberman had the last word on that piece.

"So why would I speak to you at all?" I asked. But I did. I needed to make sure they heard me out about the misinformation Haberman and Vogel had written about me already.

In the middle of my tirade spewing out the facts about the inaccuracies of their reporting, my husband came through the door after a long day at work. I introduced Katie, and when I introduced Ken, I said, "Here's the ass that ruined my life!"

David took it from there. He didn't yell. "I mean no disrespect," he said, "but what the fuck?" He just calmly questioned Vogel's ethics, for writing untruths about me, defaming me, and disregarding the real story, for whatever his reasons might be, and for giving the *Times* readers a privileged woman to love to hate. "You're the *New York Times*. You maligned my wife for no reason. When you do that, you give Trump credibility when he calls you 'fake news.' In this case, you did publish 'fake news,' and people got hurt."

He was my champion. Vogel and Rogers were kind of stunned, and a bit shamed.

I told them as much as I could, and we parted on good terms.

Rick Gates testified in federal court in DC at the Paul Manafort trial on August 7 and admitted for the first time in court that it was "possible" he'd stolen money from the inauguration funds. Why hadn't Trump and Barrack made Rick Gates the fall guy instead of me? He would have been more convenient than me, since he'd been under indictment since October 2017. The problem was, Gates was a wild card. While I was being set up to take the fall, Gates was hiring and firing lawyers and having meetings that would lead to his making a plea deal with Mueller on February 15, the same day the *Times* story dropped about me. The powers that be knew Gates had already agreed to talk to prosecutors and they needed fresh meat. My friendship with Melania made a great headline, and I already had enough enemies who wanted to get rid of me. I was in the pole position and muzzled with an NDA. Could you ask for more?

On August 17, 2018, the *New York Times* published a somewhat friendly article by Katie Rogers about Melania and included a decent description of the work I'd tried to do for her: setting up the East Wing, hiring staff, writing speeches, and developing the platform and its mission, in addition to overseeing the inauguration.

She also wrote that I "vehemently denied" that my departure had anything to do with the PIC. A quote from me appeared in the story: "'It unfortunately brought an abrupt end to the efforts and partnerships we'd developed to improve the well-being of children, which Mrs. Trump genuinely cares about,' Ms. Wolkoff said in an interview. 'The end outcome was not what I expected, but this had more to do with other factions of the White House.'"

Melania texted the basic pleasantries: Hi, how are you? Then "Your friend Katie Rogers did a nice story about you. Hope you are happy now." She sent a thumbs-up and wished me "a great weekend."

I responded: "Katie isn't my friend. She's a journalist doing her job, getting the facts right. I wish I could have told her more."

Mr. Fix-It

On August 18, 2018, Michael Cohen called me.

"Hello, Steph," he said. "The FBI and SDNY have the recording I made of our conversation."

"What are you talking about?" I asked. "A recording of what?"

Michael said, "I recorded our conversation to use for contemporaneous notes." I was stunned. He continued, "You need to have your lawyer get in touch with my lawyer to talk about whether the conversation is privileged or not."

"Privileged?" I asked. "What do you mean? Which conversation?"

"When you were crying," he replied.

Wait a second. I needed to digest what Michael had just told me.

He had a recording of our conversation?! The tape that was seized in the FBI raid? When did he tape me? He came to my house that one time and wore a trench coat! OMG, if that tape went public . . .

"Michael, why the fuck did you tape our conversation?" I asked, beside myself. I had asked Michael for his legal opinion, not to record our conversation without telling me.

He explained, "I couldn't sit down with a notepad. I wanted to make a memo in order to strategize to exonerate you and clear your name. They destroyed you for no fucking reason at all, other than someone else took a lot of money and buried it in their pockets. And you had to be the fall guy. Same way I'm the fall guy for [Donald] getting his putz licked by a porn star."

I couldn't deny that.

I asked how he was doing. He said, "It's rough and going to get rougher. It's been nineteen weeks since they've gone through every aspect of my life. It's destroying [my wife] and the kids. You know what's coming next. First they deny. They discredit. They demean, distract, and digress. That's not how the political world is supposed to work."

He continued, "I wanted to help [Donald] so [Melania] wouldn't kill him. For what? I'm being turned upside down. I didn't tape you for a gotcha. It was so we could sit down and create a memo to get your name cleared and let those who did wrong suffer. It shouldn't be you. The fact that you were crying really bothered me. [The Trumps] are not crying and you are."

That was the cue for me to start crying *again.*

"Look at what they did to me," I said, glancing at the state of my house, my face, my whole life.

"Look at what they're doing to me every day!" said Michael. "Every *Wall Street Journal* article. You think I don't know who's putting it out? Jared, Abbe Lowell [Ivanka and Jared's lawyer], Don Jr. How do I know? People have told me. Who owns the *Wall Street Journal*? Rupert Murdoch. Fox News is state-run media. All I want is the same thing I was trying to do for you. Clear my name. Let them eat shit, which is what they should have been doing instead of throwing it on everyone else's back."

"They'll get away with it," I said.

"What they did [on the inauguration] was criminal. When I saw your binders, I said to myself, 'This is not someone who is doing something wrong.' The level of precision, it's beyond anal. I'm super anal. You're beyond."

I laughed. "They wanted me to think I was crazy," I said. Melania and her downplaying, her "don't be so dramatic," as if my reputation had just been dinged a bit. As if the stress of witnessing the inauguration self-dealing hadn't put me in the hospital.

"Shame on every single one of them, all the people who watched out for them, to throw us under the bus. That one article said you took money from the inauguration. Who do you think created that story line?"

"You know who did," I said. "It was a PIC and White House–approved effort, all of which I have documented, going from day one. Heather Martin and Tommy Davis gave the story to Maggie Haberman. Those motherfuckers threw it on me. I wasn't willing to keep my mouth shut, so they said, 'Let's knock her off her high horse.'"

He said, "They threw you not just under the bus but under a train."

Michael warned me that, because of what I'd said on our recording, I might be called to testify in the investigation. "Which investigation?" I asked.

"Take your pick," he said. "They might subpoena your binders. There has to be an end to all of the bullshit. *Everyone* can't be a fall guy for their malfeasance and corruption. [Donald] is the worst version of himself I've ever seen."

Coming from Michael, who'd worked for Trump for over a decade, that was saying a lot. I broke into a cold sweat at the thought of being involved in an investigation.

"You should take solace in knowing that if the FBI or Southern District really thought you stole money from the inauguration, you would have gotten a phone call. How is Jared not behind bars? It makes no sense. Our intelligence community is the best in the world, and they don't know he's playing the Qataris against the Saudis for money?"

That triggered a memory. Once, when I was at a meeting at Colony Capital, I saw Jared come in, dressed in his white sneakers and blue blazer, for a meeting with a roomful of Middle Eastern men in headscarves. I started to dial Melania's number before I even got out the front door. "Guess who I just saw . . . ?!" I said to her at the time.

Michael said, "I asked people for money every day for the inauguration. Friends of mine. And for what? So they can walk away with eighty million dollars? It's disgusting."

"It's so wrong. I want my life back."

"You and me both."

Omarosa Manigault Newman had just released her book, *Unhinged*, about working in the White House, and she'd released a recording of her conversations with Lara Trump, Eric's wife, who'd offered her a high-paying job on the reelection campaign in exchange for her silence about the Trump family. Michael said, "It didn't bother me one iota when Omarosa dropped the tape of Lara Trump. She married at third base and thinks she hit a triple."

Three days after this phone call, Michael pled guilty to eight charges of tax fraud, tax evasion, and illegal campaign contributions. We spoke again on September 2, 2018.

"What happens next?" I asked.

"I can only surmise that it's not going to go well," he said. "They're going to come after me with everything they've got. Threats. Intimidation. Fifty, sixty, eighty counts of different violations for three hundred years in prison. I'll be on the inside. But you, Steph, will be on the outside telling the truth. You will make this happen."

I actually had to leave the house to go to my lawyer's office to listen to the Cohen recording. We sat in his office with a couple of other associates to listen to it. Every time I spouted "fuck," "shit," "douchebag," and "motherfucker," I sank a bit deeper into my leather chair. The lawyers heard Melania's and my nicknames for some of the biggest players, like Dopey and Tuberculosis.

I wanted nothing more in the whole wide world than the human right of being allowed to defend myself against the false accusations that had tarred my name and reputation. But I was muzzled by an ironclad NDA agreement. The contents of the tape were not made public. I was not allowed to comment on it in the press or discuss it.

As Michael had predicted, the recording did catch the attention of interested parties in the media and law enforcement, and an excerpt with me complaining about the Trumps charging way too much for a Trump Hotel venue surfaced.

Bless the Rain

Melania and I were in loose touch in September.

"The summer went too fast," Melania texted on September 5. "Wishing you all a successful year."

On September 12, she wrote, "Hope you're well. I guess you were at Fashion Week."

Did she seriously think I was going to Fashion Week? I was barely functioning. "No Fashion Week for me. I'm dealing with back-to-school, doctors, and paperwork."

The paperwork in question: collating and compiling a complete record of every email, text, and phone log from the day I joined the PIC until now for the US District Court for the Southern District of New York. "I'm always thinking of you my dear sweet friend, I miss you," I said.

On October 2, 2018, I received a grand jury subpoena from the US Attorney's Office for the Southern District of New York; I also received a Sealed Order issued by the US District Court for the Southern District of New York that prohibited me from disclosing, among other things, the fact of the subpoena for 180 days. The nondisclosure order from the SDNY did not expire for "180 days unless otherwise extended by the Court. The order will therefore remain in effect until early April 2019."

I couldn't breathe a word to anyone but my husband and children for months, because this had to be kept confidential from the PIC and the White House. The investigations were under way, and they couldn't know. I wasn't allowed to tell anyone, and that included Melania.

October took Melania to Kenya, where she wore a pith helmet reminiscent of colonialists from Europe. She said her sartorial choice offended the "liberal media." "I googled 'what to wear on safari,' saw the outfit, and liked it. So I bought it," she said. "I wasn't making a comment on colonialism." Our last voice conversation was all about how little she cared about what people thought of her.

On November 6, 2018, I received a surprise call. "Stephanie, Tommy Davis with Tom Barrack. I'm in New York as of Tuesday. Can you give me a ring when you get this call? I want to touch base with you on a couple of things, and yes, it's time sensitive."

I didn't call back. My lawyer from Paul, Weiss, Rifkind, Wharton & Garrison contacted Davis and informed him that he could address all his communications to him and to refrain from contacting me directly.

After I'd been subpoenaed, I didn't feel like chatting so much with Melania. It felt dirty. Texts and calls with her had slowed to a trickle after that. Right around the 2018 midterm elections, which brought a "blue tsunami" into the House of Representatives, she texted as if nothing major were going on. "Happy Thanksgiving. Hope you are well! I'm sure you're preparing for a feast there." I didn't reply.

On December 13, 2018, the news came out that Manhattan federal prosecutors had opened a criminal probe into the inauguration's spending and into whether some of the committee's top donors had traded cash for access to the Trump administration. The accounting didn't delineate where and how the donations had come in. Investigators were looking into whether extravagant donation packages offered face time with officials and if selling access explained the Trump inauguration's record-shattering $107 million cost—$50 million more than any other PIC.

Melania sent holiday wishes in December, and on January 1, she wrote, "Wishing you and your family a happy and healthy New Year."

I wrote back with my own message that I hoped she would have a happy and healthy 2019.

Since then, we have not talked, texted, or emailed.

On my birthday in 2019, flowers from Melania did *not* arrive at my door. For fourteen years, she had sent something, no matter what was going on in her life. Her wedding. The swearing-in. She always remembered. I had to assume she remembered my birthday that year, too, but she sent nothing. Despite everything, I was disappointed. Our friendship didn't end with a fight. It ended with an absence.

I've thought a lot about my grandparents since my departure from the White House, the ruination of my reputation, and Melania's betrayal. I've been secluded and debilitated. While I could never compare what I've been through to what my grandparents went through— they witnessed the very worst of humankind—I do know what it's like to feel destroyed, rendered powerless. It's a feeling like no other because you are denied the human right to defend yourself.

I have tried to match my grandparents' fortitude and resilience by putting challenges in front of myself, testing myself to see what I can endure.

The force of Melania's personality blinded me to the truth about her, and Donald's, lack of character. But I wasn't the only one. They have pulled the same trick on (about) half the country. I didn't see it from the inside out, but once I was on the outside looking in, it became glaringly obvious. Now I can't believe how blind I was to the depth of their deception and lack of common decency. I put Melania's needs ahead of my own. I volunteered to break my back (literally) for her, for nothing in return, other than a bunch of emojis. And she was happy to oblige. The biggest difference between Melania and me: I would never let a friend crash and burn for my sake. Never.

I would never sit back and watch someone exhaust and sicken themselves for me, but she did. I doubt she lost a minute's sleep over it.

Her selfishness is so deep, it enables her to keep her distance from the rest of the world. It makes her untouchable; if she doesn't give a shit about things, they can't affect her. The wall around her is her defense mechanism. The secret to her happiness is to be authentically and unapologetically skin-deep. She lives through her external attractiveness and how her appearance is perceived. Her behavior hasn't changed from her pre–First Lady days; she's just more visible now.

After our breakup, I asked myself, *Did her character change or was she always like this?*

Throughout the years of our friendship, our mutual affection, maybe all I really saw was her charming, warm, grounding "personality." I gave her the benefit of the doubt about her moral character, the virtues of empathy and honesty I have taught my children. I have tried to live my life by the principle that *what* you do becomes *who* you are. I was Melania's enabler, and her using me became the basis of our friendship. I liked feeling needed. I believed she was a noble person and treated her that way, blinding myself to the truth about her to justify our long friendship.

I used to think she was different from her husband. I saw streams of daylight between them and thought Melania was more principled, kind, and honorable than Donald and all of his offspring. I was wrong about that.

A Trump is a Trump is a Trump.

All along, I thought she was one of us.

But at her core, she's one of them.

— Epilogue —

I'm Still Here

I have spent the last several years reflecting on my experiences and the wave of misleading and factually false stories portraying me in a way that I myself would have called irresponsible and unacceptable if it had happened to someone else. While I can't turn back the clock and undo the harm that this has caused to me personally, I can still try to do good in the world.

This journey has been truly life-altering and, as I continue to have a deep sense of patriotism and a desire to give back, I will do so with the knowledge that not only do I have a social responsibility, I have a political one as well. I have learned that when it comes to politics, not knowing is not okay. For many years, I was apolitical. That was a mistake. I now know that is not an option—it's a luxury. And a luxury no one can afford. One's moral values and political beliefs clearly go hand and hand, and for me to have believed otherwise was naive and foolish.

I continue working with Dr. Marc Brackett and Dr. Robin Stern, advocating for the importance of teaching social and emotional learning, which empowers people of all ages with the skills to lead a life full of well-being and success. Through SEL, people learn to be strong, kind, caring, and resilient all at the same time.

My second subpoena came from the House Permanent Select Committee on Intelligence; the third came from the District of Columbia. I cooperated fully with both. These investigations are still underway. On January 22, 2020, the DC attorney general's office filed suit against the PIC and the Trump International Hotel. The charge was misuse of nonprofit funds, which they'd used to pay outrageous fees to the family's own business.

DC's attorney general Karl Racine stated, "District law requires nonprofits to use their funds for their stated public purpose, not to benefit private individuals or companies."

The suit cited emails between me and Rick Gates. The details are stomach turning: The hotel wanted to charge the PIC $3.6 million for event space, food, and drinks, over *eight* days. The inaugural events spanned four days. The amount of $450,000 per day was "significantly more than the Trump Hotel's internal pricing guidelines for use of this event space," per the lawsuit. The filing also said that I met with Donald and Ivanka about the inflated pricing and that "the President-elect acknowledged these concerns and directed that Ivanka Trump would handle this issue," and she did, with Rick Gates.

The *Washington Post* reported, "Stephanie Winston Wolkoff, a friend of first lady Melania Trump who had previously produced the Met gala and New York's Fashion Week, expressed alarm, writing that other properties had been offered to the committee at little or no cost. She warned that one of the committee's two planned events at the hotel was for the Trump family and that 'when this is audited it will become public knowledge.' Wolkoff said the meeting space should cost a maximum of $85,000 per day. Even that was pricey compared with offers from other hotels."

The Trump Organization called the lawsuit a "PR stunt" and vigorously denied any wrongdoing. No comment from Team Barrack.

But I can say now that my official comment is, "You go, Karl Racine!"

I wish I could say cooperating with *three* different investigations is empowering. It isn't. It keeps me involved in something I want to have nothing to do with. My family would love for me to wake up one morning and say, "I'm over it. Time to move on." So would I, which is why I had to write this book. It has helped me process my feelings and make sense of this tumultuous and defining episode of my life. I had a choice: to let it destroy me, or to learn from it. I chose the latter.

On February 4, 2020, my daughter, Alexi, and I watched the State of the Union address on TV.

In the First Lady's box sat talk show host Rush Limbaugh, a bully like Trump, who uses divisive, hateful rhetoric against individuals and groups with less power to claw his way to political and cultural influence. Melania pinned him with the Presidential Medal of Freedom, the country's highest honor.

She stood there clapping with a smile plastered on her face, going through the motions, advancing the Trump agenda.

I should have listened to her when she said, "Why are you trying so hard? Why do you care so much?" She'd told me in her way that she was not part of the solution, she was part of the problem. Not speaking up, and not fighting against the problem, is being a part of the problem, and I learned that the hard way.

Every person is capable of having the courage to be heard, no matter how uncomfortable it may be. So speak up for what is just and never give up until the truth is revealed. I hope my grandparents would be proud of me today.

I'm still here.

The woman I once considered my close friend is gone.

— Acknowledgments —

First and foremost, I want to thank my family for their endless support and patience over the last several years, especially this past year of writing this book. I appreciate and love you all.

David, my husband: I love you with all my heart. Thank you for accepting me for who I am, putting up with my divided attention, and allowing me the time to get to the other side to be with you. Your love saved me.

Zachary, Tyler, and Alexi: I couldn't ask for more devoted and loving children. You are my heroes. This is as much your story as it is mine, as you lived it every day. I love you the most . . . moster . . . blahdiblah.

Barbara and Bruce Winston: My parents have believed in me and supported me always. Your influence and unconditional love guided me to where I am today. There are no words strong enough to express my gratitude. I love you always and forever.

Michele and Jerry Wolkoff: My in-laws have treated me like the daughter they never had and I'm so lucky to have them as my family. No matter when, where, or what hour, you have always been there for me and us. I love you.

Randall Batinkoff: You are an amazing brother. We've been on many long journeys together, none of which I could have done without you. Thank you for diving into this book with me, being my first reader, and for your brilliant suggestions and catches. I wouldn't have been able to express myself without you. I love you, RB1.

Hilary and Izzy Batinkoff: My sister-in-law's and niece's patience and love guided me along the way. Your insight has been invaluable to me. I love you.

Gordon Winston: My big brother—you are and always will be irreplaceable. We know we never have to face anything alone. Love you, GB.

Golnar, Niki, and Leyla Winston: To my sister-in-law and nieces, although you're not by my side, you're always in my heart. I love you.

To my family Dr. Martin, Roz, Brandon, and Devon Weiss: We've shared so much together, and I hope you know that it's always coming from a place of love. Our family is our strength. I love you.

I also want to thank my friends for their immense support and understanding, in the good times and hard times, all times. Nina Shapiro, Erica Karsch, Caryn Zucker, and Nina Davidson ("You told me so!") never let me face this alone. Jenny Ruff and Jen Goodman never let me climb this alone. Meryl Poster, Holly Phillips, and Wendy Clurman never stopped believing in me. Amanda Poses and Roxanne Palin loved me just the same. Tammy Mager, Kim Yates, and Hillary Cahn constantly checked in on me.

Dr. Dexter Sun and Dr. Roger Hartl: I am forever grateful to both of you for saving my life.

Dr. Frank Miller: Your advice will stay in my heart forever.

Dr. Roy Boorady: With heartfelt appreciation, thank you for always caring.

Dr. Marc Brackett and Dr. Robin Stern: Thank you for believing in the greater good, giving me "Permission to Feel," and teaching me how to cope with "The Gaslight Effect."

My lawyers: Thank you for your counsel and support. Forever grateful.

Andy McNicol, my agent: Thank you for guiding me through it all, and for being in my corner.

Val Frankel: Thank you for believing in me and helping me tell my story.

Zoe Weisberg Coady: Thank you for always being there for me and having my back.

To everyone at Gallery Books: This book would not have been possible without the incredible work and talent of you all. Thanks to publisher Jennifer Bergstrom, editorial director Aimée Bell, executive editor Natasha Simons, publicity and marketing director Sally Marvin, managing editor Caroline Pallotta, production editor Jamie Selzer, assistant editors Maggie Loughran and Max Meltzer, art director Lisa Litwack, interior design director Jaime Putorti, and production manager Kaitlyn Snowden. Also thanks to lawyer Eric Rayman, researcher Ben Kalin, copyeditor Aja Pollock, and proofreaders Linda Sawicki and Susan Bishansky.

Finally, to my grandparents, Bobie Ethel and Papa Joel: With all my love, I dedicate this book to you.